EARTHLY MISSION

ROBERT CALDERISI

EARTHLY MISSION

THE CATHOLIC CHURCH AND WORLD DEVELOPMENT

YALE UNIVERSITY PRESS
NEW HAVEN AND LONDON

For information about this and other Yale University Press publications, please contact:
U.S. Office: sales.press@yale.edu   yalebooks.com
Europe Office: sales@yaleup.co.uk   www.yalebooks.co.uk

Set in Arno Pro by IDSUK (DataConnection) Ltd.

Printed in Great Britain by TJ International Ltd, Padstow, Cornwall.

Library of Congress Cataloging-in-Publication Data

Calderisi, Robert.
   Earthly mission : the Catholic Church and world development / Robert Calderisi.
      pages cm
   ISBN 978-0-300-17512-7 (alk. paper)
1. Church work with the poor—Catholic Church. 2. Catholic Church—Missions. I. Title.
   BX2347.8.P66C35 2013
   261.8'5088282—dc23
                                                                            2013007110

A catalogue record for this book is available from the British Library.

10 9 8 7 6 5 4 3 2 1

2017 2016 2015 2014 2013

$35.00

Contents

Acknowledgements

THIS book draws on a broad range of research, information, opinion, and advice, including interviews with more than 150 people in twenty countries. As most of them were talking to an utter stranger about a complex and nettlesome subject, I am deeply indebted to them for their frankness and openheartedness. Only one person insisted on anonymity, but in a few other instances I have disguised the identity of my sources where I judged they would appreciate my discretion.

In particular, I want to thank Kishore Jayabalan (Acton Institute, Rome); Enrique Aguilar, Roxana Alfien, Pablo Alberto Blanco, Virginia Bouxed, Esteban De Nevares, Enrique Del Percio, Carlos Eduardo Ferré, Octavio Groppa, Carlos Hoevel, Milan Jelic, Jorge Lozano, Luis Mendiola, Ricardo Murtagh, José Maria Poirier, Arturo Prinz, Julio Ruiz, Romina Ryan, Juan Carlos Scannone, Lia Zervino (all from Argentina); Bokul Francis Costa, Robi Purification, Harold Bijoy Rodrigues, Ranjon Francis Rozario, Rozen Sahadat Ali, and Richard Timm (Bangladesh); Pere Negre (Barcelona); Michael Black, Richard Conrad, Richard Finn, Simon Gaine, John O'Connor, Michael Oborne (Blackfriars, Oxford); Jon O'Brien (Catholics for Choice); Chris Bain, Susy Brouard, Clare Dixon (CAFOD);

ACKNOWLEDGEMENTS

Tom Bamat, Mary DeLorey, Daisy Francis, Paul Miller, Joan Rosenhauer, Paul Tillman, Christine Tucker (Catholic Relief Services); Thomas Tchiage (Cameroon); Michel Roy (Caritas Internationalis); Daniel and Petra Kriener, Karoline Mayer, Miguel and Silvia Schloss, Ernesto Solis (Chile); Claudio Betti, Francesco Dante (Community of Sant'Egidio); Pierre Labine (Congregation of the Holy Cross); Joseph Figuerido (*Cor Unum*); Diarmuid Martin (Dublin); Jaime Aguilar, Claudia Blanco Afara, Juan Chopin, Jesus Delgado, Carlos Feruffino, Alberto and Nadia Harth, Victor Manuel Orellana, José Panades, Paul Schindler, Jon Sobrino, Ismael Castro Velasquez (El Salvador); Mario Negre (European Parliament); Dave Evans, Peter Howard (Food for the Hungry); Katherine Marshall (Georgetown University); Carlos Avila, Réal Corriveau, Maria Elena Diaz, Yaquelin Baquedano Estrada, Octavio Sanchez, Juan Sheenan (Honduras); James Culas, Sanjay Gathia, Soosai Pakiam, Ignatius Sabbas, Nithiya Sagayam, Valeriano Vaz (India); Samuel Pommeret, Loïc Rolland Roche (International Federation of Catholic Universities); Mauro De Lorenzo (John Templeton Foundation); Janice McLaughlin, Dolores Mitch, Ellen Pearce, Jean Pruitt (Maryknoll Sisters); John Zucchi (McGill University); Michel Camdessus (Paris); Adhemir Caceres, Joel Anaya Castillo, Ricardo Garcia, Jorge Lafosse, Beatriz Perez, Guido Maggi Poisetti, Juan Humberto Ortiz Roca, Norbert Strotmann, Elías Szczytnicki (Peru); Esperanza Cabral, Carlos Celdran, John Carroll, Marilen Dañguilan, Edelina Dela Paz, Dominique Lemay, Philip Medalla, Bong Montesa, Aniceto Orbeta, Ernest Pernia, Fely Rixhon, Cate Steains, Bernardo Villejas, Marites Vitug (Philippines); Roger Etchegaray, Anthony Frontiero, Flaminia Giovanelli, Peter Kodwo Appiah Turkson (Pontifical Office for Justice and Peace); Juan Andrés Mercado, Martin Schlag (Pontifical University of the Holy Cross, Rome); Bob Bradberry, Théotime Gatete, Emmanuel Kolini, Omowunmi Ladipo, Eric Munyemana, Moses Ndahiro, Servilien Nzakamwita, John Rucyahana, Joseph Ruzindana, Prosper Sebagenzi (Rwanda); Pierre Hurtubise (St Paul's University, Ottawa); Katy Allen, Desmond Brice-Bennett, Tone Ellefsrud, Fulgence Kazaura, Mariam Kessy, Paul-Emile Leduc, Anthony Makunde, Richard Mariki, Damian

Temere Mosha, Amadeus Msarikie, Benno Ndulu, Robert Orr, Vitus Sichwale, Louis Shayo (Tanzania); Vinai Boonlue, Thavat Singsu, Manat Supalak, David Townsend (Thailand); Musa Bungudu, Dominique Corti, Elio Croci, Gerald Bnakyanzi, John Baptist Kauta, Kapil Kapoor, Tommaso Molteni, Andrew Mwenda, Rachel Sebudde, Steven Shalita, Frederick Ssemwanga, Leonard Ssekanjakko (Uganda); Christine Allen, Philip Endean, Julian Filochowski, Ian Linden, Diarmaid MacCulloch (United Kingdom); Stephen Colecchi (US Conference of Catholic Bishops); William Sheehan (Vatican Library); Victoria Kwakwa, Anthony Nguyen Ngoc Son (Vietnam); and Pamela Cox, Peter Lanjouw, John May, Jaime Saavedra, Mark Sundberg, Quentin Wodon (World Bank).

At the beginning of the project, seven people helped me chart my course: Katherine Marshall, Michel Arseneault, Edwin Cameron, Juan Andrés Mercado, Martin Schlag, Michela Wrong, and John Zucchi. Jacques Gérin, Brian Petty, Timothy Radcliffe, and Eric Southworth diligently reviewed the entire manuscript, while Brett House, Gustave Noël Ineza, Jean-Michel Jamet, John Langan, Mario Negre, and Mason Wiggins looked at individual chapters. As usual, my agent Rick Broadhead protected my interests and those of my readers as if they were his own. Clive Liddiard copyedited the final manuscript with a degree of precision that would have pleased the Holy Office.

I am grateful to the Bodleian Library (Oxford); Concordia University (Montreal); the Library of Congress (Washington, DC); the Pontifical Gregorian University (Rome); the Pontifical University of the Holy Cross (Rome); the Institut Catholique (Paris); the Maryknoll Archives (Ossining, New York); the Benedictine Abbey at St Benoît-du-Lac (Quebec); and, most particularly, the Las Casas Institute at Blackfriars, the Dominican house of studies at Oxford, where I completed the manuscript. While Blackfriars has no responsibility for the contents, I hope they will feel that the book does justice to their hospitality and encouragement.

I owe the idea for the book to Robert Baldock and Phoebe Clapham of Yale University Press (London). Once it was drafted, Phoebe helped reshape it with a sharp eye and gentle wit. It is their book as much as mine.

For Jean Daniel,
who introduced me to a different kind of Church,
and Benoît,
a modern saint who doesn't need one

Introduction

SOMEWHERE in the developing world, a 57-year-old woman is trudging up a steep hill in the early afternoon, sorry she could not come earlier when it was cooler or delay her visit until the evening. But the person at the top of the hill needs her urgently. In another life, she could have been spending a quiet afternoon in the suburbs of Bonn, with a grandson sitting on her knee, delighting in the gentle sunlight reflecting in his hair. Instead, she squints as the tropical sun assaults her like stage lights, careening off the wet banana leaves along the path. The ground is muddy and she is slithering in her sandals, her medical case weighing her down. She should have worn her running shoes, but they seemed a luxury in this area, where people are happy to afford a pair of flip-flops.

She has no grandchildren. She is a nun and a nurse, and the woman up the hill may be dying. Like many religious people, she has recurrent doubts about God and eternity, but she is sure of what she is doing, putting into practice the ideals she learned as a young girl. After a lifetime of service, she wonders, too, about the possibility of progress. Like Sisyphus of old, she always seems to be climbing a hill. The "growth" that the World Bank health team had talked about earlier in the day, when they visited her dispensary in the valley, wasn't reaching anyone she knew. She had faith in people, and wished she could also have faith in the "development" those eager young economists had been bantering about.

Her life is part of a larger history of two great causes – some would say experiments – one dating back to the first stirrings of human conscious-ness, the other rooted in the recent past, barely as old as the Second World War. The meeting of religion and development, the government-led fight against world poverty, is one of the great illuminating moments of the human story, revealing high ambition and idealism, but also the limits of planning, technology, and religious doctrine itself. It is the story of bravery and stubbornness, of breakthroughs and setbacks, and of the steel of personal determination hitting the hard rock of prejudice, ignorance, power, and corruption. That collision throws off sparks and stories that can stir a jaded heart.

This book will tell part of that story through the lens of Roman Catholicism and the lives of real men and women who have struggled to do good in forbidding circumstances. The Catholic Church is the largest and sometimes the most controversial organization on earth. Mere mention of it can irritate those who regard it as one of the worst examples of religious excess, yet provoke deep loyalty among Catholics who have a pained understanding of its past. Catholics see traces of glory in Church history, take pride in its universal character, and regard it as a rare beacon of hope and fraternity in a fractured world. The most devout believe it to be the "Mystical Body of Christ." Most Europeans and North Americans feel little need for formal religion, but know that the Church and its offshoots have had a profound influence on Western civilization. Latin Americans are ambivalent, after centuries of being smothered and inspired by Catholicism. Outside the Philippines, East Timor, and a few Indian states, Asians see Catholicism as one of a number of competing religions, but also as a source of health and education services. Africa – the last of the continents to respond to Christian overtures – is still establishing its loyalties, torn between traditional religions, Islam, main-stream Christianity, and fast-expanding Pentecostal sects.

The Church's impact in the world's poorer societies has been the subject of thousands of books, essays, and treatises; but none seems to have approached the subject comprehensively for a general reader. This book will describe the Church's practical role and will touch on the relationship between religion and political, economic, and social progress more generally. By definition, the story will focus on the last sixty years, as the very notion of "development" is that recent.

To many people in the West, impatient with organized religion, the damage Catholicism has done across the developing world is much more glaring than any of the benefits it has brought. Christians – who make up a third of the world's population – generally view the contribution of their churches more positively, despite their own reservations about the way eager evangelizers once trampled on traditional beliefs. Even boyhood adventure heroes have disliked missionaries. Rider Haggard's *King Solomon's Mines* (1885), one of the first English novels set in Africa, has the restored king of Kukuanaland tell his white benefactors before they return home, "I will see no traders with their guns and gin . . . I will have no praying-men to put a fear of death into men's hearts, to stir them up against the law of the king, and make a path for the white folk who follow to run on."[1] Yet some scholars argue that many missionaries were modernizers rather than marauders, sowing deliberately or accidentally the seeds of a more open and prosperous society.

As an agent of Western imperial expansion, Christianity witnessed the wholesale eradication of peoples and cultures. Not all of this was systematic or deliberate; much of it was accidental, through the spread of disease, or incidental to what was considered a "civilizing" process, and the Church was rarely the principal actor. But these qualifiers mean nothing to the lives, the voices, and the traditions lost. The Church had a particularly destructive impact on Latin American cultures in the sixteenth century, with one Spanish bishop in Merida (on Mexico's Yucatan Peninsula) responsible virtually single-handedly for the destruction of the Maya tradition of hieroglyphic writing. However, other missionaries in the same period were training Maya converts to preserve their ancient literature in the Latin alphabet.[2]

Where written forms did not exist, Christian missionaries codified local languages, initially as a means of evangelization, but later as a vehicle of broader education and community action. In Uganda alone, in the early twentieth century, Catholic educators published dictionaries and grammars in Luganda, Acholi, and Runyoro. But Church behavior was often a patchwork. In the northwest Amazon of the 1970s, Catholic priests destroyed the ancestral *yurupari* trumpets of the Barasana people as supposed symbols of the devil;[3] at the same time, on the banks of Lake Victoria in northern Tanzania, French-Canadian White Fathers were preserving the ceremonial drums of the Haya people, symbols of traditional authority which the government had been destroying in the name of "national integration."[4] In some places, missionaries instilled an enervating sense of inferiority. "Many assumed that God favored them less," says Wangari Maathai, the Kenyan winner of the 2004 Nobel Peace Prize, "that God had decided not to reveal himself to them directly but only to others – the Europeans – who were now offering them God's messages."[5]

Elsewhere, Christianity appears to have had the opposite effect, giving converts a sense of purpose and dignity that transformed their lives. To many Westerners, the most important aspect of the Church's role in development has been the Vatican's views on birth control; in developing countries, most people do not understand why rich countries even worry about the subject. In short, the larger picture has as many angles as a Cubist painting. But it is often more plausible, compelling, and human.

The story of the Church's influence in the developing world is also rich in irony. In Western societies like Ireland and Quebec, once dominated by the Church, Catholicism is identified with intellectual repression. From 1879 to 1960, Quebec's bishops blocked the creation of a ministry of education, fearing it would weaken the Church's influence over the young. The Church's former subjects are exacting an exquisite revenge: in Quebec, more than half of all children are now born out of wedlock. And in 2002 its National Assembly passed its same-sex marriage law by a vote of 125–0, reflecting widespread public support, but also a backlash against Church interference. The bishops had complained that the Assembly had spent more time on debating whether Quebeckers should turn right on a red light than it did on upending a treasured social institution. By contrast, in parts of the developing world where social attitudes were more backward than those associated with Catholicism, many have seen the Church as a breath of fresh air and regarded its teaching as revolutionary.

Catholics have certainly been very practical. A striking example can be seen at the oldest Catholic mission in northern Tanzania, at Kilema on Mount Kilimanjaro, which I visited in August 2011. Before we talked, the parish priest took me into the large vegetable garden that sloped down from the church towards the sisters' residence a good way off. As we walked, I wondered why he was showing me so many cabbages. At the bottom of the hill, he pointed to six stunted bushes and asked if I knew what they were. "They're coffee trees," I said. "Yes," he answered. "But not just any coffee trees. Alsatian missionaries planted them in 1862, four years before the church was built. And it is to these six trees that the whole of the coffee industry in Tanzania can be traced."[6]

The Catholic Church's size, reach, and resources have given it special opportunities to serve the poor and influence global events. But much of this book will apply to other Christians as well, especially the "mainstream" confessions (Anglicans, Methodists, Lutherans, Presbyterians) that have tried to contribute to world progress in their own ways. In fact, this book could have been devoted to Christianity and development rather than just Catholicism; but most readers will probably agree that it is already broad enough.

What is the Church? Some see a Manichean struggle between the kind-hearted clergy, religious, and lay people at the base of the institution and the airy theologians and mean-spirited enforcers of the Vatican. "That," suggests John Zucchi, chair of the small Catholic Studies program at Montreal's McGill University, "is a story for the 1970s and 1980s."[7]

Certainly, there have been sharp divisions in the Church, with demoralizing effects that are hard to measure. But common sense and humanity have often triumphed over the letter of some Church teaching. Like all powerful organizations, the Vatican can be arrogant and clumsy, as in March 2012, when it criticized the leadership of women's religious communities in the United States, regarded by many Americans as the human face of a sometimes bewildering institution. If this had been a soccer match between the nuns and Rome, most would have described the Vatican's action as an own goal. When not embarrassing itself, Rome can be too circumspect. Many Latin Americans were shocked by John Paul II's muted response to the 1980 assassination of El Salvador's Óscar Romero, the first archbishop to be slain at the altar since Thomas Becket in 1170.

But the sometimes tone-deaf Vatican has offered some of the most challenging reflections on how to apply 2,000-year-old Scriptures to the messy social and economic issues of our age. Beginning with Pope Leo XIII's 1891 letter *Rerum Novarum* ("Of New Things") (known as an "encyclical" from the Greek for "circular") – and continuing with a series of updates of the Church's "social teaching" since then, popes have challenged statesmen, economists, and policymakers to look at human progress through different lenses. Consider the words of Pius XII (1939–58), one of the least-loved popes, in a 1951 letter to his fellow bishops: "Charity can remedy many unjust social conditions. But that is not enough. For in the first place there must be justice . . ."[8] Such teaching has sometimes put the Church's own questionable positions and behavior under a magnifying glass. It has also made uneasy partners of conservative clerics at the center and rebellious Church people on the front line.

Although I have just used the word "conservative," I will be careful not to assign ideological labels too lightly in this book, as they can confuse rather than help. Certainly, most people at the Vatican can be described as "conservative" in the sense of wanting to protect the stability, stature, material interests, and theological "purity" of the institution; but even in Rome, there are those who believe that an informed conscience is just as important as Church teaching to moral decision-making – a "liberal" notion anywhere else. Social activists do not describe themselves as "progressives" any more than strict followers of Church teaching feel that they are right wing; both just see themselves as Catholics. According to Michel Roy, the secretary-general of the Church's umbrella charity organization Caritas Internationalis, "The Church is on the 'Right' when it emphasizes morality, on the 'Left' when it stresses the social, on the 'Right' again when it has concern for the individual, and on the 'Left' when it focuses on the community."[9] In short, while its internal politics can be ugly, the Church is not a political organization in the normal sense.

Given the breadth of the subject, this book can only be an introduction to the Church's role in the developing world; and even then it will leave out some important topics (like the role of Catholic universities), a whole region (North Africa and the Middle East), and a number of significant Christian countries (like Haiti, Korea, and Cuba) that a longer book might have covered. It is not aimed at Christians or Catholics, but I hope many of them will enjoy it. Nor is it intended for scholars, although I trust it will hold water with them. It is written for a general reader with an interest in international affairs and an open mind about religion.

Writing it has been a minefield. Four years ago, I sent a brief summary of the project to a hundred friends around the world and received sharp reactions within hours. "You mention the Church's cozy relations with 'authoritarian' governments in Latin America in the 1970s," a Paris journalist wrote back. "How did they differ from simple dictatorships? Were they the ones that let their political prisoners rot away in prison, or those that dropped them from helicopters into the sea?" "You've made no reference to the Church and HIV/AIDS in Africa," a South African judge told me. "I hope you'll be covering the Church's role in the Rwanda genocide," an English journalist observed. These challenges, and others, have been bracing and helpful and have caused me to alter some of my early hypotheses in important ways.

In my thirty years working in international development (mostly at the World Bank), my encounters with religion were more haphazard than systematic; yet even then, I was exposed to amusing suspicions on both sides. After a trip to Indonesia, I was summoned to the office of my vice-president (a Turk) to explain why I had visited a Catholic bishop in an overwhelmingly Muslim country. (In the province I was visiting – the western half of New Guinea – there were very few Muslims, and Christian leaders knew the rural situation better than anyone else.) At about the same time, I was contributing money to a Jesuit think tank in Washington, DC called the Center of Concern, which, among other things, was promoting the reform of the international financial institutions. At an otherwise charming garden party for donors one summer afternoon, the director of the Center asked me where I worked. When I told him, he answered only half-jokingly, "And you expect to save your soul?" The gulf between churches and official development agencies was so wide that in 2001, as the World Bank's country director for Central Africa, I had great trouble obtaining an appointment with the Catholic bishop of Chad's capital, Ndjamena, a Frenchman who was the cousin of a friend of mine. I simply wanted to say hello and have his perceptions on local issues. He feared that, once I heard the government was paying the salaries of Catholic teachers in the country, I would recommend the practice be dropped as part of general budget cuts. I reassured him that this was an imaginative example of the public-private partnerships that were becoming the norm in international development.

In 2000, taking advantage of a new World Bank study *Voices of the Poor* (which stressed the importance of faith leaders for poor communities around the world) and a new Bank president who felt the Bank should be less aloof from the "spiritual" side of development, I organized a meeting in Nairobi between senior Bank officials and about 200 Christian leaders from across Africa, in conjunction with the Oxford Centre for Mission Studies. My first book, *Faith in Development* (2001), was a summary of that conference. My second book, *The Trouble with Africa: Why foreign aid isn't working* (2006), was half memoir, half gentle polemic about how to help the continent differently. It mentioned religion (including the role of Catholic nuns) more than I recognized at the time; but perhaps this was inevitable, given the degree of Church involvement in African development. One conclusion of the book was that, despite its own set of limitations, people-to-people aid is more likely to reach the poor and to express international solidarity than are official aid programs. Exploring the Catholic Church's role in world development seemed a logical follow-up to those earlier studies. In a constellation of world issues ranging from climate change to high-tech terrorism, none seems more important to me than the persistence of mass poverty when the world has the knowledge, experience, and resources to end it. Global institutions like the Church must be part of the solution.

Although I will keep my personal views in check until the end of the book, I think I owe the reader a word about my own beliefs. The Catholic Church is such a lightning rod that my effort to treat it with some balance may itself become an object of controversy. In writing this book, I have tried to respect both those with deep religious convictions and those with none at all. But I identify with those somewhere in the middle, whose faith is hopeful, hesitant, and humble rather than heroic. In 1968 I left the Catholic Church for ten years, following the publication of the papal letter on birth control, distressed about the damage it would do in the developing world. I have written an "Open Letter to the Pope from a Gay Catholic" (2005) and *A Marriage of True Minds* (2009), a memoir of my husband who died in December 2008 of ALS (Lou Gehrig's, or motor neurone disease). Both may be found on my website: www.robertcalderisi.com

I believe the Church will only rise to the full height of its Founder's ideals once all of its 5,000 bishops (not just a hundred or so cardinals) have elected a woman as pope. In the meantime, I think the Church deserves to be criticized – sometimes quite severely in the light of its own professed ideals – but also respected for the good it does, sometimes despite itself. In the same spirit, not everything that it strives to achieve before a woman does finally step out onto the balcony of St Peter's Basilica should be dismissed as worthless and hypocritical.

The book begins with the story of two Church leaders (Hélder Câmara of Brazil and Denis Hurley of South Africa) who struggled with their own institution, as well as with the moral issues of their time. Chapter 2 looks at Church history since 1870, when the institution was shaken to its foundations; deals with issues (like the Church's wealth) that undermine its credibility; and explains features of Catholicism which distinguish it from other faiths, including other Christian confessions. Chapter 3 surveys the social teaching of the Church: what can be gleaned from the Gospels, what popes have said on the subject, and the Catholic role in formalizing human rights law in the twentieth century. Chapter 4 analyzes the links between religion and development, the progress that has been made in reducing the number of "absolute" poor in the last thirty years, and possible ways in which the Church may have helped or hindered that progress. The central chapters describe the Church's role in Africa, Asia, and Latin America – a sequence slightly at odds with historical chronology (even though Portuguese missionaries reached the Congo a few years before Columbus set foot in America) so as to emphasize the Church's three broad contributions to development: education, basic services, and advocacy. While Catholics everywhere have been active on all three fronts, each region illustrates one of these contributions best, with Africa exemplifying the Church's foremost contribution to modernization: education. The Church's role in the Rwandan genocide is so shocking and particular that it is covered in a separate chapter. Chapter 9 takes up the history of the Church's position on contraception and its impact on population growth and the fight against HIV/AIDS. This is followed by a chapter on Catholic "charity," which has moved away from the original notion of humanitarian relief towards longer-term assistance and the promotion of social justice. The book has two concluding chapters. One identifies issues that may affect the Church's continued effectiveness in fighting poverty; the other assesses its overall impact.

Throughout the book, I have drawn on the accounts of people I have met in fourteen developing countries: Argentina, Bangladesh, Brazil, Chile, El Salvador, Honduras, India, Peru, the Philippines, Rwanda, Tanzania, Thailand, Uganda, and Vietnam. I have also tried to heed the advice of an English free thinker and former Franciscan professor of philosophy named Joseph McCabe (1867–1955) who left the Church in 1896 and wrote critically about it thereafter:

> It is an amiable and graceful pastime to turn over the pages of past history and pick out here and there a picture of some upright abbot or bishop who, for a few decades, saw that justice was done in his little area, some saint who really acted as if all men were his brothers. But it is a poor sort of education when there are a thousand narrowly fanatical or unjust or dissipated abbots or bishops for every one whom we can admire.[10]

I hope the story that follows, told through the lives of some remarkable individuals and a few scoundrels, will pass that hurdle of "amiability" and shed real light on the positive and negative aspects of the Church's role in the developing world.

CHAPTER 1

• • • • • • • • • •

Two Troublemakers

CHRISTIANS believe that people are more important than dogmas, structures, scriptures, and rituals. So one way to introduce the role of the Catholic Church, but also its contradictions and limitations, is to look at the lives of two remarkable men who exemplified what was best in the Christian tradition and yet paid a price for it. Like the imaginary nun at the start of this book, they did not spend a lot of time weighing the "pros" and "cons" of throwing themselves into the struggle. Even less did they worry about what their superiors would think of them. Both were senior churchmen who saw their personal prominence as yet another reason to live out the Gospel, rather than as a stepping stone to higher office. Neither was typical of people in their positions, but they inspired two generations of Catholics – and Christians more broadly – to expect more of themselves, as well as of other Church leaders. One lived in Brazil; the other in South Africa.

By today's standards, it is hard to see why Hélder Câmara was regarded as a threat to the established order – even if he wanted to be. The archbishop of Recife (Brazil) certainly flirted with radical chic. In a speech in Paris just days before the French students' revolt of 1968, he told young people: "Instead of planning to go to the Third World to incite violence there, stay home and help your countries realize that they need a cultural revolution, too, a new hierarchy of values, a new world vision, a global strategy of development." Describing working conditions in Brazil as "sub-human," he urged the Church to side with the "underdeveloped masses" and support non-violent action against "landowners who are still living in the Middle Ages." "What's the use of venerating pretty images of Christ, if we fail to see him in those who need to be rescued from their poverty? Christ in the northeast [of Brazil] is called José, Antonio, Severino . . ."

Câmara was fearless in the face of personal attacks: "If people in power describe Catholic bishops as 'subversive' when we are simply defending broken human beings, how will they treat our priests and laity if we let them?" He was not overly worried about Communism, feeling that it would collapse once spiritual leaders abandoned their "Machiavellianism" – apparently referring to the Church's material interests – and promoted human rights. He said this in Rome in November 1965, during the Second Vatican Council – the twenty-first gathering in history of all the bishops of the Church – and may have been considered naïve for doing so. But at least one other person there, Karol Wojtyła, the cardinal archbishop of Kraków, may have been having similar thoughts, unaware that he would be able to act on them as Pope John Paul II. Câmara did not think mere charity would solve very much. In cases of emergency, obviously one had to help; but generosity and "slight reforms" would not fix broader injustices: "The true Christian social order must be founded not on assistance, but on justice."[1] He was impatient with labels: "When I give food to the poor, they call me a saint. When I ask why the poor have no food, they call me a Communist."[2] Peace and order, he said, were not an excuse for authoritarian rule. This was a direct shot aimed at Brazil's military governments (1964–84). He was also suspicious of intellectual fashions and overbearing advice from overseas: "Anyone who claims that the secret to development is birth control needs to have his head examined."

Latin American Christians, he thought, were responsible for the injustice around them. They had condoned the slavery of Indians and Africans and failed to defy the rich and the powerful: "Aren't we just drugging our consciences with church building and social projects? Haven't we proved Marx right by being passive in the face of tyrants?"[3] Like many saints, he could be self-righteous and tiresome, complaining that an early session of Vatican II had not been down-to-earth enough and should end in "penitence" rather than "thanksgiving." But, despite his doubts, he was loyal to the Catholic Church. Asked by a young Frenchman how he could bear reading the starchy, authoritarian documents issued by the Vatican, Câmara replied: "There is always something good to be found there, as if the Holy Spirit had insisted on slipping in between the lines."[4]

In Recife he tried to live up to the idea of a "Church of the Poor." He stopped wearing his purple archbishop's sash, abandoned the pretentious palace of his predecessors for a humbler residence next to the old cathedral at Olinda, had supper at the taxi-drivers' stall across the road, and hitched lifts into town instead of using an official car. More substantively, Câmara donated Church land to those who needed it, set up a credit union for the poor, involved clergy and laity in the running of the diocese, told seminarians to live in local neighborhoods rather than their colleges, and set up a theological institute where lay people and future priests were trained by women as well as men.[5] Câmara was part of a progressive generation. Between 1959 and 1964 (when the military took power) the Church set up more than 6,500 literacy schools in northeastern Brazil, using Catholic radio programs and a textbook called *Viver e Lutar* ("To Live is to Struggle") which challenged current income and land distribution in the country and advised people against selling their votes. The Church organized farmer unions, sixty of them just in Câmara's state of Pernambuco by 1962. Small Christian communities were also established, and the first nation-wide conference of these grassroots bodies was held in Rio in 1966.[6] All of these initiatives anticipated the call that the Second Vatican Council in 1962–65 would make for the Church to be more active in the world.

Remarkably for a churchman of the time, Câmara did not shy away from economic subjects, recognizing that people's lives could be transformed through a radical change in international trade policy. He recommended a regional common market to compete with the rest of the world: "Perhaps the moral force of the Church can help Latin America overcome its adolescent vanity and accept interdependence. Otherwise, we will be stuck fighting an unequal battle against international greed and selfishness."[7]

The Brazilian military tried muzzling him, preventing the media from interviewing or quoting him, and forbidding him to speak in public. A young associate, Father Henrique Pereira Neto, was tortured, killed, and left hanging on a tree as an apparent warning to the Archbishop. On another occasion, Câmara answered the door to find a hired killer with his gun drawn. "I have come to assassinate you, Dom Hélder," the man said. The Archbishop answered, "Then you will send me straight to the Lord." The man lowered his gun and burst into tears. "I can't kill you," he sobbed. "You belong to God."[8] Undeterred, students invited him to their meetings and graduation ceremonies, and his reputation spread around the world.

On his retirement in 1985, the pastor and prophet was succeeded by a canon lawyer, part of a generation of appointments that, in many people's eyes, would choke the breath out of a reforming institution, like a blanket of carbon monoxide. But even worse, Câmara would now be tortured by his own Church in a way that the Brazilian military could only have dreamed of. In September 1988, his successor shut down the Documentation and Public Information Service in the diocese and, a few months later, the Center for the Defense of Human Rights as well. He ordered the Justice and Peace Commission to stop using diocesan stationery. A year later, on his recommendation, the Vatican closed the Theological Institute that Câmara had founded and that had been a center of "liberation theology" for twenty years. The new archbishop also tried to close the Salesian Institute of Philosophy, but the Salesians (a religious order dedicated to teaching) protested successfully to Rome. In the face of such demolition work, Câmara was instructed to remain silent.

In December 1989, the new archbishop dismissed the pastor of the Shrine of the Immaculate Conception (one of the most important pilgrimage sites in the country) and suspended him from the priesthood because of his "left-wing" politics (speaking out in defense of the poor) and his public criticism of the archbishop. Thousands took to the streets and local residents blockaded the shrine for months to prevent the installation of the new priest. (The doors were finally forced by a large squadron of military police.) In February 2012, I talked to an elderly woman who was still a staunch defender of the former pastor, more than two decades after he had been fired. The supposed rabble-rouser lives in a small house next to the church with his wife and two children (he married two years after being disciplined, apparently believing he had nothing left to lose) and says mass to a dwindling parallel community. "I decided not to follow him into his new Church," the woman told me. "But it was very hard. It was like choosing between a Christ one can only imagine and someone in the flesh who was his most perfect representative on earth."[9] In August 1991, the archbishop stayed away from the mass celebrating Câmara's sixty years of priesthood. In return, only twenty-five of the diocese's two hundred priests attended meetings called by the archbishop.[10]

Câmara died in 1999 and is buried in the second-oldest church in Brazil (built in 1540), high up on a hill at Olinda, overlooking the skyscrapers of modern Recife in the distance. His tomb is a slab of black marble in front of the main altar, inscribed with his signature and a dove in bronze. On either side are immense bouquets of white and yellow carnations, which are replaced every week. No other bishop is buried in the church – the remains of his predecessors lie in an ossuary behind the cathedral – and undoubtedly there will be some debate about where to place his successor.

* * *

On the other side of the Atlantic, 4,500 miles southeast of Recife, during the same period, the Catholic archbishop of Durban (South Africa) was also irritating the authorities. Unlike Câmara and his future comrade-in-arms, the Anglican Desmond Tutu, Denis Hurley was a great bear of a man. (It would later be said of him: "When you're in the hurly-burly, it's good to have the burly Hurley."[11]) He grew up on Robben Island, where his father was the lighthouse-keeper (and where Nelson Mandela would spend most of his years in prison). He studied in Ireland and Rome and soon overcame the racism that most young South African whites grew up with at the time. In 1938, when Hitler visited Rome, excited fellow students called Hurley up onto the roof of the seminary to see the German chancellor reviewing a parade nearby. But the young South African stayed where he was. Pius XI (1922–39) had left the city for his summer residence so as not to have to meet Hitler, and had also closed the Vatican Museums; Hurley was simply following the Pope's example.[12] In 1947, he was appointed bishop of Durban, choosing an episcopal motto (taken from St Paul's Second Letter to the Corinthians) that was a sign of things to come: "Where the Spirit is, there is freedom." At the age of thirty-one, he was the youngest bishop in the world, and would stay in the diocese for forty-five years, becoming archbishop in 1951.

A year after he took office, the National Party won power and began to introduce the notorious apartheid laws. Hurley did not muse very long about what to do. When the Bantu Education Act (1953) withdrew government funding from church schools so that the state could control black education, Hurley organized a fundraising campaign to keep Catholic schools open. In 1957, when the government tried to outlaw racially mixed worship, he denounced apartheid as "anti-Christian" and told his clergy to ignore the order "regardless of the consequences." In the uproar that followed, the legislation was withdrawn. As one observer put it, "This was language and action never before seen from a Catholic leader in South Africa."[13]

Hurley played a prominent role at the Second Vatican Council (1962–65), where he met activist bishops from other countries and grew even bolder, talking about a "global church struggle for justice." In 1968, as part of a national plan to create separate black "homelands," people were forcibly removed from their village in Natal to a barren area known as Limehill. Hurley showed up on the day of the removal to express his solidarity, and then ministered to the uprooted community. When the government denied that children had died from malnutrition and dirty water in the new settlement, the Archbishop counted every child's grave, noted their names and ages, and released the list to the media. In 1981, as president of the Southern African Catholic Bishops' Conference, he issued a statement opposing the celebration of South Africa's twentieth anniversary as a republic, pointing out that "the vast majority of the people see no cause for celebration, since they are deprived and oppressed in the land of their birth."[14] He also backed conscientious objectors who refused to be conscripted into the army to fight the racist government's regional wars. Described by one politician as an "ecclesiastical Che Guevara," he was placed with Desmond Tutu and others on the list of opponents of the state, rendering him open to being smeared or harassed by the security services. Yet, later, he regretted that he had not done more to fight the system: "Had we been better politicians, we would have known that they were more afraid of us than we of them."[15]

In 1971, the South African Church did not look very different from the rest of society. It had 170,000 white members and a million blacks; but whites had a priest for every 120 parishioners, while blacks had just one for every 6,600. There were twenty-five white bishops and only one black one.[16] But Hurley's moral leadership was so strong and his opposition to apartheid so persistent that many wondered why he was never named a cardinal.

They did not have to look very far for the reason. Like his opposite number in Brazil, Hurley could be a thorn in the Church's side. Successive papal nuncios and his fellow prelates urged him to be less confrontational with the government. He believed in open intellectual debate and was impatient with the repressive role of the Vatican's Congregation for the Doctrine of the Faith. At the Second Vatican Council, in front of 2,200 bishops, he praised the "vision" of the French theologian Pierre Teilhard de Chardin (1881–1955), who had been forbidden to speak or publish anything for the last twenty years of his life. And in 1985, when Rome silenced the Brazilian liberation theologian Leonardo Boff, Hurley accused the Vatican of violating its own principle of "subsidiarity," which held that important decisions should be taken at the lowest possible level of an institution. Although it was a key feature of the Church's social teaching, "we do not always find it easy to practice ourselves." He was deeply disturbed by the Church's restatement of its position on birth control in 1968 and told the Pope as much to his face – Paul VI, a usually gentle man, was furious.[17] When colleagues criticized him for taking a public position on the matter, Hurley said he was ready "to lose my mitre" over it.[18]

In 1974, he was almost barred from an important meeting in Rome after writing an article on contraception in an American Jesuit magazine. "No authority has the right to command the impossible," he had said, and he warned the Church against earning Christ's rebuke: "You load on men burdens that are unendurable, burdens that you yourselves do not move a finger to lift (Luke 11:46)."[19] When Hurley threatened to make public his disagreement with the Pope's staff, the Vatican backed down and let him attend the Rome meeting. Even if his superiors had been able to accept his outspokenness, *realpolitik* would probably have got in the way of making him a "prince" of the Church. Throughout the 1970s and 1980s, Vatican diplomats wanted to maintain good relations with the racist government of South Africa, in the same way as they were subduing moral qualms about communist regimes in Eastern Europe and military dictatorships in Latin America. Making Hurley a cardinal would have been tantamount to giving him a Nobel Prize.

It is not clear that he ever sought such a distinction. In 1951, just four years after becoming bishop, he contrasted Christ's large-heartedness to the Church's "arrogant claims," "crusty dogmatizing," and "regimented religious drudgery." Fortunately, he said, most Catholics remembered the simplicity and beauty of Christ's ideals:

That is why many men, many of them old and broken, gentle in their upbringing, studious in their pursuits, retiring in their habits, humble of mind, timid by nature perhaps, have stood up like the wrath of God and raised their voices till the thunder shook the world; for the Church that spoke through them was far greater than they.[20]

Like a chrysalis beginning to quiver in its cocoon, the Church was about to break out of the crust that Hurley had complained about.

CHAPTER 2

The Catholic Church: "Seven Inches of Condemnation and One of Praise"

THE English philosopher – and towering humanist – Bertrand Russell (1872–1970) would have liked Câmara and Hurley and, knowing them, might even have toned down the opinion he expressed in 1927 to a London branch of the National Secular Society. He told it that he could think of only two contributions that organized religion had made to human civilization: the development of the calendar and the ability to predict eclipses. "I do not believe that there is a single saint in the whole calendar whose saintship is due to work of public utility."[1] At about the same time, the English Catholic writer G.K. Chesterton (1874–1936) expressed a very different view: "Christianity, even when watered down, is hot enough to boil all modern society to rags."[2] In the developing world, Chesterton may have been closer to the truth than Russell, if only because the largest single Christian confession had the resources, the structures, and the outlook to influence events.

Non-Catholics associate the Catholic Church with the Inquisition, the persecution of Galileo, quaint rituals involving incense and satin vestments, the opulence of the Vatican in Rome, an "infallible" pope, its opposition to artificial birth control, and more recently the sexual abuse of minors. Catholics look beyond these surface impressions and try, like other Christians, to focus on the teachings of a man they believe was the Son of God. They are not blind to the Church's failings; indeed, they can be the Church's own fiercest critics. "Who," asked the German theologian Hans Küng, "can imagine Jesus coming back to say Mass in St Peter's?"[3]

Whatever its remaining faults, few would compare the modern Church to what it was in the Middle Ages and Renaissance – an institution deeply corrupted by temporal and material ambition. For most of its history, the Church's spiritual focus was obscured by its secular power. It could depose kings and excommunicate entire cities (like Venice) for such "sins" as failing to contribute to papal armies; in the process, it undid itself. The Vatican itself has occasionally been eager to turn the page. In December 1809, Napoleon decided to bring the whole of the Vatican Archives to Paris as part of a larger scheme to house the greatest art and documents of his empire on French soil. When he was overthrown in 1814, the new French government wanted to return them, but money was scarce, and so the Vatican asked its various departments to decide what they could do without. The Holy Office abandoned many of its records of the Inquisition, prepared to try to blot out one of the ugliest chapters in human history.[4]

The Church has changed profoundly since then. The first upheaval followed a foolish act of aggression by France's Emperor Napoleon III, who declared war on Prussia in 1870. The Germans crushed the French armies and were on the outskirts of Paris within months. But the Italians probably cheered more loudly than the Prussians, as the war forced the French to withdraw their troops from Rome, where they had been protecting the last remnant of the Papal States, the Eternal City itself, from Giuseppe Garibaldi's patriotic troops. Within days, Italy gained a capital and the Church lost the last of its claims to direct political authority. By chance, all the Church's bishops were meeting in Rome for the first time in 300 years. Pope Pius IX (1846–78) hastily wrapped up the First Vatican Council, which had declared him "infallible," and retreated from the opulent Quirinal Palace to his humbler apartments on the other side of the Tiber. Accepting this reluctantly, he and his successors over the next fifty years pouted about being a "prisoner of the Vatican" until they settled their differences with the Italian government in 1929. Later, this clipping of the institution's wings would be seen as a form of liberation, forcing the Church to reconnect with its original mission.

One of the consequences was that by the end of the nineteenth century Catholic leaders were able to look beyond the interests of the Church itself and engage with larger issues, like the "social problem" caused by the European Industrial Revolution. Some churchmen, like the English Cardinal Henry Manning (1808–92), became national celebrities. Lytton Strachey devoted the opening essay of *Eminent Victorians* (1918) to the man, and G.K. Chesterton was later to recall, as a boy out strolling with his father, seeing the august figure on London's Kensington High Street. A crowd of people were kneeling on the pavement as a dark carriage arrived: "Out of it came a ghost clad in flame like a great crimson cloud at sunset, lifting long frail fingers over the crowd in blessing. [His] face was so extraordinary that for a moment I even forgot such perfectly scrumptious scarlet clothes." Chesterton's father backed up the boy's sense of awe: "He'd have made his fortune as a model," he quipped.[5]

Manning had other admirers. He supported the workers and helped mediate a settlement in the 1889 London Dock Strike, a milestone in the history of British trade unionism. He also set an aspiring nurse on the path to fame, by helping to persuade the British government to allow Florence Nightingale to go to the Crimea with a staff of volunteer nurses. Nightingale never became a Catholic, but she remained grateful to the Church for the rest of her life. "The Catholic Orders," she said, "offered me work, training, sympathy and help in it, such as I had in vain sought in the Church of England. In all the dens of disgrace and disease the only clergy who deserve the name of *pastors* are the Roman Catholic. The rest are only theology- or tea-mongers."[6]

The second change to rock the Catholic Church was another meeting of all its bishops in 1962–65. In a sense, May 1968 came early to Catholicism. There were no situationist graffiti along the Via della Conciliazione, the ramrod-straight street that leads into St Peter's Square, but this was an old Church shaking off its cobwebs. "Rome was one big theological 'think-in' or at least 'listen-in,'" wrote a Protestant observer. "Though we did not realize it then we were present at perhaps the greatest theological concourse the Christian world has seen."[7]

Pius XII (1939–58) had thought of calling a second Vatican Council in 1948, but abandoned the project in 1951. When John XXIII (1958–63) revived the idea, the pontifical universities in Rome rubbed their hands at the prospect of influencing the outcome. Almost a century after papal infallibility had been declared, many theologians wanted to strengthen papal prerogatives further, so as to stress the special nature of Catholicism and protect it against attacks. Roman theology was so archaic that the German scholar Karl Rahner complained that the textbooks had hardly changed in two hundred years. Theologians in Rome wanted to protect this "heritage" from modern thinking, much of it drifting in from France through the writings of Teilhard de Chardin, Yves Congar, Henri de Lubac and others. They were to be disappointed.

The trappings of the Council were old-fashioned. The language of discussion was still Latin, putting the North American bishops at a disadvantage. (Taking matters into his own hands, Richard Cushing, the cardinal archbishop of Boston, arranged for simultaneous translation at his own expense.) There was just a sprinkling of women, who grouped together at a coffee station reserved for them in St Peter's. Other refreshment points in the Basilica were nicknamed "Bar-Jonah" and "Bar-Mitzvah;" theirs was "Bar-Nun."[8] But the spirit of the gathering was new. The papal civil service (the Roman Curia), which had been preparing the draft conference documents for more than three years, was shocked when the bishops threw out the proposed membership of various commissions at the very first session and decided to reorganize them. Pope John had been lying low like a fox, tolerating the Curia's domination of the preparations rather than giving it a pretext for disowning the enterprise, but he showed his colors in his opening address. He had hinted at his views a few months earlier, when he used a ruler to measure one of the draft documents: "Seven inches of condemnation and one of praise: is that the way to talk to the modern world?"[9] He was also impatient with the slow pace of the work. Asked how many people worked at the Vatican, he replied: "About half."[10]

Diagnosed with stomach cancer, he knew he would not see the Council through to its end; but he wanted it to be a joyous event, a celebration of the diversity of the Church, and a series of positive statements. The content would be up to the 2,200 bishops to decide, as he did not want to constrain the discussion. He would watch most of the proceedings on television in his study rather than attend in person, as Pius IX had done at the First Vatican Council (1869–70). "Today," he told the Council, "the Spouse of Christ [the Church] prefers to use the medicine of mercy rather than severity." There was no need to correct "errors," which would vanish by themselves, "like mist before the sun." He told the non-Catholic observers that he felt "comforted" by their presence and that he did not claim any "special inspiration." "I hold to the sound doctrine [that] everything comes from God."[11]

The Council lasted three years and left the Church feeling like Rip Van Winkle, awaking to a new age. The liturgy was turned on its head. The priest would now face the congregation rather than the altar, no longer presiding over some secret ritual. The mass would be said in the local language rather than Latin. And Scripture ("The Liturgy of the Word") was given greater prominence. The Church was no longer to be seen as a structure, so much as "the People of God." The hierarchy was meant to serve the People rather than the other way around. Perhaps the most revolutionary of the Council's documents was the statement on Christian liberty, which put emphasis on the individual conscience. In the aftermath, some theology professors would tell their students that if they felt their religious impulses would be better satisfied in Islam, Judaism, or Buddhism, they would be sinning if they remained Catholics.

To some, this sudden liberty was heady; to others, it was dangerous "subjectivism." Depending on one's training and temperament, the Council created a vast canvas or a yawning void.

The Vatican Council had a profound effect not just on the Catholic laity, but also on religious orders and their attitude to the outside world. In 1967, half the nuns surveyed in Santiago, Chile thought that personal sanctity was more important than serving others and that God expected people to accept their social and economic conditions; only 2 percent saw helping the poor as a reason for entering religious life. Fifteen years later, four in five nuns regarded social service as more important than prayer, and many were already living with the poor.[12]

The Council also gave full vent to the cultural diversity of the Church, which still expresses itself vividly alongside the feeling of universality that unites Catholics. In Kerala, India, churchgoers leave their shoes at the door; the women sit up front, and the men at the back of the church. At the cathedral in Kampala, the capital of Uganda, the faithful break into applause at the most solemn moment of the mass, the consecration of the bread and wine, as their way of affirming its importance. Such behavior would shock American and Indian Catholics – and perhaps also the Tanzanians next door. Sermons in Africa and Latin America can last longer than some masses in the West. That diversity is part of the strength of Catholicism.

Part of the reason for its broad embrace is that, stripped of extravagant devotional practices in some countries, Catholicism is one of the most relaxed religions on earth. Unlike Hindus, Catholics are not weighed down by the consequences of past lives or concern about future incarnations; they have heard of Original Sin but only as a reason for baptism. Lent is a mild discipline compared with the rigors of Ramadan. The faithful are encouraged – but not obliged – to go to confession. Except for tourists trying to enter Roman churches in shorts, no one is told how to dress. There are no guidelines on what to eat or how many times to pray a day. And there are not very many Catholic fundamentalists. Even where the Church has strong views, it is restrained in expressing them; few priests will inveigh against pre-marital sex from the pulpit on a Sunday morning. Would-be outcasts, like gay men and women and divorced Catholics who have remarried outside the Church, do not have to wear identifying marks when they go up to the communion rail. The mother of a Pentecostal I sang with in my African-American parish in Washington, DC in the 1990s summed up the situation crisply: "How can you associate with those Catholics? They're allowed to do anything they want. Drink, dance, gamble . . . The only thing they're not allowed to do is eat meat on Fridays." (Even that was no longer true.) Most Catholics are now gentle believers. They do not take pride in being "born again" – except in the sense of continually trying to refresh their faith. This exposes them to the charge of being tepid or wishy-washy. But in a world of suicide bombers and attacks on abortion clinics, it seems quite forgivable to be wishy-washy.

In fact, compared with what they have in common, the differences between Christian denominations are rather minor. Protestant suspicion of Catholic "idolatry" – the use of visible aids to meditation and prayer – is hardly surprising. The worship of the Blessed Sacrament is indeed strange to people who do not believe in the real presence of God in the Host. (And even lifelong Catholics have felt quite "Protestant" seeing Portuguese women licking the stone steps of holy places, Filipino pilgrims being crucified or flagellated during Holy Week, or Greek Orthodox women throwing their bodies on the Holy Sepulcher in Jerusalem.) Believing that the bread and wine consecrated at mass is actually Christ's body and blood is hard, even for serious Catholics, and many make a conscious effort to revive that faith each time they receive the Eucharist. The difference boils down to how one interprets Christ's words: "Do this in remembrance of me." Catholics take the *doing*, not just the remembering, seriously, while Protestants believe they can only imitate Christ's actions at the Last Supper. Neither interpretation makes one Christian better than another.

Another stumbling block is the supposed "infallibility" of the pope, who is considered to be the direct descendant of the first "head" of the

Christian Church, St Peter. Even the most arrogant holder of that office would not claim to be personally infallible. The doctrine – adopted at the First Vatican Council and bitterly contested by many bishops at the time (who regarded it as overreach by centralizing members of the Roman Curia) – limited the notion to statements on issues of faith and morals made by the pope explicitly as the guardian of the teaching authority of the whole Church. Papal infallibility has been used only twice – once in 1854, to proclaim the "immaculate conception" of the mother of Christ (i.e. that she was born without sin); and then in 1950, to declare that, after her death, she was assumed body and soul into heaven. Neither of these dogmas is central to the Catholic faith or has any detectable bearing on how most Catholics lead their lives.

The very fact that there is such a thing as a pope offends Christians who believe that their churches should be governed "democratically." But formally the pope is "only" the bishop of Rome, the "first among equals," and his authority is derived primarily from tradition and history rather than doctrine. He may be the "absolute" head of the minuscule Vatican State, but he is elected by his peers. Some modern popes have been autocratic, but the forces of decentralization or "collegiality" resurfaced strongly in the twentieth century, reaching their apogee in the 1960s and 1970s, and still color how many educated Catholics view the institution. Benedict XVI (2005–13) suggested that the pope "can only be first together with others," and he was fond of quoting St Bernard of Clairvaux's reminder to an earlier pope: "Remember that you are not the successor of Emperor Constantine but rather the successor of a fisherman."[13] Protestants may not like "to be told what to do;" but neither do many Catholics, and they certainly do not have to agree with everything the pope says. Of course, it would be odd if they did not respect most of his advice, drawn as it is from Scripture, tradition, experience, and common sense; but it is a rare Catholic who feels intellectually captive to developments in Rome. Many American Catholics did not share the Church's firm opposition to the US invasion of Iraq in March 2003; others still balk at its absolute condemnation of capital punishment.

Inevitably, the papacy has been the focus of hopes and disappointment. Even in the modern era, there have been very few pleasant pontiffs. Most have been austere, withdrawn, rigid, intellectual, worried; none has giggled in peaceful merriment like the Dalai Lama. Although he was the first to use the mass media in his annual Christmas radio messages, Pius XII personified this other-worldliness. His sobriety explains in part why many still vilify him for failing to do more to protect the Jews during the Second World War. That he helped to save large numbers of them, and ordered convents and monasteries across Europe to shelter many more, weighs lightly in current historical opinion. But he appears to have been a complex rather than callous man, trying to protect his ability to influence events rather than be sidelined or imprisoned (as his predecessor Pius VII was by Napoleon).

Paul VI (1963–78) is famous for restating the Church's opposition to artificial birth control; in fact, he was a "liberal," although a highly tortured one. John Paul I (1978) seemed a light-hearted pastor rather than a disciplinarian, but he only lived a month. His successor, John Paul II (1978–2005) astounded the world with his vigor and energy (he was fifty-eight when elected) and his flair in front of the cameras. His numerous trips around the globe drew millions to hear him, and his World Youth Days attracted audiences that no rock star could match. But he also irritated millions of other Catholics, hopeful of a more open and egalitarian Church in the wake of the Second Vatican Council, who saw his appointments and pronouncements as a reassertion of control over doctrine, decision-making, and debate. He was arguably harsher than Christ on "social" issues (refusing to give papal decorations to anyone who had been divorced), and he was headstrong in the pursuit of his beliefs. That steadfastness served Eastern Europe well in the twilight years of Communism, but it interfered with his ability to explain rigid Church positions to bewildered Catholics in the West. The last time the world saw him, days before he died, he was beating his fist in the window of his apartment overlooking St Peter's Square, frustrated at not being able to pronounce a sentence into the microphone because of his terrible physical debilitation. Just days later, people would brandish banners with the slogan "Santo

Subito" ("Make Him a Saint Immediately"), but his last public gesture was a reminder of his stubbornness rather than his saintliness. He has been described as conducting a Vatican I pontificate in the language of Vatican II, embracing "consensus" and "dialogue," but dictating the conclusions. "It is all rather Orwellian," wrote the Irish diplomat and author Conor Cruise O'Brien. "And it seems fitting that the pontificate of John Paul II should have included the year 1984."[14]

Elected in 2005, Benedict XVI inherited the frustrations of many Western Catholics, with an additional edge. As prefect of the Sacred Congregation for the Doctrine of the Faith, he had penned most of the positions that offended women, divorced Catholics, social activists, health professionals, gays, and anyone still interested in greater "collegiality" within the institution. The only pope whom almost everyone loved was John XXIII, the first Roman pontiff to describe himself as "the servant of the servants of God" and to address himself not just to Catholics but to "all men" – and, by implication, all women – "of good will." Until the March 2013 election of Pope Francis (who seemed to resemble him in important ways), John's papacy seemed to many older Catholics like an oasis in a theological wasteland.

Yet Catholics are generally united in their respect for the head of their Church. The devout regard him as the "Vicar of Christ" and will not question his opinions, but even the more independently minded cannot dismiss him as a relic of the past. He may disappoint them at times, as real fathers do, but deep down most want to revere him. When John Paul II berated Nicaragua's minister of culture on the airport tarmac in 1983 for being a politician-priest, the man's mother wished the Pope had been more paternal. "But he *did* treat me like a father," the minister answered. "He just didn't treat me like a *mother*."[15] And, as we shall see in Chapter 3, the social teaching of popes has been important to Catholics seeking to promote a fairer distribution of wealth in the world and respect for human rights.

Two matters, however, disturb many Catholics as much as outsiders: the limited role of women in the institution and the Church's great wealth. (Other concerns, like the sexual abuse of minors, are outside the scope of this book.)

With the exception of some Protestant confessions and reformed Jews, no major religion in the world gives women a leading role in its rituals or governance; yet the Catholic Church attracts particular criticism on this point. In a sense, this is only fair, given Catholic teaching on the dignity and equality of human beings. Some early Church writers expressed opinions that now seem crass. Women were the "source" of sin, the worthy descendants of Eve, and a constant challenge to those who would be holy. But the cult of Mary and the growing importance of many women saints overtook this small-mindedness. In the words of a British religious skeptic, William Lecky (1838–1903): "No longer the slave or toy of man, no longer associated only with ideas of degradation or of sensuality, women rose, in the person of the Virgin Mother, into a new sphere . . . [This devotion] is the origin of many of the purest elements of our civilization."[16] As early as the Middle Ages, the Church allowed women to enter religious life, signaling that marriage and raising children were not the only reasons for a woman's existence; as a result, large numbers of (admittedly upper-class) women were able to exercise their talents and have careers as administrators, writers, artists, theologians, and abbesses. Of course, convents could also be dumping grounds for the undesirable, the un-beautiful, and the troublingly intelligent person whom fathers and suitors found difficult to manage.

Since 1965, as vocations to the all-male priesthood have declined in the West and pastors in the developing world have tried hard to keep pace with the expansion of their congregations, women have become more prominent as spiritual models and crucial to the running of many parishes. Yet they remain shut out from a proper role in the leadership and liturgy of the Church. The case against ordaining women is paper-thin, rooted in ancient precedents rather than modern principles, or hanging on confused interpretations of traditional images. One of the supposed obstacles is the attractive metaphor that the Church is the Bride of Christ. How can a woman stand in for the Groom? Just as easily, one would think, as men until now have been included in the image of the Bride.

Women put up with this contradiction as part of their membership in a worldwide community of faith. But senior clerics test that patience at times. In November 2009, the cardinal archbishop of Paris, André Vingt-Trois, was asked on a Catholic radio station about a greater role for women in the Church. He replied that most women did not have the necessary theological training to assume higher responsibilities: "It's not enough to have a skirt; what's important is to have something in your head."[17] And in July 2010, in another breathtaking display of insensitivity, the Vatican declared that ordaining women to the priesthood would be an "ecclesiastical crime" as serious as the sexual abuse of minors. Yet, ironically and persistently, across the developing world – well before Western feminists began laying siege to the all-male hierarchy of the institution – the Catholic Church (and Christianity in general) has been a powerful force in improving the rights, the roles, and the lives of millions of women.

Clerical celibacy – another distinguishing mark of Roman Catholicism – is often seen as the main source of the Church's awkwardness with women. Many Protestants, acquainted with the devoted role of clerical wives, find the Catholic Church intimidatingly male. But this is largely a Western concern. In Africa, Asia, and Latin America, where the Church's celibacy rules are less strictly observed and women's rights movements are still embryonic, concern about gender within the Church is less strong. And most would recognize the great benefits that celibacy – both male and female – has brought to the Church's social mission. Although Protestant missionary couples once served for long periods in a single country, after about 1960 family issues (particularly schooling) appear to have reduced their average stays quite sharply. In remote parts of the developing world, it is usually Roman Catholics who have the most local knowledge, after decades of uninterrupted service. And the largest reserves of energy, expertise, and initiative (not to mention low-cost labor) are the three-quarters of a million nuns still active around the world, a unique feature of the Catholic Church.

What about the Church's wealth? Hard-nosed realists defend it as the basis of the institution's independence and influence. As it is inconceivable that the Vatican's treasures would be sold, most have been valued at zero for accounting purposes. Defenders of the status quo ask their own set of questions: Who would want to buy St Peter's Basilica? How many low-income housing units could be built in its place? Why destroy one of the greatest masterpieces of baroque architecture and decoration, or disperse one of the most splendid art collections on earth, open to the general public six days of the week? "For sheer financial security," a senior Curia official told me, "the Vatican would gladly trade places with an average diocese in Germany. Its total endowment is no more than that of a mid-sized US college. It cannot even pay its own professional staff properly. It could sell some land and treasures, and then what? However, it is true that priests and nuns should try to live soberly and not all do."

Others observe that much of the Church's real wealth is tied up in land and buildings owned by religious congregations around the world. Neither the pope nor the local bishop has any legal claim on it, and most of the related income is used for charitable purposes and the retirement needs of thousands of priests, brothers, and nuns. Many Catholics see the Church's facilities around the world not as a sign of its wealth, so much as a mark of its reach, experience, potential, and commitment to serving others. However, there is no doubt that it can also be corrupting.

The Church's wealth disturbs those who see it as inconsistent with a professed commitment to the poor. Parishioners in Latin America, Africa, and Asia may accept that their pastor has a "family" on the side; some will even welcome it, unless he is seeing several women at once. But they will take exception to his living too comfortably or accumulating unexplained wealth. In some countries, the Church is the largest landowner, and this, too, seems paradoxical, even painful, especially where land reform has been slow and the Church is suspected of complicity with the governing class. As one African priest complained:

I have heard of seminarians who, instead of studying, spend their time looking for a rich patron for the day of their ordination, who will give them a thick envelope. How shameful! I'm not saying that priests should serve only the down-and-outs, or dress in rags and eat nothing but grasshoppers and honey like John the Baptist. What I do denounce is looking for money by any means, losing one's freedom and critical spirit, and no longer proclaiming the Gospel with all one's strength, praising idiots, defending the indefensible.[18]

There is nothing new about the Church's materialism or the efforts to fight it. During Vatican II, a discussion group at the Belgian College in Rome reflected regularly on the "Church of the Poor." One day, a Brazilian bishop recounted how he housed a number of poor families in his episcopal palace. His colleague from Malta was perplexed: "If I did that, what would happen when the Queen of England came to spend the night?"[19] And it is not just poor people who resent the contradiction between ideals and practice. The Fate Bene Fratelli (or Order of Hospitallers) runs medical facilities throughout Europe and the developing world. "They have two passions," a disgruntled former employee told me in Rome. "Financial management – which they excel at – and food. At Easter, they were always very careful to feed frozen lamb to the patients and reserve the fresh lamb for themselves."

In 1965, a French sociologist compared the Church to a rich corporation:

It has the mentality of an owner, with a spectacular abundance of earthly possessions that shock people. Certainly, this reflects the age of the institution. It is organized, focused, sure of itself. These qualities give it its strength but also its particular outlook. It is the opposite of that of the poor, who live in insecurity and isolation and do not know where they are heading. The enduring Church, the Church triumphant, the conquering Church, these are the faces the poor see most often; not the praying Church or the suffering one.[20]

Shortly after those words were written, at a conference of Latin American bishops at Medellín (Colombia) the pope endorsed a "preferential option for the poor" – a roundabout way of saying that the Church had not forgotten its mission to help the distressed. But the institution has not always lived up to its lofty ideals, and reformers are constantly reminding the hierarchy of the continuing need for self-criticism and self-renewal. The Burundian Marguerite Barankitse, who has been described as an African Mother Teresa for establishing a network of shelters for over 10,000 young people, has said that she has two "sick relatives" – her country and the Church.[21] If the pope spent half the year in Rome and the other half in a village in Haiti, Mali, or Laos, public impressions might change.

But amid the debates, the disappointments, and occasionally the distortions, two key strengths of Catholicism are often overlooked. In contrast to some Protestant confessions that stress individual salvation, Catholic tradition emphasizes the importance of collective well-being. Like the southern African principle of *ubuntu* ("People are people because of other human beings"), the Catholic notion of the dignity of the human person is rooted in relations with others. Catholics also care about material progress. Unlike Martin Luther, who believed strongly in the separation of the spiritual and secular "kingdoms," or the Orthodox, who see the world as irreparably broken, the Catholic Church believes in the possibility of creating some semblance of the Kingdom of God on earth. This is not to suggest that all Protestants are pessimistic, or that they are less interested in serving others (the American Social Gospel Movement of the late nineteenth and early twentieth centuries is abundant proof to the contrary); but the importance of social action and an essential optimism about the world have been at the heart of Roman Catholicism. Church efforts to build hospitals and self-sufficient rural communities in northern Mexico in the sixteenth century, the autonomous indigenous settlements set up by the Jesuits in Paraguay in the seventeenth and eighteenth centuries, and the initiatives of missionaries in Africa and Central America to introduce new agricultural practices and vocational training in the nineteenth and twentieth centuries all attest to the importance that the Catholic Church attached to the material – not just the spiritual – well-being of the people it was trying to serve.

The other important aspect of the Catholic tradition is the role of Reason, which John Paul II regarded as "the most marvelous of God's creations." "As the Doctors of the Church and saints have pointed out from the start, Christians are invited to 'believe in order to understand' but also 'to understand in order to believe.' "[22] Even the Church's approach to theology has been rational, drawing not just on Scripture but also on the views and interpretations of successive theologians and popes. Intellectual battles fought in the European Middle Ages are still relevant today. The French theologian Pierre Abélard (1079–1142), who lost his manhood for loving Héloïse, was just as headstrong, arguing that "revealed religion must be busily and constantly supported by reason." The great monastic reformer Bernard of Clairvaux (1090–1153) opposed this view quite vehemently and, in the words of one scholar, would have regarded the work of Thomas Aquinas (1225–74) a century later to be an "exhibition of human pride and intellectual self-sufficiency."[23] Clairvaux lost the argument, quite decisively, but some Protestants have echoed his discomfort in the succeeding centuries. In 1938, the author of a highly influential missionary handbook complained that the Roman Catholic conception of a "natural theology" was an "unpardonable mistake." For him, Divine Revelation remained the bedrock of Christian faith; it was not a "supplement" to Reason but "the crisis of all religion and all human reasoning."[24]

This debate will surprise those who see religion as irrational or even anti-rational; but the importance of Reason in Catholicism is not just long-standing: it has governed Catholic education and behavior profoundly. With the mild exceptions of African-American Catholics moved by gospel music or small "charismatic" groups trying to break out of traditional tones of worship, Catholicism has never had its Holy Rollers. Catholic priests do not ask people living with HIV/AIDS to stop taking their medicines and simply pray to be cured, as some Evangelical Protestants have done in East Africa, because they do not believe blindly in faith healing. In fact, the Church has certified less than a hundred of the thousands of reported cures at Lourdes since the reported apparition of the Virgin Mary there in 1858; and the last case was investigated for fifty years.[25]

In *The Victory of Reason* (2005), the sociologist of religion Rodney Stark has suggested that, with some striking exceptions (like Galileo), Catholicism promoted the development of Western science by believing in a rational God and an orderly universe that could be understood better through proper inquiry. (Even Galileo was condemned not so much for postulating that the sun was the center of the universe, as for changing the standards by which such a theory was to be proved.)[26] In contrast, many Muslims do not believe in natural or immutable laws, as those would imply that God was no longer able to act freely. Stark has made a career of swimming against the stream (he has even defended the Crusades) and he occasionally overstates his case, suggesting that while other civilizations dabbled in astrology and alchemy, Westerners transformed these subjects into astronomy and chemistry; but the core of his argument appears sound. Like others, Stark is impressed by the view of Alfred North Whitehead, the co-author with Bertrand Russell of *Principia Mathematica* (1910–13), who wrote that "The greatest contribution of medievalism to the formation of the scientific movement [was] the inexpugnable belief that there is a secret which can be unveiled [and that the] search into nature could only result in the vindication of the faith in rationality."[27]

The speech that Benedict XVI gave in Regensburg, Germany in September 2006, which raised the hackles of the Muslim world, was devoted essentially to the same argument: Christians had a duty to use their heads. "Not to act in accordance with reason is contrary to God's nature," the Pope said.[28] Such "reasoned faith" is a good inoculation against fundamentalism, which has been the subject of papal condemnations. John Paul II complained that, in countries ruled by zealots, religious "freedom" meant imposing the "true faith" on every citizen.[29] And Benedict XVI suggested that those who want to promote justice and peace should "banish every form of discrimination, intolerance, and religious fundamentalism."[30]

What the Church's engagement with the world and its commitment to rational discourse has meant for developing countries will become plain in the chapters that follow. But its worldview would be almost irrelevant if it did not have the numbers, the structure, and the independence to exercise influence around the globe. In this respect, history has been a friend rather than a scourge.

First, the numbers. More than 17 percent of the world's population, or 1.2 billion people, are Catholic, including almost 90 percent of South Americans, 65 percent of Central Americans, 40 percent of Europeans, 25 percent of North Americans, and 20 percent of Africans. Only 3 percent of Asia is Catholic, but it has more Church members in absolute terms (125 million) than North and Central America combined. The size of the institution is mirrored in the numbers of those in its service: 5,000 bishops, 400,000 priests, another 120,000 studying for the priesthood, and 730,000 nuns, 40 percent of whom work in Africa, Asia, and Latin America, providing the backbone of the Church's services to society. Those services are provided in 140,000 schools, 5,500 hospitals, and 18,000 clinics around the world, not to mention 16,000 homes for the elderly and handicapped, 10,000 orphanages, 12,000 nurseries, and 37,000 centers of informal education.[31] Some 65 percent of Catholic hospitals are located in developing countries, and to this day, one American in six receives medical care at Catholic facilities.[32]

The structure of the Church is also unique. Roman Catholicism is the only religion with a formal leader (elected for life) who is also a head of state. This may seem an historical accident, even anachronism, but it has profound implications for what the Church can do and for the coherence with which it can speak on global issues. With less than half a square kilometer and a population of 900, Vatican City is the smallest state on earth, created in 1929 when Benito Mussolini and Pope Pius XI (1922–39) ended the political stalemate that had been in effect since 1870, when Italian troops occupied Rome. When the United Nations was created in 1945, the Vatican was refused admission (as it had no army for collective peace-keeping efforts), but it began attending UN conferences in the 1950s through its membership of the Universal Postal Union and the International Telecommunication Union, and was later granted permanent observer status. Since the 1960s, the General Assembly has invited all states to participate in world conferences with full voting rights, blurring the distinction between observers and full members. As the UN aims at consensus rather than explicit votes, the Vatican and other small countries have acquired disproportionate influence at such conferences. The 1994 UN Population Conference in Cairo was a painful example. There, the Vatican delegation stood firmly in the way of resolutions designed to promote "safe motherhood." The Church's structure is not just an advantage for Catholics. "Who else but the pope can speak for all of us?" asked former Archbishop of Canterbury George Carey (1991–2002). "He is the only one who can make decisive and symbolic gestures on behalf of all Christians."[33] If so, he speaks for a third of humanity. A good reminder of this was the attention paid, even in the West, to the election of Pope Francis.

Like all global institutions, the Church is undergoing profound change as it tries to adapt not just to an age of instant communications and challenges to traditional authority, but also to rampant materialism, individualism, and skepticism in the West. One line of defense has been a closing of ranks and a "purification" of young clergy, who are expected to re-center Catholic life on spiritual and moral matters rather than "worldly" ones. There has also been a hardening of positions in the Vatican. Its corridors may never have teemed with avuncular clerics like Father Brown, the bumbling hero of G.K. Chesterton's detective series. But younger members of the Curia now seem as if they would be quite at home at military academies like West Point, Sandhurst, or Saint-Cyr, toeing the line, quoting the higher command, avoiding any expression of the slightest personal opinion, their eyes fixed on moving steadily up the ladder. Vatican officials can be as sober and earnest as Iranian mullahs or some of the more long-faced American Evangelicals. Over coffee, genial zealots will suggest that the Church is trying too hard to "please" people. They keep drawing you back to the sacrifice and teachings of Christ. Visitors wanting to discuss the nuts and bolts of individual papal programs, the implications of a recent Curial appointment, or problems with the Church's public image, can be surprised by this focus, as it seems to contradict the hard-headedness and even *realpolitik* one expects in the upper reaches of the hierarchy; but one soon learns to accept it, like a modern corporation brandishing its mission statement. Sometimes it can be disarming. At my first meeting in the Vatican, I asked for reactions to the book outline I had circulated ahead of time. The senior person in the room (a woman) almost gulped: "Well, I was surprised that you would refer to the Church as an 'organization.' Obviously, we have to manage the institutional aspects of the Church's work, but honestly it embarrasses us at times as it distracts us from our mission."[34]

What that mission is – or should be – now provokes some controversy. Five decades after the event, there is even debate about what "really" happened at Vatican II. As a result, it is difficult to tell where the Church is headed. But it is certainly possible to explore its actions in parts of the world where making a distinction between material and spiritual concerns still seems an absolute luxury. Such actions drew heavily on the consciences of thousands of individuals, but just as much on a rich body of Catholic social teaching.

CHAPTER 3

♦ ♦ ♦ ♦ ♦ ♦ ♦ ♦ ♦

Social Teaching: From Caesar to *Centesimus Annus*

CHRIST'S most famous "political" statement – "Render to Caesar the things that are Caesar's and to God the things that are God's" – seems to have been a clever way out of a rhetorical trap rather than real advice; and even if it was intended as guidance, it was sibylline and unsatisfying. Despite claims that the Church's social teaching is firmly rooted in Scripture, there are very few specifics to be found there. In fact, the early Christians were not particularly concerned about the way human societies were organized, as they believed the world was about to end. One sign of this was the destitution of the first Christian community of Jerusalem, which sold its possessions and shared the proceeds without preserving any capital; St Paul had to raise money to help it.[1]

Christ spurned earthly honors and power ("My kingship is not of this world") and he warned against the corrupting effects of material possessions ("It is easier for a camel to go through the eye of a needle than for a rich man to enter the kingdom of God"), but he was realistic ("You always have the poor with you") and apparently more concerned about people's outlook than their income ("Blessed are the poor in spirit for theirs is the kingdom of heaven"). Yet, he cared deeply about what was happening around him. His first public acts were to relieve the suffering of people he encountered. He urged all "masters" to act as "servants," but did not preach revolution or even civil disobedience. On the contrary, he sometimes urged submission: "If any one forces you to go one mile, go with him two." He was not a pacifist either. The incident that made Jesus a national figure – and apparently also a fugitive – was his expelling of the traders and moneychangers from the precincts of the temple.[2] Later, he submitted to Pontius Pilate's authority and his imperial obligation to judge him according to the law.

His disciples followed suit. In the Acts of the Apostles and the Epistles of Paul, we see them obeying the religious and political authorities of the time, so long as doing this did not interfere with their ability to spread Christ's teaching. They urged obedience to just laws and to those charged with enforcing them. And Paul used his Roman citizenship as a shield in carrying out his missions.[3] But, apart from living together and sharing each other's goods in a form of primitive communism, a rich strand of egalitarianism, and the obligation to serve the poor, there is very little in early Christian example to guide modern economic and social policy. In the late twentieth century, Latin America's "liberation theologians" would find more substance in this slender record; however, they would be accused of imputing their own ideas to Scripture, "politicizing" Christ's example, and forgetting that his "kingdom" was to be one of solidarity, without power, money, prestige, groups, or classes.[4] Others would draw different, even bizarre, conclusions, with proponents of a "gospel of prosperity" suggesting that Christ led such a comfortable life that, after his death, Roman soldiers were eager to compete for his superb robe.[5]

The Dutch Protestant Hendrik Kraemer, in his influential book *The Christian Message in a Non-Christian World* (1938), was categorical about the limited political implications of Scripture:

> Although Christianity is exceedingly ethical – more ethical than any other religion – and although it is concerned with a "Kingdom" and with a new order of life, in the New Testament there is no

definite guidance in regard to the political, social, cultural, and economic spheres of life ... The ever-changing character of historical and cultural life requires ever-changing programs. There is universal agreement as to the value of man, the sanctity of righteousness, etc. [but such abstract agreement] does not carry far.[6]

Claims about the positive impact of Christianity on Western society have also been disputed, with one critic pointing out caustically that "if our modern civilization was the outcome of Christianity, the length of time between the cause and effect had no parallel in history."[7] In fact, by the standards of the time, the Roman Empire in which the first Christians lived was relatively enlightened, humane, and effective. One black mark against it was slavery, which affected about 200,000 people in Rome alone (a fifth of the city's population), most of them Teutonic and Slavic captives of war. Stoic and Epicurean thinkers argued for improving their conditions, and some Roman statesmen called for the practice to be abolished; but no Christian did. Neither Christ, nor St Paul, nor any of the early Church Fathers made an issue of it – St Augustine (354–430) even defended slavery as a just punishment for sin – but they treated slaves as equals within their own community, once they were baptized.[8]

After that, the record is mixed and the Church's influence was not very decisive. One religious order, the Trinitarians, was set up in 1198 explicitly to redeem slaves in Muslim lands, particularly North Africa; by the seventeenth century they had released 900,000 and were running hospitals for them in Algeria and Morocco. The Spanish Jesuit Peter Clavier (1580–1654) cared for 300,000 slaves in his lifetime in Cartagena (Colombia). Popes in five successive centuries – Pius II (1402), Paul III (1537), Urban VIII (1639), Benedict XIV (1741), and Gregory XVI (1839) – condemned slavery, a sure sign that they were not being listened to. Even the Roman Inquisition objected to the use of slaves (1686). Yet the papacy itself was still using them in its Mediterranean galleys up to the French Revolution (1789); the British Society for the Propagation of the Gospel (an Anglican body) owned slaves in the West

Indies as late as 1830; and the Portuguese bishop of Luanda (Angola) was baptizing captives bound for Brazil in the 1870s, forty years after the British had banned the international trade in human beings.[9] If the Christian record on slavery is so poor, some wonder why we should expect a clear connection between Church teaching and any elements of modern civilization.

In fact, social issues appear to have been much less prominent in early Christian philosophy than were matters of personal morality. The Church "Fathers" Augustine and John Chrysostom (347–407) preached about the "corruption" of riches and the "virtues" of poverty, but – like Christ – seem to have been more concerned with a spirit of materialism than differences in people's incomes.[10] It was medieval thinkers like Thomas Aquinas in the thirteenth century who first considered specific issues like property rights systematically. And it was not until the Italian Renaissance that the renegade Dominican friar Girolamo Savonarola set up the first "Christian" republic in Florence; it lasted only four years (1494–98). In the words of an eminent Anglican historian, "that legacy of a particular and rather frightening Christian vision of reform has become one of the most important political ideas of the modern world."[11]

Between the sixteenth and the eighteenth centuries, drawing on ancient Greek tales and the Acts of the Apostles, writers like Thomas More (1478–1535) and François Fénelon (1651–1715) imagined Utopian societies ruled by a philosophy that the Russian revolutionary Lenin would later adopt: "From each according to his ability, to each according to his need." Around the world, inspired by these writings or by the sheer force of circumstance, priests and nuns conducted real-life experiments in Christian living – with mixed results.[12] In South America in the eighteenth century, first in Brazil and then in the southeastern Spanish territories, Jesuits tried to protect their Indian converts in large structured settlements called "Reductions," but treated their protégés so paternalistically that no local leaders emerged when the Jesuits were expelled from the Americas in 1767: as a result, the communities fell apart.[13] The Sisters of St Joseph de Cluny and later the Franciscan Missionaries of Mary experimented with "Christian villages," like the one set up in French Guyana by Anne-Marie Javouhey (1779–1851), commissioned by the French navy to look after slaves freed by their vessels on the high seas.[14] But these were disparate rather than connected efforts and, beyond monasteries and convents, there was no equivalent to the Amish and Mennonite traditions of community life that would survive into the twenty-first century.

This does not mean that Catholic theologians tiptoed around political theory. Curiously for an institution run like an absolute monarchy, the Church long argued for limits to royal power. Aquinas was quite blunt on the subject: "A king who is unfaithful to his duty forfeits his claim to obedience. It is not rebellion to depose him, for he is himself a rebel whom the nation has the right to put down."[15] For expressing similar views, Francisco de Vitoria (1483–1546), Robert Bellarmine (1542–1621), and Francisco Suárez (1548–1617) had their books burnt publicly in London under King James I (1603–25). At the other end of the spectrum, the Church was also uncomfortable with what it regarded as the "new absolutism" of individual freedom proposed by John Locke (1632–1704), Jean-Jacques Rousseau (1712–78), and John Stuart Mill (1806–73), which it thought could turn into "self-love" without regard for neighbor.[16] And popes were inconsistent. Innocent III actually annulled the Magna Carta of 1215 (not that his opinion affected anything); and the Jesuits were suppressed between 1773 and 1815 in part because Latin American landowners had complained about their defense of Indian rights.[17]

The nineteenth century was a period of rapid economic, political, and technological progress in Europe and North America, but the Church resisted it. Gregory XVI (1831–46) regarded science and modern thought as a "wild boar" that could destroy "the vineyard of the Lord."[18] He opposed elected assemblies, freedom of the press, freedom of conscience, and the separation of Church and state, describing representative government as a "pernicious opinion."[19] Even railways and gaslight were introduced slowly into the Papal States. Pius IX (1846–78) was so rattled by the new ideas that he declared "modernism" itself an evil in his 1864 Syllabus of Errors. One of the reasons, no doubt, was that three years after he became pope, his secretary was shot dead by revolutionaries and he had to flee his palace disguised as a servant. Even in death, he could not escape the modernists: during his funeral procession, irate Romans threw mud at the cortège and tried to throw his coffin into the Tiber.[20]

Perhaps because he never had to face down a bloodthirsty mob, Leo XIII (1878–1903) was more open to new ideas and technology. "Does not something like the spark of the Creator manifest itself in man," he asked, "when he summons the light and orders it to illuminate the darkness of the night?"[21] A few days after Leo's election, a Frenchman named Isaac Pereire wrote to him to suggest that the revolutionary movements sweeping across Europe were aimed at protecting the oppressed, and that the Church should take a leading role in the ferment rather than worry about a wave of secularism.[22] But it took time for Leo to warm to the idea. In 1881, he conceded that political leaders "may in certain cases be chosen by the will and decision of the multitude, without impugning Catholic doctrine."[23] Ten years later, however, he wrote an encyclical that seemed to set the Church on a different course.

One of the great ironies about *Rerum Novarum* (1891) is that Leo was immediately denounced as a "socialist" by those who felt he had gone too far in defending the interests of the workers. Certainly, he used language that might have heartened Karl Marx. "Working-men," the Pope wrote, "have been surrendered, all isolated and helpless, to the hard-heartedness of employers and the greed of unchecked competition." Another burden on the poor was the "rapacious usury [high interest rates] . . . still practiced by covetous and grasping men." As a result, "a small number of very rich men have been able to lay upon the teeming masses of the laboring poor a yoke little better than that of slavery itself."

But fifty years after the French socialist Pierre-Joseph Proudhon (1809–65) described property as "theft," Leo XIII also spoke up for the importance of private ownership. Most of his arguments were not particularly strong – that God gave the earth to all men; that the family existed before the community or the state; and that most countries already protected private property. But his main fear was about what would happen if it was abolished: "The sources of wealth themselves would run dry, for no one would have any interest in exerting his talents or his industry; and that ideal equality about which [socialists] entertain pleasant dreams would in reality be the leveling down of all to a like condition of misery and degradation."

The encyclical was a great balancing act. Many commentators suggested simplistically that the Pope was charting a "third way" between those who felt all productive property should be owned by "millionaires" and those who thought it should belong to the state. (The Church believed that landed property, at least, should be distributed widely among many small owners.) Yet few capitalists or socialists would have recognized themselves in the polar opposites portrayed in this argument. And the practical meaning of papal sentiments was hard to perceive in an environment where industrial labor – not agriculture – was bearing the brunt of modernization and competition.

More central to the Pope's compromise was a call for "moral" behavior, an avoidance of violence and oppression, respect for both rich and poor, and a just sharing of society's "surplus." The state's role was to promote "public well-being and private prosperity" and "safeguard the welfare and the comfort of the working classes," who had no other means of defending themselves. "The object of governing a State is not the advantage of the ruler, but of the ruled."

The encyclical opposed child labor, the employment of women in unsuitable occupations, and excessive taxation; it urged the introduction of a "living wage" (enough to support a "frugal and well-behaved working-man" and his family), the acquiring of land by working people, and – fifty years into the life of the labor movement – the setting up of trade unions. Preferably, these should be Christian organizations, as they were more likely to avoid the internal "strife which ever accompanies poverty when unresigned and unsustained by religion." The encyclical ended with a gentle call to arms: "Every minister of holy religion must bring to the struggle the full energy of his mind and all his power of endurance . . . They should never cease to urge upon men of every class, upon the high-placed as well as the lowly, the Gospel doctrines of Christian life [and] try to arouse in others charity, the mistress and the queen of all virtues."[24]

The international reaction to the encyclical ranged from surprise, through bemusement, to relief. Until his election in 1878, Leo XIII had had an undistinguished career, rising steadily through the hierarchy on the strength of his seniority and capacity not to rock the boat. Like a highly popular pope eighty years later, John XXIII (1958–63), no one expected much of him. Some worried that his eighteen previous encyclicals showed reactionary tendencies. But, like John XXIII, who convoked the momentous Second Vatican Council in the 1960s, Leo seems to have been pushed by circumstance into rising beyond his modest past. *Rerum Novarum* transformed his reputation, strengthening his spiritual and social authority and that of the Church as a whole. The hero of George Bernanos's *Diary of a Country Priest* summed up the reaction: "We felt the earth tremble under our feet. This simple idea that work is not a commodity subject to the law of supply and demand, and that one must not speculate on salaries, on the life of men, like wheat, shook our consciences."[25]

This admiration was not confined to Catholics. The prominent British journalist and social reformer William Thomas Stead (later to die on the *Titanic*) eulogized Pope Leo in 1903:

He had no fellow while he lived, and in his death he had no peer. [He] spent his life – the whole ninety-three years of it – in an honest, weariless attempt to bring heaven down from the skies, so that even here and now the toil-worn children of men should realize something of the peace and joy of Paradise. Protestant, Freethinker and Catholic sorrowed as brothers at the tomb of their common father.[26]

For Stead, *Rerum Novarum* was a "new declaration of the Rights of Man" and the Pope had used the whole force of his influence to turn the Church into "an instrument for improving the condition of the people."[27] Leo had demonstrated "the immense possibilities for good that lie latent in what might be termed the central headquarters of the Intelligence Department of the moral sense of mankind [i.e. the Vatican]."[28]

Of course, the encyclical did not emerge from a vacuum. In 1887–88, Cardinal James Gibbons of Baltimore headed off a papal condemnation of the first American trade union (The Knights of Labor), and in England in 1889 Cardinal Henry Manning supported the London Dock Strike. A benevolent French industrialist, Léon Hamel, organized annual workers' pilgrimages to Rome during the 1880s. The controversial German theologian Hermann Schell (1850–1906) argued that God was fully present in one's own life only when one struggled to transform society through Christian values.[29] And the new German emperor, Kaiser Wilhelm II, tried to seize the initiative on the "social problem" by inviting the Pope to a Labor Congress in Berlin in March 1890. Leo declined, but felt added pressure to develop a Church position on the subject.

The call to social reform extended beyond Roman Catholicism. At Cambridge in 1894, the Anglican bishop of Durham preached that the human person "cannot reach his own perfection except through social action … Wealth in every form, material, intellectual, moral, has to be administered for the common good."[30] At the same time, many of the great social reformers of nineteenth-century Europe – those who struggled for the vote, national education, and the emancipation of women – were not Christian at all, but were atheists or deists at best. In the words of a disgruntled ex-Catholic, "It was only when the majority of us were convinced that war is evil, that the poor must be uplifted and so on, that the Churches discovered that the ethic of Jesus implied these things."[31] Robert Owen (1771–1858), the founder of the British cooperative movement, opposed organized religion for putting too much emphasis on individual responsibility; he believed that human faults were the product of bad institutions and a poor environment that could be corrected through education.[32]

But the Church's new views were momentous. One of the keenest promoters of the *Rerum Novarum* message was a French priest named Jean Léon Dehon (1843–1925), who worked in the northern industrial town of St Quentin. Calling himself the Pope's "little phonograph," introducing young priests to a broader social ministry, and mobilizing the Catholic vote in the 1898 elections, he helped foster a whole generation of French Catholics concerned with political and social issues. When the Pope and his entourage began worrying that they had unleashed a political genie in the ranks of the clergy, Dehon the "phonograph" continued to blare out a message that may have grated on papal ears. In a sense, he was prefiguring the heated debate fifty years later on the subject of "worker priests," committed to living and working with the industrial poor and even dressing and behaving like them so as to be more credible. The priest, he argued, must intervene in "the current social disorder," not just to fend off socialism, but also from "a strict sense of justice and charity and the faithful fulfilling of his pastoral mission."[33] He was ahead of his time. For the most part, the Church in France in the nineteenth century was more interested in training a pious clergy than in confronting social issues. But Dehon's views appear to have had a profound effect on French Catholic opinion, as well as on the sense of purpose that many young clergy carried to their new parishes and to the missionary fields of Africa.

In more remote parts of the Catholic world, the implications of Leo's encyclical took time to percolate through. Well into the 1930s, the bishops of Costa Rica were opposing strikes by the country's banana workers, fearing the onset of communism. It was not until the 1940s that a plucky archbishop in the capital cooperated with a progressive government to help introduce a welfare state.[34]

The United States had a mixed reaction to the encyclical. Although there were Catholic signatures on the Declaration of Independence (Charles Carroll of Maryland) and the American Constitution (Thomas

Fitzsimons of Pennsylvania), most Catholics kept their heads low, knowing they were associated with the forces of reaction and monarchy that the colonists had rebelled against. But, as immigration increased the numbers of Irish, Germans, and Italians, Catholics went from appearing "backward-looking" to being suspected radicals, importing dangerous notions from the Old World. To fend off such criticism, the Church tried calming some of its livelier spirits. In 1887, a priest named Edward McGlynn was excommunicated for spreading the views of Henry George, who opposed private property and wanted a "single tax." In 1889, two years before *Rerum Novarum*, the Vatican condemned George's writings; but shortly after, steadier minds prevailed and McGlynn's excommunication was reversed. Said a Curia official: "There is no right or wrong implied in the question. If you people in the U.S. want [a] single tax, why take it; it is nobody's business but your own."[35]

Back in France, in the course of an extraordinary life, one man was to extend the principles of *Rerum Novarum* to what were soon to be termed the "emerging" nations. A native of St Malo (Brittany), Louis-Joseph Lebret (1897–1966) served in the French navy during the First World War, and then entered the Dominican order, one of several religious congregations re-establishing themselves after the wave of anti-clericalism in France earlier in the century. In the late 1920s, for health reasons, he returned to Brittany, which was in the throes of the Depression and reeling from the collapse of the cod fisheries. Unemployment was widespread, as were malnutrition and tuberculosis; there was no system of social security; and quite naturally, religion was being abandoned in favor of the Communist Party. Lebret went straight to work – "Religion is about life," he said[36] – and took a lead in strengthening various fishermen's unions along the coast. With another priest, Ernest Lamort (1890–1958) from Cancale, he drew attention to the issues facing France's fishing industry in a stream of studies and reports that resulted in the setting-up of formal channels for consulting fishermen on national policy.

Unlike most of the Catholic hierarchy, Lebret and his "St Malo Movement" supported the left-wing Popular Front government (1936–38), which introduced fixed working hours and paid holidays. Branded a "Red" by ship-owners in St Malo, and distrusted even by some who listened to him preach in the cathedral there, Lebret was being true to the principle of the "common good" enunciated by another Dominican, Thomas Aquinas, centuries before him. Aquinas fascinated him in another way. Just as the thirteenth-century theologian had incorporated the "pagan" philosopher Aristotle into his thinking, so Lebret wanted modern theology to reflect the latest advances in the physical, biological, and social sciences – and to confront the challenge of Marxism. He was said to spend fifteen minutes a day reading the Fathers of the Church and three-quarters of an hour studying *Das Kapital*.[37] To support the cause, he set up an association called Économie et Humanisme.

In 1941, he was about to publish a colleague's book on "the meaning of Marxism" when the Holy Office forbade Catholics from joining the Communist Party and defending Marxist thought. Lebret issued the book anyway, as it had received all the necessary permissions (known as *imprimaturs*) from senior Church figures. At first it was greeted with total silence; but as the months wore on it created a backlash, and Lebret was summoned to explain himself before the head of the Dominican order in Switzerland. According to one French bishop, the book lacked "the balance of a Christian and the clarity of a Frenchman" and the Vatican instructed the French hierarchy to look into its procedures for issuing *imprimaturs*.[38]

Accused of going too far in marrying Christian and Marxist values, Lebret was forced to take a new tack. He now studied British, Scandinavian, and Dutch social democracy and began linking Christianity and international development. He wanted to listen to "ordinary" people – who "in fact are the only ones who really know what is going on." He contrasted their "rich" knowledge with "our cacophony of formulas drawn from books" and wanted them actively involved in finding solutions to economic and social issues.[39] His faith in the "masses" may now seem naïve to some, but it was faithful to Catholic ideals of human dignity and responsibility, and better than the heavy-handed technocratic approach being taken by many governments at the time. He was a precursor of "participatory approaches" in development planning, and in a long series of overseas consulting assignments in Brazil, Chile, Colombia, Peru, Senegal, and Vietnam in the 1950s and 1960s he advised governments on how to use local knowledge to combat poverty.

His international experience attracted interest in Rome and he was made an adviser and confidant to Cardinal Giovanni Battista Montini, the Vatican secretary of state, who was to become the next pope. It was Montini, with John XXIII's support, who insisted that the Second Vatican Council prepare a document spelling out the Church's relations with the "modern world," and it was Montini again (as Paul VI) who appointed Lebret as one of the outside experts for that task. His influence on the resulting document *Gaudium et Spes* (Joy and Hope) is unmistakable, and he was also involved in the drafting of Paul VI's 1967 encyclical *Populorum Progressio* (The Development of Peoples), which appeared the year after Lebret died.

For Lebret, charity alone would not help the poor. He wanted to see changes in economic and political structures and a new international order capable of promoting justice among individuals and nations.[40] At a meeting of the United Nations Conference on Trade and Development (UNCTAD) in Geneva in 1964, he may have looked back ironically to the day he had defended himself before the Master of the Dominican Order. As Paul VI's representative at the conference, he was given a standing ovation. The only other person to be accorded that honor was Fidel Castro's envoy, Che Guevara.[41]

While Lebret was organizing fishermen, issuing pamphlets, and doing international consulting work, the Church was adapting its social teaching to new developments. Since 1931, popes have tried to mark every tenth anniversary of *Rerum Novarum* with a new statement of the Church's economic and social views. In doing do, they have been careful to stick to broad principles and avoid making specific recommendations, although – in some people's minds – Paul VI came dangerously close to doing so in 1967.

The first of these modern encyclicals, *Quadragesimo Anno*, issued on the fortieth anniversary of *Rerum Novarum* in 1931, was not widely read outside theological circles, but Pius XI (1922–39) introduced a number of key principles. The first was the notion of *subsidiarity*: "It is an injustice, a grave evil and a disturbance of right order for a larger and higher organization to arrogate to itself functions which can be performed efficiently by smaller and lower bodies." A second principle was the right of people with similar interests to form associations to promote the common good. A third (which the Pope labeled "social justice" or "social charity," and would later be called "solidarity") required the state to protect citizens from the "headstrong and vehement power" of the market: "Free competition, though within certain limits just and productive of good results, cannot be the ruling principle of the economic world."[42]

Much of the encyclical now appears dated, including its preoccupation with attracting working people back to the Church from socialism; but the three principles that Pius XI stated in 1931 would endure into the twenty-first century. Although he was never regarded as a progressive, the Pope could occasionally stand up to vested interests. The year before the encyclical, a number of French industrial barons complained to him about the bishop of Lille, Achille Liénart, who had taken sides with unionized workers in an industrial dispute; Pius XI responded by making the 46-year-old Liénart the youngest cardinal in the world.[43]

Pius XII (1939–58) has been accused of speaking and writing too much, and of being incoherent as well.[44] None of his forty encyclicals could be described as "social," and only a few touched on world issues, like the war in Palestine (1948) and the Soviet crushing of the Hungarian uprising (1956). But in his 1939 Christmas address, he anticipated the charter of the United Nations by stating "five premises for peace" – the right to life and independence of all nations, gradual disarmament, international judicial institutions, respect for ethnic minorities, and a sense of responsibility based on a "hunger and thirst for justice."[45] His opinions on international issues are significant because of how backward some of his other pronouncements now seem. In a dyspeptic encyclical letter of 1950, entitled *Humani Generis* (or otherwise "False Trends in Modern Teaching"), Pius complained about an "unwholesome itch for modernity," described some ecumenical thinkers as "hot-headed supporters of appeasement," and referred to the "bulwarks of the true Faith." "Let those fall, and the world may indeed be united, but only in a common ruin."[46]

In a radio address on the Feast of Pentecost in June 1941, the fiftieth anniversary of *Rerum Novarum*, against the backdrop of war, the Pope appealed for a "just distribution of goods" in the world and suggested that a nation's wealth should be measured not by abundance but by its ability to support "the fair personal development" of its citizens.[47] In March 1951, in a radio address to Spanish workers, he called *Rerum Novarum* the "Magna Carta" of labor rights and suggested that most social legislation in the "world" – apparently meaning the West – was essentially an application of Church principles. He renewed Leo XIII's call for a "just wage" and appealed again for a "better distribution of natural wealth," while also suggesting that class harmony, sacrifice and mutual respect, and a simple life were crucial to social progress.[48]

As radio and television turned popes into "personalities," the impact of their words on social issues was linked to their reputations. John XXIII was in a class of his own. Pius XII had been as austere as a pope could be (there is certainly no anthology of his collected wit), but his successor was the polar opposite: affable, outspoken, and ready to set the cat among the pigeons. Already, as a young man, he had written about Christ's preference for "the disinherited, the weak, and the oppressed," anticipating the major theme of Latin American "liberation theology" by about fifty years. He was also a *bon vivant*, down to earth, and capable of seeing the ridiculous in life. In the late 1940s, as papal ambassador in Paris, he could be spotted at diplomatic receptions with a cigarette in one hand and a glass of champagne in the other. On one occasion, a woman is said to have come up to him with a very low-cut dress, mountainous breasts, and a crucifix suspended between them. "Quel Golgotha [What a Calvary]!" he said wickedly.[49]

His encyclical *Mater et Magistra* (Mother and Teacher) (1961) was long and solemn, like a treatise rather than a letter, covering matters as detailed as industry, farming, taxation, credit, social insurance, and foreign aid. But its central claim – "*Individual human beings are the foundation, the cause, and the end of every social institution*" – was all the more powerful because of the kind of human being John was known to be. This was also the first encyclical to refer to gaps in wealth among nations, to call for the free movement of goods, capital, and people across borders, and to demand respect for the individuality, traditions, and customs of poorer nations. In helping the less fortunate, the Pope said, "the more advanced communities . . . must beware of forcing these people into their own national mold . . . Every nation has its own genius, its own qualities, springing from the hidden roots of its being. The wise development of that genius does no harm." He also reflected on the Church's positive impact around the world, with new converts "feeling obliged to improve their own institutions and environment." The Church's social teaching, he said, was "an integral part of the Christian conception of life," demanding a commitment to improving – not withdrawing from – this "passing world."[50] In *Pacem in Terris* (Peace on Earth) in 1963 he suggested that the principal role of government was to safeguard human rights, borrowing words from St Augustine: "Take away justice, and what are kingdoms but mighty bands of robbers?"[51] He appealed for an end to the arms race and the banning of nuclear weapons, for greater assistance for poor countries, and for the creation of a worldwide "political authority" to promote the common good (implying that the United Nations had neither the power nor the resources to do that properly).

So what did Catholic social teaching amount to at this stage? Most encyclicals repeated the general nostrums of "our illustrious predecessors," suggested innocently that governments could slow down structural changes like the disappearance of the family farm, and called for a strong state role, while warning against socialism. Newcomers to papal encyclicals could find them circuitous, their wording worthy of a Grecian oracle, but habitués could spot changes in nuance that were "electrifying."[52]

Some commentators regarded *Mater et Magistra* as a "bombshell" – the Paris newspaper *Le Monde* announced on its front page that the "hegemony" of the German Jesuits at the Vatican was over (apparently, more down-to-earth Frenchmen had taken over). The encyclical's approving reference to "socialization" – the coming together of citizens to advance social causes – was confused with "socialism" and condemned by the American Right.[53] And behind the placid surface, bruising battles were being won and lost. The American Jesuit Philip Land helped draft a statement on "Justice in the World" suggesting that the Church should not speak out on the subject unless it was seen to be practicing justice itself. One cardinal objected that the Church did not commit injustices and, when the final document included the passage, another told Land that he was "destroying the Church."[54]

Paul VI's *Populorum Progressio* in 1967 extended the Church's social teaching to the problems of the world at large. Although he was never a media "star" like John XXIII or John Paul II, his views did carry weight, as he was the first pope in history to travel outside Europe: to Africa, Latin America, Australia, India, the Holy Land, and New York (to address the UN General Assembly). According to French Cardinal Paul Poupard, the Pope wanted to contrast a world in need and a "Christian" world (the West) drowning in abundance. "Years later," Poupard wrote in 2008, "I still hear the bitter cry of a Chinese priest, 'You have kept Christ for yourselves and left us the Cross.' "[55]

Paul VI did not mince words. "The world is sick," he said in the encyclical, referring to the lack of brotherhood among people and nations.[56] In one of the simplest definitions of development ever, he recognized that human beings sought "to do more, know more, and have more, in order to be more."[57] This meant promoting the good of every person and the whole person. Although they could be helped or hindered by their education and those around them, people were responsible for using their own intelligence and free will, and for helping others do the same. He restated the Church's long-standing position that the right to private property was not absolute and that it should be subordinated to the common good. This led him to approve of the expropriation of land from large private estates in developing countries that were not being managed properly, and to condemn the export of capital by the rich "purely for their own advantage." He called for "fair trade" rather than free trade, especially where differences in economic capacity put countries at a disadvantage in the open market. And, while discouraging it, he opened the door to political violence. "Except where there is manifest, long-standing tyranny which would do great damage to fundamental personal rights and dangerous harm to the common good of the country," revolutionary uprisings, he said, engendered new injustices.[58] Many people in Latin America felt that the elaborate caveat applied to them.

For some, *Populorum Progressio* marked the beginning of a conscious effort by the Church in developing countries to become more involved in economic and social issues. The 1968 conference of Latin American bishops at Medellín (Colombia) applied the encyclical to regional circumstances, adopting a term ("a preferential option for the poor") which now seems relatively tame, but was tantamount to a declaration of divorce from the Church's traditional allies in the political, business, and military establishments. In Africa, individual dioceses began establishing justice and peace commissions to focus on development issues, modeled on the Pontifical Council of the same name set up in Rome in 1967. But progress was slow. In 1981, African bishops admitted that they had not done enough to promote Catholic social teaching.[59]

John Paul II (1978–2005) issued three anniversary encyclicals, two in memory of Leo XIII (1981 and 1991), and one to mark the twentieth anniversary of *Populorum Progressio* (in 1987). He was unable to deliver the first of these, as he was shot two days beforehand. That assassination attempt and his fearless confrontation of totalitarian regimes in Eastern Europe raised him to a level of moral leadership almost without parallel in modern history. As an American journalist observed near the end of his reign, the Pope never received the Nobel Peace Prize, but it hardly mattered as he seemed larger than the prize itself.[60] He was a complex man – "filling our public spaces during his visits," one Latin American bishop told me, "but emptying the hearts of our young people because his moral teaching was so hard to follow."[61] However, young – and older – people listened to him on international issues.

He also had a human side that was not always evident in his public appearances. Late in his papacy, an American priest in his entourage spotted a beggar on the steps of a church in central Rome. The man looked familiar and turned out to be an old friend, also a priest, who had fallen on hard times. Lending him some clothes, the American invited the beggar-priest to dinner with the Pope the following week. After the meal, John Paul II motioned to everyone except the newcomer to leave the room. Twenty minutes later, as he emerged from the dining room, he was asked what had happened. "You won't believe this," he told his friend, "but the Pope asked me to hear his confession. Then, he instructed me to resume my priestly duties and minister to the beggars of Rome."[63] Almost instinctively, readers of John Paul II's encyclicals sensed this humanity and humility in him, which gave his views a power greater than any catechism.

But none of his encyclicals would add much of interest to developing countries, and they became vaguer and more conservative in some readers' eyes. *Laborem Exercens* (1981) was an elaborate essay on the nature and dignity of work. Borrowing from liberation theology, *Sollicitudo Rei Socialis* (1987) talked about "structures of sin," implying the need for radical social reforms. The Pope's even-handed criticism of communism and capitalism led the US ambassador to the Holy See to complain that John Paul II was putting cancer and a common cold into the same basket.[63] And the 1987 encyclical contained a moving summary of Church teaching on human dignity: "Solidarity helps us to see the 'other' – whether a person, people or nation – not just as some kind of instrument, with a work capacity and physical strength to be exploited at low cost and then discarded when no longer useful, but as our 'neighbor,' a 'helper,' to be made a sharer, on a par with ourselves, in the banquet of life to which all are equally invited by God."[64]

Quite appropriately for the hundredth anniversary of Leo XIII's encyclical, *Centesimus Annus* (1991) was the most wide-ranging and sophisticated letter yet, and the first to be taken seriously by international organizations. The World Bank arranged a detailed discussion of the document at its Paris office, attended by numerous ambassadors. Because it described the positive aspects of the market system, the Catholic American thinker Michael Novak thought it had "exploded across the Roman sky like a sonic boom."[65] But it was as toothless as *Rerum Novarum* had been daring a century before. It still swam against the stream, resisting Western triumphalism following the collapse of the Berlin Wall, criticizing socialism and capitalism alike; but it was more a summary of existing teaching than a new departure. This may have been deliberate. As a Vatican insider who wished to remain anonymous told me: "A cynical reading of the evolution of the Church's social teaching is that with the collapse of communism in Europe, the risk of 'losing' the working class to socialism receded and the institution no longer had to appeal to anti-capitalist emotions." But the central principles of that teaching remained powerful. "It was not just a prop," says Julian Filochowski, the long-time head of the Catholic Agency for Overseas Development (CAFOD), the Catholic charity for England and Wales. "Its principles were clear. All men and women were equal in God's eyes, members of the same family (no one could be excluded), and within that family the poor were to receive particular attention. In our work, we progressed from charity to development and then from development to justice. Promoting justice was part of being faithful to the Gospel."[66]

Not everyone, however, found the Church's views enchanting. Peter Bauer, the iconoclast of received opinion on development, described Catholic social thinking as "immoral" and "incompetent," and said that Paul VI, in particular, had surrendered blindly to intellectual fashion on foreign aid, land reform, debt cancellation, and international commodity agreements. Bauer also objected to the idea that wealthy countries were somehow responsible for the misery of others. To believe that was to promote envy rather than equity among nations, which was un-Christian and dangerous. He also objected to the notion (in the 1967 encyclical) that governments always intervene "with care for justice and with devotion to the common good."[67] An American Catholic, Michael Novak, was just as withering, believing that democratic capitalism was the only path to "modest" world progress and that the Church had adopted a "preferential option for the state."[68]

At the other end of the spectrum, left-wing critics thought the Church's views on society too neat, even naïve, appealing to the good will of the elite rather than backing a grassroots struggle for justice. And not all clergy were in step with papal teaching. Benoît Bouchard, a colorful Québécois missionary in Côte d'Ivoire, told two researchers in 1986 what he thought of the Church's "social mission":

> I didn't come here to do material things. To do that, I could have stayed home! I'm here to teach catechism to young people, not till the soil. Others will do that better. I've spent twenty-five years trying to help Africans, but helping does not mean doing other people's work. My predecessor imported a tractor, which he drove instead of the farmers. I've played Santa Claus in my time, but now I've learned to act differently.[69]

But most priests, brothers, nuns, and lay activists in the developing world, particularly after the Second Vatican Council (1962–65), appear to have been fortified by the Church's social teaching, including its strong commitment to human rights. On this subject, most historians acknowledge the importance of Thomas Aquinas's teaching on the dignity of the human person; but few credit Christian sources exclusively, preferring to trace the roots of modern rights back to older faiths like Stoicism and Confucianism as well. However, the Catholic role in formalizing human rights law in the middle of the twentieth century was striking. One of the first prominent uses of the phrase was in Pius XI's encyclical *Mit brennender Sorge* (1937), in which he condemned Nazi attitudes to religion. "Man as a person," wrote Pius, "possesses rights that he holds from God and which must remain beyond the reach of anything that would tend to deny them."[70] The Church's tendency to think of society as an "organic" system with specific but honorable roles for everyone might have led to a kind of Christian caste system; but Church teaching on the equality of all human beings prevented that. In the words of the British economist Barbara Ward, "Between the Brahman refusing food because the shadow of an untouchable has crossed it and the Christian king setting aside his crown to kneel and wash the beggar's feet is a gulf so vast that no superficial resemblance of class or social or economic structure can bridge it."[71]

The most important Catholic figure in the human rights debate was Jacques Maritain (1882–1973), a French theologian and philosopher who was marooned in New York when the Germans overran France in May 1940. In 1942, at the request of the US Office of War Information and General de Gaulle, Maritain wrote a book called *Christianity and Democracy* (1942), copies of which were printed on Bible paper and dropped by parachute over France by US planes. The basic message was straightforward: "The notion of democracy is the lay expression of the Christian ideal."[72] His exile in the US made him a fervent admirer of American civic values: "One of the springs of American civilization is the dignity of each person in everyday life, and it is to achieve that dignity more completely, not just on their own soil, but also everywhere else on earth, that they have accepted the war, and begun to build a new world."[73] Drawing on his American experience, Maritain argued that a society with fervent religious beliefs could also embrace strong civic values, and that "materialism" and "secularism" were not the necessary outcomes of an open society.

After the war, he worked with Julian Huxley, the first director of the UN Educational, Scientific and Cultural Organization (UNESCO), to study international precedents for defining "universal" rights across different cultures, ideologies, and legal systems. After spending only a month in Argentina in the 1930s, he had a profound effect on political debates across Latin America.[74] More crucially, his arguments were on the minds of Latin American politicians at the 1945 San Francisco

Conference, which set up the United Nations. When the draft Universal Declaration of Human Rights was debated in the UN General Assembly in 1948, a prominent UN official complained that the "speeches were laced with Roman Catholic social philosophy, and it seemed at times that the chief protagonists in the conference room were the Roman Catholics and the communists, with the latter a poor second."[75] Even Angelo Roncalli (the future Pope John XXIII) worked behind the scenes on the draft Declaration when he was papal ambassador to France during the 1940s.[76]

In fact, Maritain's most important convert to modern values was the Vatican itself, which until then had associated modern liberalism in Spain, France, Italy, and Latin America with secularism and anti-clericalism. (Not very long before, during the Spanish Civil War, the Republicans had murdered 7,000 Catholic priests, brothers, and nuns.)[77] As a result, even before they were elected, John XXIII and Paul VI were among the twentieth century's most influential advocates of human rights. Ten days before he died in 1963, John XXIII told some visitors: "Now, more than ever, we are called to serve Man as man, and not just Catholics; to defend the rights of the human person, not the Catholic Church . . . It's not the Gospel that has changed. It's we who are beginning to understand it better."[78] Human rights was also a central theme of John Paul II's papacy much more than it was in official Protestant circles.[79]

Maritain, however, was not naïve about the likely impact of the UN Declaration:

> The function of language has been so perverted in our day – even the "truest" words have been made to lie – that people will have no faith in beautiful and solemn declarations. It is by putting these declarations into practice that people will be won over, and I have my doubts on that score.[80]

As Maritain suspected, the Universal Declaration remained almost a dead letter for twenty years; but the involvement of prominent Catholics in drafting it, and the Church's promotion of the dignity of the human person, raised the importance of human rights in Catholic seminaries, religious communities, and papal documents, deeply affecting the way Catholic and other opinion leaders thought about these issues around the globe. Amnesty International, whose 1977 Nobel Peace Prize signaled the coming-of-age of international human rights, had Christian roots. Its founder, Peter Berenson, was a convert to Catholicism, and his close associate, Eric Baker, was a Quaker.[81] And as early as the 1950s, the Lebanese activist Charles Malik wrote:

> There is nothing that has been proclaimed about human rights in our age ... which cannot be traced to the great Christian religious matrix. Even those in our own day who carry, on a non-religious or even anti-religious basis, the burden of human rights with such evident passion and sincerity ... owe their impulse, knowingly or unknowingly, to the original inspiration of this tradition.[82]

Today, in political science and international relations courses, in learned journals, and in national and global debate, a single-minded emphasis on human rights is being challenged. Even left-wing politicians now stress the complementary importance of human duties and responsibilities. This revisionism would have seemed a luxury a century ago and is an eloquent expression of the real progress that has been made in expanding human liberty in the world. Was the Church right to promote such values? Plainly. Did it help to put human rights firmly at the center of the international agenda after the Second World War? That, too, seems clear. But more important than whether the Church was right or successful on the international front is the impact that Catholic social teaching had on hundreds of thousands of Christians – not just Catholics – who were fighting injustice and trying to give the poor the means to lift themselves out of their misery.

There was nothing radical about this. In fact, from *Rerum Novarum* onwards, Catholic social teaching lagged behind major breakthroughs in liberal or social democracy by about fifty years. What was significant was that, once the Church adopted these values, it went from being a protector of the established order to a proponent of change, and all the more convincingly because of its stodgy, even reactionary, reputation. Its presence in almost every corner of the world ensured the spread of these ideas – rather quickly in Latin America and Asia, and more slowly in Africa – and gave Church people around the globe the encouragement they needed to follow their instincts, based on the Gospels or the harsh facts they were facing. For the young Denis Hurley, future archbishop of Durban, "We ate and slept and pondered over *Quadragesimo Anno*, the encyclical of 1931. And then the encyclicals of Pius XI against communism, against fascism and against Nazism. These things were our bread and butter."[83] Of course, not all Catholic missionaries or teachers or nurses read the encyclicals; but they saw or heard digested versions and appreciated the support for what they were doing.

The Protestant Hendrik Kraemer was right. The universal principles of the Gospels – and papal encyclicals for that matter – could not dictate answers to the complicated problems facing individual societies. But Catholic social teaching gave priests, nuns, brothers, and even lay people, previously shy about expressing "political" opinions, a convenient entrée into debates that might otherwise have seemed outside the scope of Church responsibility, and it inspired countless men and women to serve and even die in the cause of greater justice in the world.

In Africa, I asked a foreign nun who had spent her entire adult life there whether she had felt supported in her work by the Church as a whole. She winced: "You're asking the wrong person. The Millennium Synod did not have a single woman present." Was her religious congregation important to her then? "Certainly, because it is constantly renewing itself with fresh expertise and perspectives and challenging us to think of new ways of serving those at the edges of society." And was Catholic social teaching an inspiration? "Absolutely," she said. "I was attracted to being a nun because our founder wanted us to be 'contemplatives in action.' But it was the Church's equating of our mission as Catholics with the pursuit of justice that gave me the greatest energy, purpose, and satisfaction in life." The relationship between that mission and economic and social progress in the world over the last fifty years has many facets and remains the subject of much debate.

CHAPTER 4

Religion and Development: "A Task of Fraternity"

THE taxi driver at Paris airport started it. "What were you doing in Rome?" he asked. Research for this book, I told him. "Are you Catholic?" "Yes," I replied. "A practicing one?" "Yes," I answered. "And you?" "Muslim," he declared. "Practicing?" I shouldn't have asked. "Of course!" Then he picked up the thread. "Do you believe that Christianity is a universal religion?" "Yes," I told him. "I don't," he replied. "I think Islam is the only universal religion." This puzzled me. "If that is so, why are there so few Muslims in Latin America?"

Now it was the taxi driver's turn not to understand. "Oh, you're speaking of geography," he said. "What are you talking about?" I asked. "Islam is the only religion open to everyone. Christ preached only to the sons of Israel." I couldn't let him get away with that. "You mean Mohammed preached outside Arabia?" "Well, no," he answered, "but he sent people to do that." "Christ did that, too," I pointed out. "They were called the Apostles. Besides, if Islam is open to everyone, why am I not allowed to visit Mecca?" The taxi driver was suddenly accommodating. "You are – if you convert to Islam." I seized on the point. "Well, you know, you don't need to be a Christian to visit St Peter's in Rome."

There was a hushed silence in the car and then the driver delivered the following very slowly: "You . . . compare . . . St Peter's . . . to . . . Mecca? St Peter's was built by men. Mecca was established by the Prophet Abraham."

*   *   *

Although religion has always been inflammatory, "development" was safer ground until recently; but it, too, now has its high priests, heretics, and quarrels. To quote just one "atheist," the Canadian anthropologist Wade Davis, "development for the vast majority of the peoples of the world has been a process in which the individual is torn from his past, propelled into an uncertain future, only to secure a place on the bottom rung of an economic ladder that goes nowhere."[1] Like any soft jargon, development can mean a range of things: modernization, economic diversification, improvements in human well-being, the creation of equal opportunities, and poverty reduction. But despite frequent confusion on the subject, development is not the same thing as economic growth. Growth is generally considered necessary for development, but how much is enough and what kind of growth it should be is unclear. In some places, the two do not seem connected at all. For example, the most populous country in Africa, Nigeria, is still struggling to share the benefits of its oil wealth with the majority of its population, while Cuba has had one of the best education and health systems in Latin America, despite decades of economic stagnation.

While growth is important for development, few scholars have suggested the same for religion. In fact, many have thought the opposite. The Swedish economist Gunnar Myrdal, best known for his book *Asian Drama* (1968), argued that religion was a drag on human progress. Wangari Maathai, the Kenyan winner of the 2004 Nobel Peace Prize, agreed with him:

As Christianity became embedded in Africa, so did the idea that it was the afterlife that was the proper focus of a devotee rather than this one – a legacy that continues to affect development. Such an attitude allows institutions and powerful people to encourage people to remain passive. They sit and wait for their MP [Member of Parliament], the church, an aid agency, or a foreign government to solve the problem. They devalue their own capacity and responsibility to act.[2]

Matthew Parris, a former British member of parliament who grew up in southern Africa, has a different opinion. In December 2008, he wrote an article for *The Times* of London in which he summarized a return visit to the region. It was entitled "As an atheist, I truly believe Africa needs God." When he was growing up, he reflected,

The Christians were always different. Far from having cowed or confined its converts, their faith appeared to have liberated and relaxed them. There was a liveliness, a curiosity, an engagement with the world – a directness in their dealings with others – that seemed to be missing in traditional African life. They stood tall.[3]

In short, the effect of religion on development, for better or worse, is highly contested.

Whatever its effects, religion remains central to the lives of most people in the world – to a striking extent in developing countries, but also in the United States, one of the few Western countries that still takes religion seriously. In 1997, religion was regarded as "very important" by more than 90 percent of people in Nigeria, 80 percent in Ghana, Bangladesh, and Pakistan, 70 percent in the Philippines, and 60 percent in Turkey, South Africa, Venezuela, and Brazil. The result for the United States was 54 percent, with Ireland (48) and Poland (49) close behind. The scores were remarkably low for supposedly "Catholic" countries like Italy (31), Spain (24), Portugal (17), and France (14). In China, which has been trying to stamp it out since 1949, only 3 percent thought religion "very important."[4] A 2009 Gallup poll asked people in 114 countries a similar question. The median result per country was 84 percent, with as many as 99 percent of people in Bangladesh, Indonesia, Sri Lanka, Malawi, and Burundi saying religion was important to them.[5]

A quick look at these numbers might suggest that there is an inverse relationship between religion and development; but that would be rash. Western countries were still religious at the time of the Industrial Revolution, and widespread secularism is a relatively recent phenomenon, more likely the result of development than its cause. Whatever its past influence, religion is no longer very influential in international decision-making. In their memoirs, two men who were at the center of development policy at the beginning of the twenty-first century – James Wolfensohn, president of the World Bank (1995–2005), and Mark Malloch-Brown, administrator of the United Nations Development Programme (1999–2006) – make only fleeting reference to the role of religion. Malloch-Brown mentions Cardinal Jaime Sin's support for the 1986 People Power Revolution in the Philippines and the rising international menace of Islamist terrorism.[6] Wolfensohn cites John Paul II's Apostolic Letter of 1994 as the seed for what became the Jubilee 2000 international campaign to reduce poor-country debt.[7] Wolfensohn's silence on other aspects of the subject is rather strange, considering that he was the first World Bank president to regard religion as a central factor in human progress and set up a World Faiths Development Dialogue to consider its role more seriously. His staff reacted to the initiative as if it were radioactive, finding it faddish, irrelevant, and contrary to the non-confessional character of international organizations. The religion unit at the World Bank has since been closed.

Before 1950, few Westerners outside the Church – and certainly very few states – worried about what was happening to people in the developing world. Some economists even objected to talking about poor countries as a group. "What is there in common between, say, Papua New Guinea and Mexico, Indonesia and Peru, Malaysia and Lesotho, India and Chad?" asked the skeptical Hungarian-British economist P.T. Bauer, whose cranky opinions eventually entered the mainstream. "In most Third World countries, people often do not even know of the existence of other Third World countries. Much less do they think of these populations as brothers."[8] Although not termed "development," there were calls for spreading world prosperity well before the Second World War. In 1931, at a Paris meeting of the international Human Rights League to discuss colonialism, one speaker was lyrical: "To bring Science to people who do not have it, to give them roads, canals, railroads, cars, telegraph, telephone, to organize public health services for them, and – last but not least – to communicate the rights of Man to them, is a task of fraternity."[9] But there was little practical follow-up to such appeals.

The real impetus for international action came from very unsentimental quarters: the desire of the Western Allies in 1944–45 to stave off the kind of slump in international trade that had occurred in the inter-war years. Rebuilding the war-torn economies of Western Europe and Japan, opening markets, and investing in poorer countries – this was seen as the recipe for making everyone better off. Poor countries would act first as suppliers of raw materials, then as markets for the industrialized countries; but as their skills and infrastructure improved, they would take over some of the simpler manufacturing industries (furniture, textiles, shoes, etc.) that the rich countries abandoned as they moved into more sophisticated sectors. In the 1980s, the process was working well in East Asia, but stalling in Latin America. In the 1990s, South Asian economies (especially India) began responding to better public policies and Latin America started to reassert itself. Only Africa seemed shut out of the process. The driving force was private investment and open markets, with foreign aid helping the poorer countries to overcome constraints like power supplies, transport links, and the shortage of necessary skills.

Development has proceeded at such a pace that the world has now been transformed. The best news of all is that the world's most populous country, China, is looking after itself. Between 2007 and 2012, its economy expanded by close to 60 percent.[10] More generally, there has been striking progress in fighting poverty. In 2012, for the first time in thirty years, the number of "absolute" poor – those lacking even the minimum needs for a decent life – declined in every part of the developing world. In East Asia, which was the poorest region in 1981, the number dropped from 77 percent to 14 percent, and in South Asia from 61 percent to 39 percent. In Latin America, the starting point was lower (14 percent), but absolute poverty was more than halved (to 6 percent). Even Africa improved, but not by much, to just under half the population (47 percent), down from 51 percent thirty years before.[11]

China and India are the most spectacular cases of successful development, but other countries have done well, too: Vietnam, Brazil, Peru (in the last ten years), and Chile (where poverty is now comparable to the rate found in the US). Even Bangladesh, once thought to be doomed to perpetual misery, has reduced extreme poverty to less than 40 percent of the population. Unfortunately, Africa is still in a class of its own, despite several years of sustained growth – another reminder that development is not the same as increases in national income. "The continent still doesn't fit into standard world graphs or indicators," Jaime Saavedra, chief of poverty analysis at the World Bank, told me. "For example, access to individual toilets is so rare in Africa that we can't use it as a measure of progress, as we do elsewhere."[12] Good as they sound, the global poverty numbers need to be put into perspective. While the number of people living on less than $1.25 a day has dropped, the number of those earning less than $2.00 a day – 2.5 billion or 43 percent of the population of the developing world – has hardly budged in thirty years.[13] Basically, improvements in human welfare have barely kept pace with population growth.

Surprisingly, there is no consensus on how to guarantee growth or development. Most economists believe that governments must promote the private sector and use markets and globalization to wean economies away from dependence on natural resources. But that is as far as they are prepared to go. The specific tools to be used will vary with the setting. "Recipes for success do not travel well," says one prominent scholar. It is the "broad vision" behind them that is important.[14] A stable economic environment – low inflation, reasonable interest rates, predictable rules, and so on – is clearly essential. Political stability is also important, although there is controversy about just how much is necessary.

Authoritarian regimes have usually been stable; but some have been modernizing (China, Indonesia, Korea, and Taiwan), while others have not (Africa). Even more significantly, economists have moved away from the broad strategies – like agricultural mechanization, import substitution, and export-led growth – that once dominated the development debate to more "micro" solutions. While about 70 percent of Brazil's success in reducing poverty can be attributed to growth, the other 30 percent was achieved through cash transfers to poor families, conditional on keeping children in school and having them vaccinated once a year. Some economists now argue that these and other shortcuts – like the right kind of nutrition and deworming children – will have a greater impact on the lives of poor people than will indirect measures to promote higher incomes.[15]

Paralleling this pragmatism has been a broadening of the notion of development, spurred by the Indian economist Amartya Sen's 1999 landmark book *Development as Freedom*. Income by itself was never regarded as a good measure of progress, because it disguised wide variations in standards of living. Consequently, economists have tracked other aspects of welfare, such as life expectancy, literacy, school enrollments, and access to health care. Even then, these were crude yardsticks that said nothing at all about the actual quality of people's lives. Furthermore, people in different cultures want different things, so the development profession now focuses less on meeting "basic needs" (shelter, food, clothing, water) than on enlarging the range of human choices. Longevity, knowledge, and a higher standard of living are no longer regarded as ends in themselves, but as means of ensuring that people will have the freedom and opportunity to lead lives they value.[16] (Interestingly, this comes very close to the Catholic Church's definition of human development.) This is not to suggest that economists have suddenly become starry-eyed or sentimental. Income levels still account for most of the disparities in life expectancy across countries.[17] Health, education, and clean water will in themselves make people better off; but in theory they should also lead to higher productivity and incomes, and higher incomes are still the most direct way of increasing human choice. Both aspects of fighting poverty are now considered important: raising income and improving access to basic services.

Outlooks may have changed, but certain fundamental facts remain the same. As the World Bank's chief economist, Lawrence Summers, a brilliant man famous for making unfortunate statements, issued a policy paper that no one took exception to. Educating girls, he claimed, was the single most effective investment in promoting social progress. Improving basic health and education services was a central part of the successful East Asian development "model" and is on most economists' agenda for spreading the benefits of economic growth. Even the draconian right-wing regime of General Pinochet in Chile (1973–90) recognized the importance of investing in child nutrition and early learning development, which helps explain the country's successful emergence from poverty under later democratic governments. In short, open markets and good economic policy are not enough to guarantee development; basic services for the poor and political stability are also important.

Let us now turn to the role of religion. With the exception of Japan, the first countries to "develop" were all Christian. This was no accident, according to the German sociologist Max Weber, whose book *The Protestant Ethic and the Spirit of Capitalism* (1905) sparked a lively debate about the impact of different Christian denominations on the emergence of modern economies. Weber held that Protestant values (especially Calvinist ones) accelerated the growth of capitalism in places like England, Holland, and the United States, and that Catholicism slowed it down in southern Europe (Italy, Portugal, and Spain). Weber was not the first person to comment on differences within Christianity. Alexis de Tocqueville (1805–59) believed that Protestantism helped explain why Great Britain escaped major political upheavals from the eighteenth century onwards, despite stark differences in income: Catholics were obedient but expected fairness, whereas Protestants valued personal independence more than equality.[18] Many scholars think that the Weber thesis is too tidy and underestimates the importance of the Italian city-states (Venice, Florence, Genoa) and the large monastic farms of the Middle Ages as breeding grounds for capitalism. But there is little controversy that Christianity as a whole nurtured the emergence of capitalism and that other belief systems did not. For example, Islamic partnership rules, inheritance laws, and even polygamy may have blocked the development of the joint-stock company in North Africa and the Middle East.[19] In one respect – the Catholic Church's discomfort with profits and markets – the Weber thesis may still be relevant to the story of world development, and we will come to that a little later.

Important as Christianity was for the rich countries, most scholars downplay the significance of religion elsewhere. This seems paradoxical, given the general influence of culture on economic ambition and organization. Objective factors – geography, natural resources, population density, climate, insects, and disease – certainly play a major role in the creation of wealth. So, too, does history, including the advantages of a head start and the persistent effects of regional inequalities. Yet personal values, cultural norms, and political choices can sometimes triumph over physical obstacles. There is nothing pre-determined about the development process, unless you are in the middle of the Sahel or the South Pacific, where there are clear limits to economic potential. Singapore and Mauritius – two islands with few inherent advantages – have exceeded any hopes that a reasonable person might have had for them back in the 1950s. And although Indonesia and Africa faced the same constraints of disease and climate, Indonesia cut poverty from 60 percent to 20 percent of its population during the same period (1970–90) that Africa was losing half its foreign markets – to countries like Indonesia.

A striking example of the effects of culture comes from the memoirs of a Catholic priest who spent his entire professional life in Bangladesh. At a conference in Malaysia in the 1980s, Dick Timm learned that the government was providing special opportunities to the native Malay population (known as *bumiputra*, or "sons of the earth") to help them catch up economically with the more enterprising Chinese. This policy included pushing many Chinese into the rural areas to make room for Malays in towns and factories. Timm was surprised to hear that the Malaysian Chinese were farmers. They weren't, he was told, but despite that they were already growing three crops a year. To Timm, this reflected "a truth that is often overlooked in development – that it is not the reform of socio-economic structures alone which will mean progress for the poor. Certain personal virtues: zeal, self-discipline, self-reliance, [and] sharing [are] even more important."[20]

Christianity's historical influence in the developed world was conveyed over many centuries through education and the spread of common values rather than direct intervention in economic and social matters. The idea of a Christian "social mission" overseas arose rather late, in the nineteenth century, as missionaries fanned out into tropical countries and ran up against inequalities and hardship that begged for solutions. As modern technology (including medicine) opened up new possibilities for improving the lives of the poor, Christian activism became more pronounced. An English Methodist bishop working in South India in the 1950s described the political effects this had: "In the West, the Church is largely middle-class: here it is chiefly rooted among the labourers. Communism is appearing in the villages, but it is the Gospel which has created the ferment and which still has the greater hold." But he pointed to the risks of pressing the social mission too far: "There is a terrible danger that the Church should become a large social service organization with its centre in a modern streamlined office rather than God's family with its centre in 'the apostles' teaching and fellowship, the breaking of bread and the prayers.' "[21] Michael Ramsay, a progressive archbishop of Canterbury (1961–74), expressed a similar concern. During his tenure, the Anglican Church was being pushed to take stands on international peace and economic reform, if only to appear more up to date:

But the New Testament suggests that the right answer begins at a very different point, for the relevance of the Church of the Apostles consisted not in the provision of outward peace for the nations, nor in the direct removal of social distress, nor yet in any outward beauty of the Church itself, but in pointing to the death of Jesus the Messiah, and to the deeper issues of sin and judgement.[22]

Most Catholics – and many Anglicans – have behaved very differently, even if they, too, occasionally had doubts about their priorities. In the 1960s, a Muslim professor in Indonesia asked an American Maryknoll Sister how she thought the nuns could ever win converts: "Christians are nurses, social workers, and teachers, and not interested in the things of God." "Our work," the sister concluded, was "not visibly grounded in the worship and praise of God." Other sisters felt they should be more political than evangelical: "We dealt with the effects of poverty, but because we did not question the structures that sustained it, we became ourselves part of the problem."[23]

Now we come to a feature of Catholicism that is consistent with the Weber thesis, but not the usual subject of international headlines. In Chapter 2, we saw how fundamentally rational and rooted in the world the Catholic tradition has been; but neither of those virtues has made the Church comfortable with economics, an intellectual discipline with very secular roots. For many devout Christians, not just Catholics, it is a leap of faith to "believe" in the market; it seems too capricious, irrational, and unfair to be set on a pedestal. The most they can do is accept reluctantly that the market system may have improved the lives of millions around the world – for now. Even that "success" is not very comforting in the face of gross inequalities in the world. What is the point of developing a smarter smart phone when 800 million people do not have clean water and 2.5 billion lack proper sanitation? Other Christians see no contradiction at all between free enterprise and the Gospel, citing the parable of the talents (Matthew 25:14–30) as the basis of a broader view. In that story, the master reprimanded one of his slaves for burying the money he had entrusted to him rather than investing it and earning a return. Some Evangelicals even preach a "gospel of prosperity" which suggests that

Christ expected his followers to grow rich and that material success is a sign of virtue. (Most Biblical scholars would probably find scant support for such a view, but hope springs eternal among some readers of Scripture.) Suffice it to say that very few Catholics are ardent supporters of the last two schools of thought. Robert Sirico, founder of the US-based Acton Institute for the Study of Religion and Liberty, tells of receiving a letter from a Catholic businessman who had discovered Sirico's views in *Forbes* magazine: "It was a shocking and emotional experience – shocking, because in all of his Roman Catholic school education and regular church attendance, he had never before heard a priest speak insightfully of the responsibilities, tensions, and risks inherent in running a business."[24]

In some developing countries, Catholic discomfort with private enterprise and profit appears to have been reflected in public policy. Tanzania's Julius Nyerere (president from 1962 to 1985) attended mass almost every morning and based his "African socialism" more on the Acts of the Apostles than on Karl Marx; but his sense of Christian fraternity had its limits, as he allowed the state media to call even honest businessmen "criminals." The international development profession was sometimes tarred with the same brush. In 1998, the Guinean archbishop of Conakry, Robert Sarah, who now coordinates the Church's charity work around the world, denounced "development" as the mere acquisition of material possessions; economists as the "priests" of a "new religion;" and management schools as the new "missionaries." He even grumbled about the "Gospel" of John Maynard Keynes – a curious target for the socially conscious – by quoting him out of context: "Avarice and usury and precaution must be our gods for a little longer still. For only they can lead us out of the tunnel of economic necessity into daylight."[25] Development economists added to the confusion by referring to rural roads, agricultural services, basic health and education, and clean water as investments in individual "productivity." Many Christians saw health and education as simple human "rights." Development experts also had trouble explaining how economic "reforms" – increasing competition, reducing food and fuel subsidies, and doing away with regulations – could improve the lot of the poor. Such confusion was more than academic: it proved wide-spread and fuelled resistance to economic reform and private investment in large parts of the developing world.

Doubts about "development" squared with older Catholic concerns about economics and "progress." In 1958, a French missionary in Africa worried that

> everywhere in the world today, old and unique civilizations are being threatened, if not already dying, and despite touching efforts to revive them, we can only just barely prolong the agony. More or less quickly, they will all be submerged under that scientific and technical form of modern civilization that we can now describe as "global" and consists of Western or Christian values "gone mad." Either in the form of capitalism or Marxism, it is leveling and homogenizing most of humanity.[26]

And it was not just clerics who sniffed at modernization. Catholic artists, journalists, and commentators joined the chorus. For example, the English Arts and Crafts sculptor Eric Gill (1882–1940) thought that Christians should live a life of thrift and that mechanization was a scourge rather than a solution. A friend of Gill's (sounding like Mahatma Gandhi) told him: "Your homespun will instruct you better than the Declaration of Independence on the dignity and the rights of man."[27] In his *Outline of Sanity* (1926), G.K. Chesterton suggested improbably that everyone should be given a small amount of land to save them from the dehumanizing effects of mass production and urban squalor. Recently, that view has been updated by traditionalist Catholics opposed to globalization. To quote the American editors of a 2001 edition of the Chesterton book:

> Never mind that exporting jobs in search of cheap labor adversely affects real men who have real families to feed. Never mind that playing games with debt, finance and capital to drive [chief executives'] salaries and shareholder dividends up may at the same

time drive the average citizen's purchasing power down. Such are the consequences ... where the needs of finance and "market forces" come first and those of the Common Man barely register.

The editors prefer organic farms to agribusiness, neighborhood shops to chain stores, the country to the city, real art and literature (even good beer) to a culture of "imposed artificiality." But at the same time, they regard other anti-globalizers as a "motley composition of pacifists, socialists, communists, anarchists, the unemployable, social inadequate and the militantly nihilist."[28] This example of anti-modern thinking from the Right is a sign of how deep, long-standing, and pervasive Catholic attitudes have been. Current-day market skeptics – like the "Occupy Wall Street" movement – may find it surprising that they have anything in common with the Catholic Church; but they are treading a well-beaten path.

The most striking example of Church discomfort with conventional economic theory was the intense debate about "liberation theology" in the 1970s and 1980s. By the late 1960s, many Latin American theologians were impatient with the failure of "development" on their continent and the growing gap between rich and poor, seeing gradualism in theology as a contributing factor. Regional pride was also at work. Having studied in Europe and been exposed to the Christian–Marxist dialogue there, they decided it was time to create a "theology" for their own continent, apparently blind to the internal contradiction of having "European" or "Latin American" theologies. Much of what they produced was an echo of left-wing ideas they had absorbed overseas. The Medellín Conference (1968) had used the word "liberation" but refused to condone revolutionary violence.[29] Verbal violence was another matter. "Prepare your bomber planes," the secretary-general of the Latin American Bishops' Conference warned a conservative Brazilian colleague on the eve of a later meeting. "You must start training the way boxers do before going into a world championship. May your blows be evangelical and sure."[30]

The content of the new theology was difficult to pin down. In 1979, en route to Latin America for the first time, John Paul II was asked by a journalist what he thought of it. "Well, to begin with," the pontiff mused, "is it a theology?" In Peru, Norbert Strotmann was listening to the interview live on his car radio and his heart sank. What an unfortunate way to introduce himself to the region, he thought. (Later, he saw that the Vatican had deleted the comment from the official transcript.) A German who has lived in Peru for forty-five years and is now a bishop in Lima, Strotmann believes that the debate over liberation theology was largely one of cultural misunderstanding. Critics were reacting to Spanish rhetoric: "The German mind [implicitly referring to Cardinal Joseph Ratzinger, head of the Sacred Congregation for the Doctrine of the Faith in the 1980s] expected clear distinctions and consistency. Latin American writers, however, were willing to contradict themselves within a page or two, so long as the general drift of the argument was in the intended direction."[31]

The key texts of the movement – like Gustavo Gutiérrez's *A Theology of Liberation* (1971) – were laced with Marxist jargon and references to "the worldwide class struggle." They interpreted the story of the Exodus as political liberation rather than just spiritual salvation, saw Christ as a political figure, and regarded certain Scriptural passages, like Mary's *Magnificat* ("He hath put down the mighty from their seat and hath exalted the humble"), as a rallying cry. There was concern about "structural sin," meaning institutions, practices, and a distribution of wealth which individuals themselves could do very little about and that societies as a whole would need to change (a contemporary example might be the system of compensation for bankers). Some of their statements had no meaning at all. "History is no longer as it was for the Greeks, a remembrance," wrote Gutiérrez. "It is rather a thrust into the future."[32] Others, like the Nicaraguan Jesuit Fernando Cardenal, gave the new theology a pastoral accent: "I used to be worried about the few people who would go to hell. Now, I am worried about the millions of my fellow men, here and now, who are already in a hell of material misery. A priest can and should be involved in the struggles of his people."[33] Their views comforted and mobilized hundreds of thousands of Catholics who were impatient for change and saw collective action as their only means of fighting dictatorship and poverty. The Church had to take sides, they thought. It could not denounce injustice and at the same time support the established order.

Intellectuals living in more serene environments regarded the new theology as superficial. The US Catholic writer Andrew Greeley said it lacked even "the minimal sophistication of the social sciences" and ignored the complexity of social and political choices; on top of that, he said, liberation theologians spoke as if they were infallible.[34] And the Vatican regarded their thinking as dangerous. In August 1984, it issued the first of two Instructions – one that emphasized the negative aspects of the new thinking. Participating in the class struggle, it suggested, was a contradiction rather than an expression of charity. Christians were expected to love everyone, regardless of class. While the new writers were right to refer to sacred texts defending the poor, they were wrong to interpret them ideologically. References to a "Church of the People" were also divisive. It was one thing to criticize pastors "fraternally" for being arrogant, but quite another to challenge the Church's entire hierarchical structure, "which was willed by the Lord Himself."[35] Later that year, referring to the thousands of small Christian communities that had been set up across the continent, the Pope talked about the "serious danger" that they would foster a "Church of poor people" separate from the Church as a whole.[36]

The Vatican's second Instruction on liberation theology (1986) was more balanced, even positive, and many regretted that it had not been issued first. The 1984 document bore the imprint of Cardinal Ratzinger (the future Benedict XVI); the second was reportedly the product of the more personable Frenchman Roger Etchegaray, the long-time president of the Pontifical Council for Justice and Peace, who was sensitive to the links that Latin Americans were drawing between the Gospels and their fight for justice. In fact, the debate in Rome was a sideshow – except, of course, for those theologians being censured. More powerful than the language of liberation theology was the moral example it inspired and the serious risks that people were taking to live up to a new sense of what it meant to be a Christian. Under interrogation in the 1970s, blindfolded and handcuffed, an Argentinian priest was told by a senior officer: "You are not a guerrilla fighter. You are not in the violence. But you do not realize that by going to live [with them], you unite the people, you unite the poor, and uniting the poor is subversion."[37]

One of the saddest episodes of misunderstanding was the Pope's visit to Nicaragua in March 1983. Although it lasted a mere eleven hours, it reverberated around Latin America for years. Because of his general criticisms of capitalism, his presence at the 1979 Puebla Conference in Mexico (which reaffirmed the "preferential option for the poor"), and his brave efforts to stand up to the communist dictatorship in his native Poland, some regarded John Paul II as the ultimate "liberation theologian." But he dashed those hopes during the visit. Unhappy that three ministers in Nicaragua's "revolutionary" government were priests, he rebuked them as soon as he arrived, with the whole country watching. The minister of culture, Ernesto Cardenal, was not just a priest: he was also one of his country's most distinguished poets. Taking off his black beret, Cardenal knelt on the tarmac for a blessing; instead, the Pope pointed his finger at him and gave him a tongue-lashing, reducing him to tears. That evening, at a mass attended by 600,000 people (a quarter of the country's population), the Pope called the idea of a "People's Church" absurd and dangerous. During his sermon, some people in the crowd shouted out slogans and, testily, he told them to be quiet. He left many Nicaraguans – and Latin Americans – saddened and confused.

The Jesuit Juan Carlos Scannone was one of the fathers of Argentinian liberation theology, which lacked a Marxist flavor altogether as there was no Communist Party in the country. Like others, he was puzzled by the Vatican's fears: "None of us recognized ourselves in their summary of our thinking. I had written to Cardinal Ratzinger to explain that there were at least four currents of thought that could be identified under the general heading. But I never got an answer. It was important that we engage with the realities of Latin America as Vatican II had been too optimistic about the state of the world." Did he resent the Pope's criticism, despite the strong political stance he was taking in Eastern Europe? "No," replied Scannone mildly. "He was worried about the communist threat, which still seemed real across large parts of Latin America."[38] Another Argentinian, a former ambassador to the Holy See at the time, minimized the whole debate: "Let the professional historians do their work. Even thirty years later, it's too early to come to a judgment. John Paul II had a long reign and bigger problems to deal with. While that discussion was going on, he was trying to straighten out the record on Martin Luther, the Inquisition, and the persecution of Galileo. Now, those were real issues."[39]

In fact, the Pope's views had many layers, and they evolved. In 1980 in Brazil, and again in 1981 in the Philippines, he urged the poor to "struggle for life," to be actively involved in shaping their own destiny, and to be "artisans of their own progress."[40] In October 1981, at the urging of sympathetic voices in the Vatican, the Pope read Gutiérrez's work late into the night and suggested to Cardinal Ratzinger the next day that he water down a statement he had drafted for the Peruvian bishops to sign. The Pope also refused to condemn Gutiérrez when he visited Peru in May 1985.[41] Shortly after the second Instruction (1986), Réal Corriveau, a French Canadian bishop working in Honduras, asked him: "Setting aside what the official documents of the Church say, what do you think personally about liberation theology?" Replied the Pope: "It was necessary."[42]

Whether belittled or feared, liberation theology had a profound effect beyond Latin America. James Culas, a priest in the Indian state of Kerala, felt something was missing in his ministry until he attended a 1974 Jesuit course in Bangalore on social analysis and community development. It looked critically at economic and political structures, the social foundations of India's different political parties, the role of the World Bank and International Monetary Fund, and the nature of poverty:

This was a major shift in my life. I realized that solutions were not to be found in the mainstream parties, including the Communists. To use Arnold Toynbee's term, we needed a "creative minority" within the Church to fight against poverty. Some of us decided to focus on Kerala's one million fishermen and, with the bishop's support, we worked on a number of fronts to help them improve their lives.

Their first priority was to campaign against fine-mesh trawling by the commercial fisheries, which was depleting stocks for the traditional fishermen. Neither the Congress Party nor the Communists regarded this as a priority, but eventually the battle was won. Later, he and his team pressed for better housing and credit. Separately, Culas worked with a Catholic women's forum that fought domestic violence, the demeaning dowry system, and sexual harassment. At another course in Thailand, organized by the Columban Fathers, one of the lecturers was the Salvadoran Jesuit and liberation theologian Jon Sobrino. Culas found his stride: "I had considered taking a sabbatical leave from the priesthood to rethink my life, but now I was convinced that I could be a priest and social activist at the same time."[43]

It is impossible to measure the impact of Church teaching, including the anti-market skepticism of the "social" encyclicals, on economic policy, but it almost certainly reinforced resistance to economic reform, complementing nationalism, self-interest, and a fear of the unknown with a convenient sense of Christian fairness. It is surely no accident that the world's economic "tigers" emerged in East Asia in the 1970s rather than in Latin America, and that no "Catholic" country has set records of economic growth and better income distribution. In fact, until recently, the greatest gap between rich and poor was in Brazil, the largest Catholic country on earth.

But this is only part of the story. Catholic condescension on modernization, private investment, free trade, and economic reform, like Church teaching on birth control (to be discussed in Chapter 9), may have done real damage in developing countries; but Catholics (and other Christians) made major contributions to world development in three very concrete ways – through education, basic services for the poor, and global advocacy.

Let us begin with education. Even before the Reformation, there were eighty universities in Europe; but the religious congregation established by Ignatius of Loyola (1491–1556) gave new impetus to the notion of Catholic education. Its beginnings now seem improbable. After his conversion, Loyola lived as a mystic, fasting and beating himself, begging for food in the streets, and letting his hair and fingernails grow long. As a student, he was imprisoned twice by the Inquisition, which decided he was bizarre rather than dangerous. In the founding papers of what was to become an important teaching order, there was no mention of schools at all. But the Society of Jesus grew fast – from ten to 3,000 members in twenty-five years (1540–65) – and spread out across Europe, India, Japan, and Brazil.

Francis Xavier, who roomed as a student with Loyola in Paris, was so zealous that he set off to evangelize India even before the Society was properly constituted. Yet centuries later, the phrase "trained by the Jesuits" would not mean to be consumed by a passionate faith, so much as to be able to stand on one's own feet, be critical of inherited truth, discern and exploit important distinctions in meaning, debate confidently, and admire knowledge and culture. Jesuits were also indulgent confessors. From the very start, they were urged to be "sweet, approachable, and sensitive," to show "compassion and kindness," and avoid self-righteousness. Their moral judgments could also appear rather convenient, which is why the word "Jesuitical" has never been a compliment in the English language. Inspired by the humanist ideals of the Renaissance, they wanted to produce good citizens, not just good souls. One Jesuit wrote to Philip II of Spain: "All the well-being of Christianity and of the whole world depends on the proper education of youth." Thanks to Francis Xavier, their first school (for about 600 boys) was established in Goa in 1543, and by the time the Society was suspended by papal edict in 1773, the Jesuits were running more than 800 universities, seminaries, and secondary schools around the world.[44]

Since then, dozens of teaching orders have been founded, including the Christian Brothers (1808), the Marists (1817), the Congregation of the Holy Cross (1837), and the Salesians (1873), not to mention the many teaching congregations of nuns. Their impact was far greater than the instilling of knowledge. More broadly than spreading the Gospel, missionaries were proud bearers of modern values. In the words of a 45-year veteran of the Blantyre Mission of the Church of Scotland (in modern-day Malawi), writing in 1932: "When the Native medical student sits at the microscope prying into the secret forces of disease in the form of germs and parasites, there can hardly be room for that most deadly of all superstitions, belief in the power of witchcraft." The writer was proud of other developments, too. "The Christian house in an African village is easily noted from its neatness, cleanliness . . . But better than all, the husband and wife will sit together with the family at meals – a revolution indeed in native society, for it means that his wife now takes her place as the equal and the helpmate of her husband, instead of being largely his chattel."[45] Christian missionaries also pitted individual free will and personal dignity against the sometimes paralyzing forces of fatalism in traditional cultures.

In the words of a contributor to the *Oxford History of the British Empire* series, "It is impossible to imagine what education might have been like without the presence of Christian missions. They so dominated the provision of educational services for indigenous populations that in many lands the term 'native elites' was synonymous with 'Christian-educated.'"[46] In India, nineteenth-century mission schools filled up quickly – not only because of the opportunity to learn English, but also because they were open to all social classes. In Madras, as early as 1838, half of all students enrolled in Christian schools were girls; the Medical College opened its doors to women in the mid–1870s (ahead of most institutions in Europe and North America); and in 1933, 56 percent of Bachelor of Science degrees were being awarded to women. In Africa, literacy programs that introduced the Bible to students made some of them eager to escape their own Babylonian captivity. The first newspaper published in an African language – the Yoruba *Iwe Irohin* – started as a mission journal in Nigeria in 1859.[47] While not confined to the governing class, Christian education was fundamental in transforming outlooks and challenging elites to adopt a more responsible role in society.

A second contribution of the Christian churches has been the provision of basic services for the poor, including primary education, health facilities, clean water, and credit schemes. These services have been all the more valuable where governments have been slow to establish national networks for such purposes. As we saw above, progress on basic education and health is one of the few common factors explaining success in reducing poverty around the world. In this respect, as in others, evangelists were trailblazers. Before most European states had committed themselves to public education, Christian missionaries were teaching young people free of charge, pioneering co-education, and offering free medical care as well. One scholar has even suggested that missionaries were the forerunners of the welfare state and international philanthropy.[48] In some African countries, the Catholic Church is still providing 30–50 percent of such services. Quentin Wodon, who headed the now defunct religion-in-development unit at the World Bank, estimates that the Catholic Church's role still averages 10–15 percent across the continent. These services do not always reach the very poor, and they are not always cheaper than the alternatives; but they are among the best.[49] A 2003 World Bank survey found that government health staff in six developing countries did not work 35 percent of the time (43 percent in India). Schoolteachers were also away quite often (20 percent); and in India, even when they were on the job, they were reading newspapers and drinking tea half the time. Private-school teachers (including Catholic ones) are more reliable.[50] That the Church still plays a large role suggests how much more important it was at an earlier stage in saving or molding the lives of millions of people otherwise beyond the reach of modern health and knowledge. In 1956, on the eve of African independence, 90 percent of education on the continent was in the hands of missionary bodies.[51]

The Church's third contribution to world progress – speaking up for developing countries as a group or for isolated or oppressed communities in individual countries – builds on the close ties that exist between poor people and their faith leaders. Such ties may seem odd to Westerners, who value their personal independence and see no need for intermediaries with "God" or anyone else. Yet, where political systems are weak and multinational corporations, foreign aid experts, and humanitarian officials have a heavy hand in decision-making, the poor need advocates or go-betweens. Imams, priests, and pastors living among them are usually their first choice, as they tend to know local issues up-close. Take the aid profession, which is now so large that it has been the subject of anthropological studies. Even development staff who have spent much of their lives abroad and seem at home in difficult environments can paper over the differences between countries or regions.[52] Religious leaders can remind politicians, local officials, and foreign experts alike what those differences are and can help spread the benefits of national programs and international projects more widely. The Catholic Church has been careful not to claim any particular technical expertise in solving concrete problems, but it has not been shy about representing the rights of the poor. In the words of the final document of the Medellín Conference (1968), "these problems receive their logical and human strength from a conception of human life which only religion can provide: that all men are sons of the same heavenly Father and, hence, brothers."[53]

Given its reach and size, the Catholic Church has had a particularly rich opportunity to represent the interests of the poor. In its social teaching, its support for human rights, and its political mediation, and through Catholic radio and newspapers, the Church has been one of the clearest voices for redressing economic and political injustices in the world and for appealing to the consciences of developed countries. During the Algerian uprising (1954–62), for example, the archbishop of Algiers, Léon-Étienne Duval, denounced France's torturing of prisoners so often that the French settlers nicknamed him "Mohammed Duval."

Spearheading the Church's effort over a quarter of a century (1973–98) to promote social justice around the world was a remarkable Frenchman named Roger Etchegaray, first as papal emissary and then as a senior Vatican official. Etchegaray received me in his apartment overlooking the hills of Rome, on top of an office block in Trastevere that is officially part of the Vatican. He shares his eagle's nest with four other retired cardinals, including an Argentinian whose potted oleander trees almost block the outside gallery giving access to the apartments. A ceramic plaque outside the door suggests (in French) how unpretentious he is: "I move ahead like a donkey . . ." He is also the only cardinal (and before that bishop) to refuse a personal motto and coat of arms, which he regarded as a pretentious survival of a time when prelates were nobles. But he is proud of his age. "Do you know how old I am?" he asked. "Eighty-eight," I said, and his eyes twinkled. He is hard of hearing now and limps from a broken femur suffered when a deranged woman jumped on Benedict XVI as he walked up the aisle of St Peter's on Christmas Eve 2009. His apartment is decorated with gifts from foreign governments, including elephant tusks from Vietnam. Over coffee, he offers me *amaretto* cookies from a wicker basket made in Burundi. But the object that catches my eye is a large, unframed photograph of himself and Fidel Castro on the far wall of his sitting room. "He sent that to me," Etchegaray says, as if to head off suspicions that he was an admirer; but it is the only picture of a foreign leader in the room.

A native of France's Basque country, he was archbishop of Marseille when John Paul II named him to head the Pontifical Council for Justice and Peace in 1984. In that role, circling the globe, he lived through highs and lows. Possibly the most galling moment was when he had to watch the Ugandan dictator Idi Amin belly-dance on a table. Among the most painful was a dinner in Rwanda at the height of the 1994 genocide, when the minister for the family, the district governor, and other local bigwigs lifted their glasses in a toast to peace; afterwards, he learned, some of the guests went down to a local prison to murder the inmates. "My missions often plunged me into the absurdity of wars and catastrophes that make it difficult to accept the silence or self-effacement of God," he wrote in his memoirs. When he visited Vietnam in 1989, the first papal representative to do so since the country's reunification in 1975, more than a million people attended his events. The cathedral in Ho Chi Minh City was so crowded that Etchegaray himself had trouble getting in. And he seldom passed up an opportunity to bear witness to the Church's social values.

In June 1985, he visited Chile, still under the dictatorship of General Pinochet. While there, Etchegaray meditated in the room where a French priest, André Jarlan, had been murdered in his presbytery nine months before. The Bible he had been reading was still stuck to the table in the man's blood. Later, behind closed doors at the Vatican embassy, Cardinal Etchegaray met with a representative of the families of political prisoners.

Visiting Burma in 1992, he was told that he could not mention human rights or democracy or even the name of Aung San Suu Kyi, the opposition leader who was under house arrest; so he spent an evening in the street in front of her house, to the annoyance of the military police.[54]

Key to Catholic influence has been the knowledge that the Church's information is usually sound. The Canadian Dominican Philippe LeBlanc spent twelve years at the United Nations in Geneva, appearing often before the UN Commission on Human Rights and drawing attention to government abuses around the world. "They knew what we were saying came from the field, and not from some newspaper article, because we had people in more than 100 countries," explains LeBlanc.[55]

At the ground level, individuals have also been important. In 1970, a Maryknoll nun from Pittsburgh named Janice McLaughlin became the Catholic Church's spokeswoman in Nairobi. One of her first assignments was to arrange a press conference for an American priest deported from white-ruled Rhodesia (now Zimbabwe). During the next few years, she became deeply involved in the southern African liberation movement. In 1977, she moved to Salisbury (now Harare) to work with the Catholic Justice and Peace Commission, documenting the brutality of government forces against the civilian population. Shortly after, she was arrested, put into solitary confinement, and accused of supporting terrorism. Excerpts from her diary were read out in court, infuriating the white authorities but delighting the African public. "If I had a black skin," one entry ran, "I would join 'the boys' [i.e. the nationalist rebels in the bush]." It was a public relations disaster for the white racist regime. American newspapers ran the headline "US nun held in Rhodesia" and her trial was covered on prime-time evening news. Maryknoll nuns demonstrated in Hong Kong, sparking headlines in Asia, too. McLaughlin was convicted and quickly deported. Years later, she recalled a phrase that the Shona people of Zimbabwe used for God: "The One Who Turns Things Upside Down."[56] She seems to have adopted it as a motto, continuing her involvement in promoting human rights in Zimbabwe, but now against the increasing brutality of the former independence leader (and now president) Robert Mugabe. In 2010, she was elected head of the Maryknoll order.

As an educator, provider of basic services to the poor, and political and moral advocate, the Catholic Church has left its mark across the developing world. But, as we shall see in the next three chapters, its emphasis and impact have varied in Africa, Asia, and Latin America.

CHAPTER 5

Africa: "No One is Opposed to a School"

THE greatest surprise about the Church in Africa is how long it took to take root. There had been sporadic Portuguese contacts along the coast in the sixteenth and seventeenth centuries, a short-lived Christian kingdom in the Congo, and almost fruitless missionary efforts in Senegal and Madagascar. But at the beginning of the twentieth century, Catholicism was largely absent from Africa. In 1900, there were only 1.5 million Catholics in the whole of the continent; by 1958, the number had grown to about 16 million; now there are 180 million. The Sacred Congregation for the Propagation of the Faith (sometimes described irreverently as the Vatican's "ministry of colonies") had overall responsibility for the missions; but the process was laborious. "We used fishing rods rather than nets," explained one missionary in 1958, "and in many places that's still true now!"[1]

The early missionaries rode roughshod over local customs and imposed blocks of superficial beliefs. As a result, after the 1789 Revolution in France, Catholicism disappeared in French-speaking Africa like "a pile of straw in a fire."[2] The missionaries of the last half of the nineteenth century were more enterprising. They came largely under their own steam (rather than on account of political patronage), went deep into the interior at great personal risk, learned local languages, and tried linking their teaching to the deep spiritual beliefs already guiding African lives. But their numbers were never very large, and many died of disease and exhaustion. The average missionary of the Holy Spirit or "Spiritan" (a French order of priests in West Africa) died at the age of thirty-five.

As a result, the mustard seed spread very slowly. According to the Nigerian novelist Chinua Achebe, Anglican missionaries came to Onitsha in 1857 and reached his own village – just seven miles away – thirty-five years later, averaging one mile every five years. "That is no whirlwind," he observed.[3] One reason was that missionaries ministered to the few rather than preached to the many. In fact, seeing priests and nuns helping the sick and the outcast, most people felt that Christianity was not intended for them. Some missionaries would have engaged more with the local elites, but most of the money sent to them by Rome was earmarked for releasing slaves. As a result, much of it was spent on cotton, salt, and even gin to purchase their freedom, since most slave owners distrusted paper money. The missionaries were actually breaking the law in doing this, because the British judged that any payment – even to free a slave – helped maintain a market value for human beings. But the alternative was to leave the slaves in bondage. Another preoccupation of the missionaries was the killing of children. Among the Igbo people of southern Nigeria, infants with birth defects (like six fingers or toes) and even twins were considered "deformed" and thrown into the bush to be devoured by ants or wild animals, since accepting them was considered an insult to the spirits. Missionaries helped end this. By 1950, adult twins were relatively common among Catholics; less so among non-Christians.[4]

But the missionaries' greatest contribution was education. For decades, in many countries, mission schools were the only teaching establishments. The first Catholic missionary in Gabon set one up in 1845; the first state school opened in 1909, sixty-four years later.[5] A sparkling example of this commitment to education was the Irish missionary Joseph Shanahan, the so-called Apostle of the Igbo. When he arrived in

1902, the region was regarded as one of the most hopeless missions on earth. As Shanahan wrote: "Man after man had gone out, determined to do or die – and had died without even the consolation of feeling he had done anything worthwhile."[6] Two years into his stay, Shanahan described what his "lion-hearted" predecessors had had to put up with:

> The natives would give [us] nothing – they were bitterly Mohammedan and the villagers for miles around were also followers of the Prophet. They would not even let us into their homes, so that we were obliged to buy fifteen slaves to have a little Christian community. Slaves were cheap in that part of the world, where food was so scarce. I often saw them sold in the open market for a bowl of corn.[7]

In 1908–09, Shanahan walked a thousand miles, making new contacts, encountering chiefs, and opening missions and schools. Rife with leopards, apes, cannibals, and headhunters, the territory was regarded as "bad bush" even by the locals. Thirty years later, his "Great Trek" was still being talked about. In 1919, he walked another thousand miles, this time to open up missions in Cameroon.

He was a little awestruck at first. "[The African] aspires to God – to All Goodness – by some inborn tendency, and the missionary has but to foster the tendency ... Once you understand and love him in Christ, [he] is a treasury of goodness and loveableness. Only those who have lived with him, and spoken to him of God from the depths of their own souls know that."[8] Soon Shanahan was setting up schools, using a cunning speech to convince local chiefs:

> Next time I come, perhaps after some six or seven moons, a black teacher trained at Onitsha will be with me and he will stay in your town; together we will show you how to build a house where Chukwu [God] will be worshipped properly. The children of your town will also learn "book" there and will know more than children in other towns. After some years, they will be fit for

government work and will make much money. When they become men they will say "Ha! The chief in our town who first met the white man was very clever. He got the white man to put a school in our town." [9]

Shanahan later claimed that every year these schools liberated thousands from "barbarism." Instead of just freeing a few hundred from literal slavery, education was giving many more genuine freedom.

In 1913, Shanahan traveled to Europe to ask for more priests, but there were none to be had. In Rome, Pius X (1903–14) received him warmly, and when Shanahan fell to his knees to ask for his blessing, the Pope knelt, too, placing his hands on the visitor's shoulders and weeping with gratitude at what the Irishman was accomplishing.[10] Shanahan was strong but not invincible: "Sometimes the missionary finds the heat intense, mosquitoes and fevers almost intolerable . . . till he begs God's mercy to put an end to it." But visits to a leper colony cured matters: "When a priest has said Mass in the leper settlement, he can never again complain . . ."[11] When he was made a bishop in 1920, he agreed to perform confirmations at the settlement, so that the lepers would be the first to see him in his new vestments. He arrived by motorcycle, carrying his miter and crozier.

He may not have had enough priests, but by 1921 he had 1,000 teacher-catechists and a good supply of motorcycles. Some criticized these as a "luxury," but when Shanahan visited the new pope, Pius XI (1922–39), he was urged on to new heights of resourcefulness. "Nothing can be too modern on a mission in the twentieth century," the Pope said. "If you have motorcycles, look forward to cars; when you get cars, think of aeroplanes. All the time, think of souls."[12] By the time Shanahan retired in 1932, the number of churches and schools in his diocese had risen from twenty-four in 1906 to nearly 1,400.

Despite his accomplishments, his life ended sadly. When he retired, he wanted to stay in Nigeria, but his successor would not allow it, apparently jealous of Shanahan's popularity among the Igbo. Then he hoped to live with a community of nuns he had founded in Ireland; but again he was rebuffed. The mother superior instructed the sisters not to write to him, see him in private, or even refer to him as their "Founder." The reason? In August 1929, Shanahan had accompanied an ailing nun back to Ireland and had shown her too much affection. Every night on the ship, he visited her in her cabin to see how she was doing and gave her a paternal kiss on the forehead. Back at the convent, the nun reported that the bishop was in love with her.[13] Cut off from his "daughters" and crippled by paralysis, he died in Nairobi on Christmas Day 1943 at the age of seventy-two. But, to the end, he was proud of his work. His words could have served as an epitaph: "I realized that the keys of the Kingdom were in the tiny hands of children."[14]

Many others shared Shanahan's strong commitment to education, often at the expense of what was seen as the more natural role of missionaries: conversions. In the 1880s, in present-day Zimbabwe, ten Jesuits died of malaria without baptizing a single person; but by the 1920s, Catholic missionaries were training more than 10,000 children in 100 bush schools and using local teachers, to the great chagrin of the white settler community, which wanted to "keep the native in his place."[15] "Where it is impossible to evangelize and teach at the same time," wrote Bishop Arthur Hinsley, who visited missions across Africa on behalf of Pius XI, "neglect your chapels and improve your schools."[16] At about the same time, the superior-general of the Missionary Fathers of Africa, visiting the African Great Lakes region, told members of his congregation: "If your educational efforts require it, go ahead and close an entire mission to concentrate on another, even if there is an outcry from recent converts, heartbroken at losing their priests."[17]

Why this single-mindedness? An Alsatian missionary in Cameroon offered an answer in 1914:

The tree of paganism is gigantic, with a thick trunk, many branches, and deep roots in the lives of the people. It is not enough to attack it with an axe. We must dig deep beneath it to deprive it of its nourishing soil, so that it will fall on its own one day. Or we can light a fire inside it that will wear it down. That fire is already burning here in our schools and beginning to spread.[18]

Even if they used the word "primitive" at times, most missionaries knew they were dealing with deeply ingrained traditions that had to be eroded over time.

Schools were also the missionaries' way of influencing society as a whole. Young people were not just malleable targets in their own right, but were also a channel for influencing their elders. The first Catholic school in Nigeria (1886) taught catechism and the three R's to boys and girls. Three years later, the missionaries added carpentry, shoemaking, tailoring, and metalworking for the boys, as well as sewing, knitting, and washing and ironing for the girls. These courses were intended to give girls alternatives to their traditional roles, but parents thought that such training was also making their daughters "too lazy, insolent, and free" and complicating the task of finding them husbands.[19] Some girls were also having children out of wedlock, confirming their parents' fears about the "benefits" of modern education. Even Bishop Shanahan faltered in the face of such opposition, arguing that girls should stay in school only long enough to master basic reading, writing, and arithmetic. "It is not good for girls at the moment to get used to going to school. We need good housekeepers, and simple, humble, submissive wives. Very often, passing through school and especially the convent turns them into strangers in their own community."[20]

Still, by 1928, Christian mission schools in southern Nigeria had three times more students than state institutions, and ten times as many girls (11,000 vs. 900).[21] In French West Africa, despite the resistance of parents and a shortage of women teachers (as men were not allowed to teach female students), in 1958 girls accounted for more than a quarter of primary school pupils and close to 40 percent of secondary school enrollments. Where Koranic schools were weak, even Muslims sent their children to Catholic establishments, preferring religious instruction to the state's secular approach. If Muslim students were in the majority, some school administrators watered down the Christian curriculum so as not to offend local sensibilities. Their commitment to education for its own sake seemed paramount.[22]

In English-speaking Africa, greater attention was paid to instilling practical knowledge of agriculture and minor trades than was the case in French Africa. In Uganda in 1881, Catholic missionaries introduced the first mango, papaya, and citrus trees, as well as wheat and rice. By 1900, each mission was essentially a technical training center, where people learned to be builders, bricklayers, carpenters, blacksmiths, and tailors, and Africans did all the construction under the general supervision of the missionaries. One particularly able carpenter was even sent to Europe in 1899 to specialize in his trade.[23] Literary and cultural development was also part of the missionary impact. In Uganda, the first catechism in a major African language (Luganda) appeared in 1881; the first grammar book in 1885; and local proverbs and stories were also published. A famous Luganda legend was translated into French in 1883, giving Europe a first glimpse of Ugandan culture.[24] Pedagogical methods were improved, too, with one priest writing proudly: "I had to suspend the Latin exercises to tackle a more rational way of teaching grammar, applying the rules first to the local language. Our young Baganda are amazed to find so many riches in the Luganda language which they did not even suspect."[25]

But not everyone was happy with the missionaries' work. Jan Christiaan Smuts (1870–1950), twice prime minister of South Africa and highly regarded overseas as a liberal statesman, criticized Christian education in a series of lectures at Oxford in 1929:

Already the African system is disintegrating everywhere over the whole African continent. Missionaries share the blame with governments; the fight against the native social ideas has been no less destructive than the deposition of native chiefs and the institution of European organs of government ... If this system breaks down and tribal discipline disappears, native society will be resolved into its human atoms, with possibilities of universal Bolshevism and chaos which no friend of the natives, or the orderly civilization of this continent, could contemplate with equanimity.[26]

Others mixed snobbery and racism in their accounts. Travel writers like Mary Kingsley (1862–1900) and Joseph Conrad (1857–1924) criticized mission education as superficial, impractical, and subversive. Kingsley thought the missionaries underestimated the differences between whites and Africans, which she thought as great as those between men and women. Conrad described a Sierra Leonean who "spoke English and French with a warbling accent, wrote a beautiful hand, understood book-keeping, and cherished in his innermost heart the worship of evil spirits." Cecil Rhodes (1853–1902) complained snidely that mission schools "seemed destined to produce a nation of preachers and editors." He wanted more "practical" and "industrial" training for the Africans.[27]

Of course, missionary methods were not always gentle. In some countries, converts were expected to give up everything they had grown up with. Secret meetings, initiation rituals, wakes, funerals, and even traditional dances were considered improper. A missionary in Cameroon insisted that converts attending such events would have to walk to a distant village to confess their sin to the bishop. "How will we mourn our parents when they die?" one youngster asked the priest. "I won't even let you beat your drums," he replied callously. In southern Nigeria, released slaves were grouped together in "Christian" villages in a new kind of servitude. Their lives were regulated like those of monks, rising, sleeping, working, praying, and eating at the same hours. The missionaries could also seem indifferent to the social consequences of their actions. It was the British government in Nigeria, not the Church, which insisted that husbands pay compensation to former wives, once they converted to monogamy.

Missionaries could also be blinded by their own self-righteousness. In October 1889, a French priest named Lutz was put on trial by the British authorities in southern Nigeria after a freed slave named Fatima complained that she had been kept in chains and flogged by her "protector." Later, the priest "sold" her to her future husband. Lutz did not deny the charges, but said he had done it all "in good faith," as the woman kept disappearing at night, presumably to engage in immoral acts. As for "selling" her, he had only asked for the traditional dowry (a practice the missionaries usually denounced as another form of slavery). He was more honest in a letter to his appalled Superior: "She was never going to convert, so I thought we should recover our money and spend it on better candidates." He was convicted, fined, and lectured by the deputy governor, who called him "un-Christian" and "immoral." Coming from an Anglican layman, this must have been the most bracing part of the sentence.[28]

Shanahan had been confident that missionary education was in everyone's interest: "If we go from town to town talking only about God, we know from experience that much of our effort brings no result. But no one is opposed to a school."[29] For example, any young person who could speak a little English was less subject to the risk of being carted off by slave traders. Looking back, however, many Africans have wondered whether such efforts were really worthwhile. The individual dignity and self-worth that Christian education instilled could also be seen as tearing away at the delicate fabric of solidarity in African society. Many regarded the foreigners – priests, colonial administrators, or settlers – as one indistinguishable lot. In the words of one, "In days of old, we had the land and they had the Bible; now, we have the Bible and they have the land."[30] Despite claims that Christian education had a leveling effect on personal outlooks, the opposite could also be true. "School," wrote a French commentator in 1965, "seems like a completely foreign place. One goes through the door and crosses a frontier, not just to knowledge but to new ways of being, feeling, thinking – making it difficult to relate to the rest of society afterwards. School is the first rung of a ladder leading somewhere else."[31] The result, in some minds, was the creation of a carefully nurtured elite that became individualist and cut-off, more interested in the pursuit of honors and material comfort than in contributing to society.

Missionaries sometimes also underestimated the painful dilemma of African parents, illustrated by the moving speech of the sister of the great chief in the Senegalese novel *Ambiguous Adventure*:

I have done something which is not pleasing to us and which is not in accordance with our customs. I have asked the women to come to the meeting today. But more and more we shall have to do things that we hate doing, and which do not accord with our customs. The school in which I would place our children will kill in them what we love and rightly conserve with care. Perhaps the very memory of us will die in them. When they return from the school, there may be those who will not recognize us. What I am proposing is that we should agree to die in our children's hearts and that the foreigners who have defeated us should fill the place, wholly, which we shall have left free ... But ... remember our fields when the rainy season is approaching. We love our fields very much, but what do we do then? We plough them up and burn them: we kill them. In the same way, recall this: what do we do with our reserves of seed when the rain has fallen? We would like to eat them, but we bury them in the earth ... [Our] best seeds and our dearest fields – those are our children.[32]

Even when their objectives were in harmony, the missionaries and colonial authorities did not always work hand in hand, and there was a delicate balance to be maintained. The occupying powers rarely had much military back-up, so they needed to respect local customs, including the authority of the chiefs. Education could upset that balance. As one colonial governor in Madagascar complained, "All we want is a labor force, and you're turning them into human beings."[33] In fact, missionaries often walked a tightrope. They needed official support, but did not want to ask too many favors. Occasionally, they had to assert their rights without appearing "unpatriotic" and offending their financial backers at home. Even after the separation of Church and state in France in 1905, the French government subsidized the construction of Catholic cathedrals in West African cities like Dakar, Brazzaville, Douala, and Yaoundé. In return, Church people were expected to act as "proper" citizens of France. When the Petits Frères of Charles de Foucauld established a mission among some of the poorest communities of northern Cameroon, the colonial governor ordered the mission closed, as "prejudicial" to French prestige.[34]

At times, the showdown between politics and religion could be electric. Charles Lavigerie (1825–92), who founded the Missionaries of Africa (known as the "White Fathers" because they dressed like the Arabs of North Africa), was a particularly hard nut to crack. In 1868, three young seminarians told him they wanted to learn Arabic and work among the local people; but the French governor objected: "We do not want the Arabs to become Christians." When the emperor of France, Napoleon III, suggested that Lavigerie (who was the bishop of Algiers) return home to a larger and easier diocese, Lavigerie stood his ground: "I want you to announce that I am free to make Jesus known to the Arabs. If you refuse me that freedom, I will be forced to take it into my own hands."[35] The Emperor backed down, and Pope Pius IX (1846–78) encouraged Lavigerie to persevere. Shortly after, he sent missionaries to Uganda, Tanganyika, and Zanzibar, and by the end of the century there were White Fathers in Mali and Burkina Faso as well. In 1882, he was named the first "African" cardinal.

Catholics were not the only ones trying to awaken traditional cultures to new truths. In the mid-nineteenth century, an Englishman named Henry Venn (1796–1873) brought the two B's – the Bible and the bicycle – to Central Africa and tried to offer practical solutions in the areas of health, agriculture, and education. He wanted a self-governing African Church. Like Bishop Shanahan, a German evangelist named Karl Kumm (1874–1930) walked a thousand miles from Nigeria to Sudan in 1909, trying to set up a barrier of Christian churches against the southern spread of Islam. His wife Lucy (née Guinness) was British, and so Karl's exploits were followed closely in England and headlines greeted his safe return at the end of the year. Lucy Kumm (1865–1906) was also influential. The daughter of a famous Irish Evangelical pastor and a world traveler and writer in her own right, she called for women's equality both at home and overseas, and drew a direct link between Christianity and social justice.[36]

Throughout this time, surprisingly enough, the Vatican was urging missionaries to respect local customs, except for those (like slavery) that violated Christian principles. The Sacred Congregation for the Propagation of the Faith even forbade missionaries to teach their own language ("Don't introduce them to our countries, just our faith").[37] Heads of religious congregations reinforced the message, with one of them saying in the late 1920s: "Cast off Europe, its customs, its spirit; make yourself Africans among the Africans [nègres in the original]; that way, you will judge them as they should be judged and train them as they should be trained, not as Europeans, but in a style that respects what is particular to them."[38] An apostolic vicar in Dakar put it more bluntly: "We are not going to establish France, Italy, or some other European country in Africa; just the holy Roman Church irrespective of all nationalities."[39] Bishop Shanahan in Nigeria echoed this in instructions to his nuns: "Be ready to move off as soon as your missionary work is done. Do not dig in permanent roots – that is not your function as missionaries. While leading others to Christ, be always careful to respect their pagan customs as an expression of the human spirit."[40]

Inevitably, there were inconsistencies in the Vatican's approach. In Asia, it condemned "ancestor worship" as superstitious, to the confusion of many Chinese, who did not see the difference between leaving food on the graves of their loved ones (as they did) and leaving flowers (as Westerners did). "When do they come up to smell the flowers?" a Chinese man teased an American nun in the 1920s.[41] And a general belief that Christianity was part of a Western "civilizing" mandate made papal Instructions appear unrealistic. The very idea that one could uproot local gods and leave the rest of indigenous culture intact now seems quaint. But papal views were repeated time and again, as in 1919, when Benedict XV (1914–22) warned against "missionary nationalism."

The frequency of these messages suggested how widely they were being ignored.

The Vatican also reconsidered arcane rules that got in the way of missionary work. Until 1936, Catholic nuns were forbidden to care for pregnant women or act as midwives, "as such acts of charity [i.e. their exposure to the biological functions of other women] do not seem to conform to their being virgins dedicated to God and dressed in religious habits."[42] With no trace of irony, the Vatican department responsible for such matters boasted that it "has always tried carefully to adapt its apostolic methods to the different demands of time and place." But the reason for the change seemed more anthropological than humanitarian. "In some regions of Africa, there are entire tribes which are dwindling steadily and seem doomed to extinction if we do not find an effective way of protecting the health of mothers and their infants."[43] As with later Church teaching on birth control, nuns must have been ignoring the rules already, because in less than ten years (1945) 6,000 children were being born at Catholic clinics in southern Nigeria, and in 1956 the number was 16,000.[44]

On the educational front, missionaries were simply ignoring the Vatican's naïve purism and proving unrepentant about changing local cultures. One Frenchman's 1931 memoir was entitled *Dominating to Serve*,[45] while another complained in 1958 about ethnologists wanting Africans "parked" in natural reserves: "What would we say if the Romans had 'protected' the Gauls and kept us at the same level as our ancestors, with drooping moustaches, drinking from the skulls of our defeated enemies?"[46] "The poignancy of African civilization at the moment," he continued later, "is that the elites preaching it have lost its secret, while the mass of the population that still has it wants to get rid of it."[47] Amadeus Msarikie, the retired bishop of Moshi in northern Tanzania, summarizes the missionary impact vividly:

> Their very arrival was a revolution. People were forced to think about themselves in new terms, wondering why these strangers

were being kind to them and trying to get to know them. And the light of Christian education was so broad and intense that it forced people to look at their bodies, their souls, and the world around them in a different way. The missionaries affected their nutrition, the way they raised their crops, their hygiene, and their attitudes to each other.[48]

A modern-day Nigerian cleric was more sober about the results: "The liberating effect of the Gospel tore women from their roots, upset traditional culture, and transformed relations between men and women. We can rejoice at the advancement of women, but also fear some of the consequences."[49]

In short, missionaries were a major part of the process of Westernization and modernization. They benefited from improved technology and transport systems, while adding to the impetus for further change. As movements of national liberation developed and more Africans were appointed to senior Church positions, relations with some colonial governments grew tense. In 1953, Madagascar's bishops called for independence, and in 1955 those in French West Africa did the same; but they suggested no target dates. Swimming against the tide, Pope Pius XII (1939–58) asked Africans to recognize Europe's contribution to their progress, and warned them against "blind nationalism" that could drag them into "chaos and slavery."[50] On the ground, missionaries were caught in the crossfire, with European settlers accusing them – correctly – of giving Africans the intellectual tools and self-confidence to dismember empires, and African nationalists seeing them as slowing progress and being the "valets" of imperialism.

By the time of African independence in the early 1960s, the Church was expanding fast but facing a number of new challenges. It might have been (as one scholar put it) still replacing "tribal cosmologies" with "rational thought" and contributing to material progress through its schools and hospitals,[51] but its presence was highly concentrated among particular ethnic groups like the Baganda of Uganda and the Igbos of

Nigeria, and the proportion of Catholics in most countries remained small. Large groups like the Yoruba of Western Nigeria remained hostile to Catholicism, while many educated Africans (often products of Catholic schools) were wondering whether they still needed "foreign" religions at all. The greatest concentration of Catholics was in French-speaking Africa, but even there they made up less than 10 percent of the population. Most lived in towns or along the coast, apart from large pockets among the Mossi people of Burkina Faso and in the central Congo. But Catholics were highly influential, especially in non-Muslim countries, where they dominated the ranks of local politicians and administrators. For their part, Catholics wondered when the African Church would emerge from its Western cocoon and find its own wings. Like everyone else, it was struggling with the effects of modernization: the meltdown of traditional morals; mass migration into already overcrowded towns; sexual promiscuity; frustrated, half-educated, unemployed youth; and glaring corruption. The Church was seen to have two missions: spreading the Gospel and improving society through justice and charity. The early reading of African politicians was that the Church may have been part of the colonial order, but that on balance its contribution had been a positive one.[52]

That view may have been influenced by the fact that, for the first three decades of independence, the Church stayed out of politics. The first president of Congo-Brazzaville was a priest and another headed the armed independence movement in the Casamance region of Senegal, but these were exceptions.[53] In a culture of graft and self-enrichment, priests were expected to be more honest; but there is little evidence that the few who entered politics bore that out. Bishops did not make political statements either, because – like the rest of the elite – they saw nothing objectionable about one-party states and were slow to link dictatorship and the growing poverty of their fellow-citizens. (In French-speaking countries, some politicians had even attended the same seminaries as the bishops, before responding to a different "call.") South Africa's Denis Hurley and Bernard Yago, the archbishop in Côte d'Ivoire, were exceptions to the Church's hands-off stance in Africa. Shocked by the waste of hundreds of millions of dollars, Yago opposed the construction of the mammoth air-conditioned basilica (modeled on St Peter's in Rome) that Côte d'Ivoire's president built in his home village of Yamoussoukro, supposedly with his own money, and tried to persuade the pope to cancel his third visit to the country, during which he was to consecrate it. Other bishops, however, kept silent, not wanting to offend the President or cut themselves off from future favors.[54]

But as Africa's economic crisis grew deeper, as international opinion about autocracy on the continent hardened, and as fledgling democracy movements struggled to make themselves heard, Catholic bishops began to issue sharp assessments of the economic, social, and political situation. In the early 1990s, in a number of French-speaking states (Benin, Congo-Brazzaville, Zaire, Togo, and Gabon), citizen groups forced the dictators to convene national conferences, and Catholic bishops were asked to chair them. This was no mere secretarial function.

In Benin, Isidore de Sousa, the archbishop of the capital, not only presided over the conference to prepare the political transition, but also served as the highest power in the land during the thirteen months leading up to the elections. Until the very last moment, he did not know whether the outgoing strongman Mathieu Kérékou would agree to step down: "At the end of the National Conference, as I waited with him in the wings before he gave his final address, I had the impression he had two speeches in his pocket, one positive, the other negative. To the very last minute, I appealed to his sense of history."[55] Benin was a small country, but it offered a giant precedent: in 1991, it was the first African state to change governments through the ballot box. In English-speaking Africa, Catholic leaders were also slow to challenge dictators, but their voice eventually proved crucial. In Kenya, first individual Anglican bishops, then the National Council of Churches, and finally the Catholic bishops criticized the government of Daniel Arap Moi. In Malawi, opposition to President Banda began with a 1992 Lenten pastoral letter by the Catholic bishops. And in Zambia, Catholics were also at the forefront of democratic reform. Some Church leaders lost their lives as a result. Bishop

Joachim Ruhuna of Burundi was killed in September 1996 for denouncing ethnic killings and urging Tutsi–Hutu reconciliation, and Bishop Christophe Munzihirwa of Bukavu (Zaire) was murdered a month later, apparently for harboring Hutu refugees from Rwanda (earlier he had sheltered Tutsis) and for denouncing the foreign-led war in the region.[56]

Few would have predicted thirty years before that the Christian churches could play such a major political role. Many expected Christianity to dwindle rather than mushroom, as mission schools were taken over by governments and people linked "Western" religion with colonialism. The Church's earlier neutrality, even passiveness, may have exasperated democrats and human rights activists; but it was one of the few institutions to preserve its resources and moral standing during the debilitating early decades of independence. Geopolitical events in the world, particularly the fall of the Berlin Wall and the spread of democracy in Latin America, and the maturing of Catholic social thought made Church intervention inevitable. It was the deep roots of the mainstream Christian confessions that allowed them to take a stand, whereas the Evangelicals, who were still trying to establish themselves, were more likely to sit on the sidelines or be obsequious rather than obstreperous. In February 1992, the pastor of the Redeemed Gospel Church in Nairobi, in a sermon attended by President Moi and broadcast on the evening news, denounced "churchmen masquerading as bishops and reverends, who were preaching their own gospel and not that of Christ." Heaven, like Kenya, had only one party. It was God who made Moi president "and God never makes a mistake."[57]

As the form – if not yet the culture – of democracy has spread in Africa, so the political role of the Church has evolved, too. Some will argue that it must remain a bastion of human equality and citizens' rights until democratic values have truly taken hold, and must act as the defender of minorities and of the poor even after that. But Catholic bishops will admit that their credibility can be punctured by bad example. "Future priests need to know," wrote a Congolese cardinal in 1988, "that ordination will not inoculate them against the worship of money. Yet, it seems that some priests can hardly wait to stake their claims, as if they were entitled to an easy life, to having their own car."[58] Some seminarians will even identify a "patron" at the start of their studies to make certain of being fully equipped when they are ordained. I asked a Cameroonian priest about this. "It's a bit of a caricature," he replied. "But priests in Africa do need a car to do their work and it is important that priests be looked up to. Ordinary people expect their leaders to behave in a certain way. They do not want them to be on a par with themselves. But, to be accepted, priests also have to be able to lower themselves to the level of their parishioners and share in their joys and their grief. That's how things work in a traditionally hierarchical society." A really humble man like St Francis of Assisi, then, would not have succeeded in Cameroon, I suggested. "No," he admitted a little ruefully.

The roles of Church and state are now quite separate. In the words of one young African:

> In an earlier day, the missionary arrived draped in all the prestige of his own culture. We didn't like what the colonial powers called "the civilizing mission of the Church." It was very ambiguous. Were they coming to preach the Gospel or to make us work in the coffee plantations? Now, when a missionary comes to an independent African country and doesn't even have to teach school anymore, his role is clearer![59]

But fortunately for the hundreds of thousands who benefit from its programs, the Church has not retreated to the sidelines of African life. In countries still struggling to build proper systems of public education and health, Christian institutions are crucial, especially in the rural areas. In Uganda, the Catholic Church is the second-largest provider of vocational, technical, teacher, and business training (22 percent of student numbers, compared with the government's 42 percent).[60] About 23 percent of primary schools and 33 percent of secondary schools are Catholic or Anglican, and Catholic providers account for 28 percent of the country's hospital beds.[61] Despite the size of such contributions, there is not a single explicit reference to the roles of faith communities in Uganda's National Development Plan.[62] In neighboring Tanzania, where the Christian missions ran 70 percent of all the schools in 1961, the first president, Julius Nyerere, set his sights on developing a proper system of public services; as a result, the Church's role is now more limited.[63] But much of the elite still sends its children to Catholic boarding schools.

Tanzania is worth looking at more closely, as an example of how the Christian churches (particularly Catholics, Anglicans, and Lutherans) have contributed to African development, and how they are struggling to assert a new role. In his retirement home near Mount Kilimanjaro, I asked a 91-year-old priest who had trained most of the country's priests and bishops whether he could imagine Tanzanian history without Catholicism. He seemed taken aback by the question, but, after a pause, was firm and clear: "Definitely. But without Christianity? Never."[64] He was referring to the Christian belief in the importance and dignity of the individual, the value of education, and the possibility of affecting one's own destiny. In a newspaper interview that week, a new Catholic bishop drew an unflattering comparison between the missionaries and recent graduates: "They did not have to come here and devote their lives and sometimes their blood to us." These days, he complained, young people preferred to be without a job in town rather than serve as teachers or nurses in remote areas without electricity or running water.[65]

Fulgence Kazaura, a former deputy minister of finance and now chancellor of Dar es Salaam University, points out that Catholics were so committed to human development from the start that they built their churches outside town, so as to have enough space to put up a hospital and school. Muslims sited their mosques in town and had little room to expand.[66] From his glass office in the highest building in the capital, Benno Ndulu, the governor of Tanzania's central bank, has a view of the city as commanding as that of the economy. The Church, he told me, had been very important in education, certainly, but also in community development. In fact, during a crucial period (1967–85), because of the abolition of traditional chieftaincies, the Catholic Church was the only national institution that could rival the influence of the ruling party. Initially sympathetic to *ujamaa* (Nyerere's "familyhood" or African socialism), Catholic leaders grew doubtful as the influence of Marxists at the University of Dar es Salaam grew stronger. Meanwhile, party officials denounced religious leaders as "exploiters and parasites," and Nyerere had to step in to calm tempers.

During the economic crisis of the late 1970s and early 1980s, the Church's ability to help those in need affected the balance of forces. But the Church toned down its criticisms of the party out of concern for its own privileges and status (including tax exemptions) and to prevent a sharper backlash from the radicals.[67] Individual Catholics were more vocal. An American Maryknoll Sister living in the Kagera region at the time wrote: "So often we had to sit through meetings in which local bureaucrats told the people to work harder, or leaders lambasted the people or threatened them for not fulfilling party or government quotas for areas of planting. Yet overwork was the reality, especially for women."[68] Ndulu highlighted new points of friction since then. The Church is a big landowner and invests a large part of its rents back into the community; but Church wealth can also cause scandal, as in the case of tenants evicted from their land when they applied for legal title. And, in an era of democracy, Ndulu felt the Church could be too political, as with the bishops' statement prior to the 2010 presidential elections. "This was supposed to be the word of God!"

That document appeared under the title *Manifesto: Proposal of National Priorities*. The bishops' language was gentle, but the message was strong. It questioned the dependence on "narrow" sources of growth like tourism and mining, and, echoing Nyerere's call forty years earlier for "self-reliance," appealed for a "transformative" process. "We must lead that process," said the bishops. Depending on others was a trap. "We must strive to seek solutions to our problems from our own initiative and our own resources."[69] The bishops then criticized the centralization of political power, calling for a new constitution, the establishment of a

Council of Elders independent of the executive (like the US Senate or the British House of Lords), and proportional representation. The document appealed to police, judges, lawyers, prison wardens, legislators, and administrators to stop acting like "bosses" and instead to be "the caretakers of the good order of our society." On economic policy: "We challenge the basic assumption that we must aim, first, at economic growth and, then, we can expand spending on social services. Our view is that we must spend more on social services so that economic productivity and growth may result from it."[70] The Manifesto faulted the government's recent handling of teacher and health worker strikes as "shameful." It suggested specific measures, like a return to free medical care and a state pension after the age of sixty, that were, in the medium term at least, impractical. Also surprising was the absence of the word "corruption."

Many Tanzanians felt the Manifesto was a miscalculation, as political parties were beginning to be identified with particular religions (as in Uganda), and the document reinforced this impression. Nyerere had managed relations between religions deftly, and the Church's action now was seen as unfortunate and divisive. Others, including non-Catholics, admired the gutsiness of the episcopal conference. "The bishops didn't back down once the controversy erupted," one senior Lutheran told me. " 'These are our views,' they said, 'and we stand by them.' " Others pointed out that the Church had always been prickly, even under Nyerere, the revered Father of the Nation and a devout Catholic, worrying that his "African socialism" might turn into Communism, questioning the violence he was promoting in the liberation struggle in southern Africa, and complaining about the government takeover of Catholic schools. The Manifesto raised eyebrows because, for the first time, the opposition seemed poised to win power and the government was nervous. Government leaders wished the Church had stuck to general principles rather than make specific recommendations, but they were simply betraying their ignorance of Catholic social teaching. None of the bishops' proposals suggested how people should vote. In the West, governments might have noted the bishops' views and moved on to other reading;

here, the authorities took them to heart as a reflection of mounting public skepticism.

Mariam Kessy is a small woman with a large heart. She works for the Justice and Peace Commission in Dar es Salaam. In her view, the Church still does not speak out enough: "Culturally, Tanzanians tend to keep their heads low, feeling that they have always lived in peace. But we are not living in peace. There are serious social issues in the country and they don't just date from the current president. We need to talk about them openly."[71] Vitus Sichalwe, who coordinates the social outreach of the national Bishops' Conference, has similar concerns:

> There were differences between the Church and Nyerere, but by and large people felt they were being looked after, and that the government had everyone's well-being in mind. Later, as the economy and political system opened up, the Church realized that people had to be more assertive and it encouraged them to exercise their political rights. But we miss the vision and solidarity that Nyerere offered. Now, it's every man for himself, income differences are widening, and we are sitting on a time bomb. The peace that Tanzania has known during its entire life could well unravel.[72]

I asked one of the drafters of the Manifesto why they had not referred to corruption, given the current president's promise to fight it and the fact that only one minor official had been sentenced during his time in office. They deliberately decided not to be "pious" about it, hoping instead that decentralizing power and promoting new checks and balances in a revised constitution would allow future governments to fight the problem from within. The Church also had to be judicious in using its influence, which was greater than its share of the population (25 percent) in part because of the universal institution standing behind it. Muslim leaders, for example, complained that the government was too beholden to "Rome." There are twice as many Muslims as Catholics in Tanzania, but they are less vocal on social and economic issues. This is partly structural, as they lack leaders who can speak for the whole community, and partly deliberate, as they prefer to focus on issues of sharia law and family planning (which they regard as state intrusion into private matters) rather than governance, poverty, and corruption.

Tanzania is special in a number of ways. It is one of a handful of African countries never to have experienced a coup d'état. (A brief army mutiny in January 1964 was put down with British help.) Its ruling party has never been voted out of office during fifty years of independence, despite the introduction of genuine elections in the early 1980s. It has been one of the largest and most continuous recipients of foreign aid, despite its early commitment to "self-reliance." And it is the only African country to have been led by a devout Catholic – as distinct from a nominal one, like Zimbabwe's Robert Mugabe. When Nyerere took up the cause of national independence, Catholic leaders assured the British that he was a "moderate" politician. Later, as president of the country, he attended mass almost every day and encouraged Catholic Sisters to work in some of the *ujamaa* villages. In fact, it is not stretching the point to suggest that Nyerere's socialism was more an experiment in Catholic social thought than anything else.

If Tanzanian socialism was a Catholic experiment, did it work? The absence of revolutions and military takeovers suggests that public perceptions of politicians were, for a long time, much more positive than in other African countries. The country's socialist policies had the same suffocating effects on enterprise and savings as anywhere else; but early progress in spreading literacy, introducing clean water, and building rural clinics and schools gave hope to people still struggling to earn a living through subsistence agriculture. Unfortunately, these early gains were largely funded by outsiders. Agriculture – the economic motor of the country – stalled in the late 1970s, as it did in most of Africa, and the gaps in the country's budget grew too large even for generous foreigners to fill. Following economic reforms in the late 1980s, poverty dropped, but progress has stalled in the last fifteen years, partly because of the difficulty of spreading the benefits of mining and tourism, and partly because old ideological reflexes are still strong. During my last visit, there were no cars on the streets, as dealers refused to sell gasoline at the new government-designated price.

Given Tanzania's ideals, leadership, and early social gains, as well as five decades of uninterrupted aid at a level that other countries could only dream of, it has to be said that the country is not very different from the rest of Africa. Social peace is its one undeniable achievement, but even that is now under strain. Some would even argue that political continuity in Tanzania has been a curse in disguise.

For the continent as a whole, the Church's greatest contribution remains an educational system that has survived the political and economic turmoil of the last fifty years and still offers skills and hope to millions of Africans. In political advocacy, the Church was a late starter, but it made up ground by acting as the midwife of multi-party democracy in several countries in the early 1990s, and since then as a conscience for governments torn between the new pressures of democracy and the old ones of patronage, high-handedness, and ethnic loyalties.

As we shall see in the next chapter, because the Church is smaller in Asia, its educational and political role has been more muted than in Africa, and individuals have been more important than institutional structures. And if education was the Church's main contribution to Africa, providing basic services to the poor has been the driving motive in Asia.

CHAPTER 6

◆ ◆ ◆ ◆ ◆ ◆ ◆ ◆

Asia: A Determined Minority

THE Indian state of Kerala became Christian in about AD 52 – reportedly at the hands of the Apostle Thomas – but it was one of the few places in Asia where missionaries made any headway at all. Overall, foreign religions fared badly in that part of the world, being persecuted or simply absorbed like interlopers in a school of larger fish. India remained Hindu despite two centuries of Muslim rule. In China, Taoism and Confucianism held their ground against Indian Buddhism, as did Shintoism in Japan. Christianity was younger and apparently less sophisticated than the older religions, so it faced a particular disadvantage. Asian institutions and intellectual traditions were also sturdier than those the missionaries would encounter in Latin America and Africa. And Western individualism and the stress on religious truth were foreign to Eastern life, which emphasized the rules and requirements of community.[1]

Recognizing these special challenges, the Vatican tried to head off yet another possible problem: patriotic resentment of foreign influences. Drawing on lessons from Latin America, it created the Congregation for the Propagation of the Faith (1622) to spearhead evangelization, allowed missionaries to adapt Christian rituals to local customs (1659), and founded the Seminary of the Foreign Missions (Missions Etrangères) in Paris (1663). By and large, these steps protected Catholic missionaries for the next 200 years from being seen as agents of European expansion. The use of French missionaries was especially clever, as France did not yet have colonial designs in Asia, and it was only in 1884 (when France occupied Indochina) that matters became confused again.[2]

But it was still an uphill struggle, even in countries where Catholics won over the ruling class for a time and tried forcing mass conversions. In Japan, in 1583, one Italian Jesuit expressed frustration that latter-day missionaries had not been granted the gift of tongues and miracles like those of the early Church, and he prayed that they would triumph despite the humiliation and persecution they were undergoing. But his prayers were not answered: by the mid-seventeenth century, the small Japanese Church had been forced to go underground.[3] To this day, the only "Catholic" countries in Asia are the Philippines and East Timor, the first colonized by the Spaniards and the second by the Portuguese, who also controlled what is now the Indian state of Goa, the adopted base of one of the first Jesuits, Francis Xavier (1506–52). South Korea is the only other country with a significant Christian population (26 percent), a quarter of whom are Catholics.

Xavier died on an island facing China, frustrated not to be able to bring his faith there. Ever since, it has seemed the largest prize for Christian evangelists. The Italian Jesuit Matteo Ricci (1552–1610) was prominent at the Chinese court, more on account of his knowledge of astronomy and mathematics and the strange objects he brought with him (clocks, musical instruments, oil paintings, prints, and maps) than for any curiosity about his faith; in fact, he had to hide his missionary purposes to avoid being expelled, saying that he had come because of the "renown of the good government of China" and intended to remain there till he died, "serving God, the Lord of Heaven."[4] Despite his fame, he probably had no more impact on his adopted country than a Chinese sage might have had at the French court. But he and other Jesuits in the country had a profound influence on how Catholic missionaries conducted themselves afterwards. Their respect for national culture, their willingness to adapt Catholic ritual to local tastes, their use of local converts to help teach the faith to others, and their skill in infiltrating the ruling class became a model to follow. In India, the Jesuit Roberto de Nobili (1577–1656) adopted a similar approach and became a Brahmin scholar (and vegetarian) to gain the confidence of the upper castes.

China was a major mission territory right up to the middle of the twentieth century, with little to show for it. Sun Yat-sen, the father of the 1911 Revolution, was a Christian who absorbed progressive ideas in Japan and the West. "I knew that the essence of such a revolution could be found largely in the teachings of the Church," he said. "Today, it is the Church, not my efforts, that is responsible for the Republic of China."[5] But he was an exception. Many missionaries ended their careers in the country feeling their meager results slipping away like sand through their fingers. The Maryknoll order of nuns, set up in 1911, became so wrapped up in social – not just spiritual – work in China that some described them as "predecessors" of the Communists.[6] But once the real Communists took over, missionaries were declared to be "foreign spies." In the Maryknoll case, there was some truth to the charge, as Bishop Francis Ford (who died in captivity) supplied information to the US government on communist troop movements. Other priests had draped their churches with the Nationalist flag during the civil war. (The Maryknoll Sisters learned their lesson from this, and in Latin America, twenty years later, would put their mission before patriotism and would find themselves at odds with their own government and persecuted by right-wing regimes for their defense of human rights.)[7] By the early 1950s, the role of Christian missionaries in the world's most populous country was over.

India was also difficult terrain. The independence leader Mahatma Gandhi opposed conversion as an invasion of "the sacredness of personality" and an offense to national pride.[8] And, as with the Maryknollers in China, it was difficult to separate social and spiritual concerns; this sometimes led to the overstepping of what many saw as a boundary. In 1951, the Presbyterian bishop of Madras, Lesslie Newbigin, wrote in his journal:

> [The Communists] are waging a thoroughly justifiable campaign to force the landlords to give a greater share of the rice crop to the cultivators. At present the cultivator provides labour, bulls and ploughs, seed, manure and everything else, and gets one-third of the crop. The landlord, who may never even see his land, gets two-thirds. The Communist demand is that this should be increased to one-half. I don't think a Christian can do other than heartily approve of this demand. A wealthy landlord was very angry with me for saying so in the train the other night.[9]

But, as in China, missionaries had little success in spreading their faith beyond the existing Catholic strongholds of Kerala, Goa, and Tamil Nadu. This lack of a large-scale presence in Asia has meant that Christian influence on social and economic development has come mainly from individuals rather than from mass religious movements or the institutional Church. The one exception is the Philippines, where few would describe Catholic influence as unremittingly positive.

That country rivals the Vatican as the most Catholic place on earth. Every school bus in Manila seems to belong to a Catholic school. To attract credulous customers, private clinics carry religious monikers (St Stephen, Sacred Heart, The Lord's Grace), advertisers play tricks with Holy Writ (Almighty Aluminum, Immaculate Complexion), and bus companies name themselves after saints, like St Martin of Tours. Filipinos are accustomed to disaster – typhoons, earthquakes, floods, fires, and bombing during the Second World War (since 1571, Manila Cathedral has been rebuilt seven times), but popular devotion has proved more resilient. Reacting to a fall-off in attendance and the inroads of Protestant Evangelical sects, pastors now schedule Sunday masses at shopping malls. And the Church has had a stranglehold on public policy. Divorce is illegal in the Philippines, except through Church-sanctioned annulments, and the Catholic hierarchy continues to oppose birth control in banners on church fronts, sermons from the pulpit, and telephone calls to politicians (and their wives). One bishop was even reprimanded by his fellow clerics for promoting *natural* methods.

In 2010, galvanizing opinions on all sides, a new government announced that it would introduce a proper program of family planning. It was a family quarrel within the Catholic elite rather than a showdown between believers and secularists; but public opinion sided heavily with the government. In September 2010, Carlos Celdran, who leads colorful walking tours of Old Manila and who is also a broadcaster and activist, protested against Church interference at a conference being held at the cathedral. He intended to dress up as a bishop, but the car delivering his vestments broke down on the way; so he put on a different costume and protested outside, until it started to rain. Then, to avoid being drenched, he walked into the church in the guise of the national revolutionary hero José Rizal, brandishing a poster with one word on it – "Dámaso" – referring to a wicked priest in a novel that every child reads at school. He attracted more attention than he expected. The mayor, the archbishop, and numerous other dignitaries looked on as the television cameras rolled. "Holy shit! If I'd known that, do you think I would have gone in?" the troublemaker confided to me one evening in his apartment near Manila Bay. By world standards, it was a mild protest. But, in a bewildering example of public relations, the local hierarchy decided to press charges against Celdran under an old law protecting people's religious sensibilities. He spent a night in jail before being granted bail and was to be tried at a later date, facing a maximum sentence of six years in prison. (Two years later, the case had still not been dismissed.)

Celdran can be quite scathing about the Church, describing the Philippines as the first "Catholic" (rather than just Spanish) colony. But he keeps a sense of perspective:

The Church has oppressed women, but let's be clear, they're not the Taliban. People like to think we lived in some Arcadian paradise before the Spanish arrived. We didn't. We were killing each other. The Church introduced some peace and order and respect for one another, and if Filipinos seem relatively laid back now, it is because we have benefited from that good order for a very long time. The Church also preserved our national languages; otherwise, we'd be speaking Spanish rather than Tagalog.

Despite his Church-imposed trial, Celdran still regards himself as Catholic. "What else could I be?" he asks. "Atheism cannot explain the beautiful mysteries of life, and Christian precepts still appeal to me."[10]

If the Church has made Filipinos gentle, it has also made them docile, according to a different kind of protester, the former minister of health, Esperanza Cabral, who distributed condoms publicly on Valentine's Day 2010. According to one bishop, she "already had a foot in hell." Others wondered whether she was still a Catholic. "All religions are the same," she told me. "Generally, they promote respect for others, but what's wrong is when they try to impose their views on everyone. I don't blame the Church for our lack of progress in family planning. I blame our weak governments." She is just as skeptical about Church positions in other areas. Land reform? "The Church is the country's second-largest landowner after the government." Corruption? "The Church is prepared to overlook a lot in order to maintain good relations with the government. They're always looking for bargaining chips. Who knows? They might even accept divorce if the government dropped the family planning legislation."

There is growing resentment in the Philippines of the Church's "meddling." According to a community worker in Mindanao, "Birth control would move forward if we changed the minds of just ten conservative bishops." A minute later, he was contradicting himself: "All politics in the Philippines are about the Church." In fact, the institution has always played a political role. Every 17 February, the Philippine Historical Society places wreaths in front of a monument in Rizal Park, where three priests were executed in 1872 for alleged involvement in an uprising against Spanish rule. Priests also worked underground to overthrow

Ferdinand Marcos. Even the communist rebels, who have killed thousands of policemen and soldiers over the last thirty years, see themselves as "children" of the Church, inspired by Latin American liberation theology. The week I was in Manila, the Catholic Bishops' Conference objected to reburying Marcos's remains in the National Heroes' Cemetery. In exquisite contrast, the mayor's office announced that an eight-foot statue of Cardinal Jaime Sin – who played a leading role in the People's Revolution of 1986 – would be unveiled the following week on the twenty-fifth anniversary of the fall of Marcos. It is ironic, even tragic, that the bishops' admirable behavior in those events may have given them a greater opportunity to block sensible public policy.

Everywhere else in Asia (except for tiny East Timor), the Catholic Church is a distinct minority and must conduct itself accordingly. Take the example of Vietnam. On the way into Ho Chi Minh City (Saigon), there are no billboards winking at Holy Writ, as in Manila. In fact, there are no signs of Catholicism at all until you reach the city center and the street splits in two to make room for the 140-year-old brick cathedral of Notre Dame. Physically, Manila and Ho Chi Minh City have much in common, but the social landscape is strikingly different. Most important of all, there are no street children in Ho Chi Minh City, and very few beggars. Certainly, the government has controlled migration from the countryside in ways that democracies would find obnoxious; but just as important is a dynamic rural economy. Vietnam produces a fifth of all rice sold in the world and is the second-largest producer of coffee. Since market reforms were introduced in the late 1980s, the country has reduced poverty from 60 percent to 14 percent of the population. Religion has not had much to do with this, according to the World Bank's country director in Hanoi, Victoria Kwakwa. "It's their industrious nature and physical assets – good soils, diverse climates, and a long coastline – that have made the difference," she explained.[11] The country is also popular with foreign donors – the World Bank alone provides $2 billion a year – but aid accounts for only 3 percent of national income. Local and foreign investors are the real drivers of growth.

The Church is booming, too. In the 2008 census, only 18 percent of the country's 86 million people declared a religion, in part because Communists (who are first in line for government jobs) are not allowed to believe in anything but the Party. There were 8 million Buddhists, 6 million Catholics, 700,000 Protestants, and 75,000 Muslims. Priestly vocations are also blossoming: about 4,000 priests, 1,200 seminarians, and another 2,000 young men waiting at the doors, in what must be one of the liveliest clerical replacement rates in the world. Mass schedules read like multiplex movie listings in the West. But until recently, the Church's social role was weak, and even now it is more akin to charity and relief work than a serious contribution to reducing poverty. After the Japanese surrendered in 1945, many Catholics went into the bush to fight French efforts to retake the country. In his first provisional government (1945–46) the independence leader Ho Chi Minh appointed a Catholic as minister of finance, and Catholics were pleased that they were no longer considered traitors. But as the small Communist Party expanded its control over the national liberation movement, and the bishops began echoing Vatican complaints about Marxism, opinions hardened on both sides.

After the French defeat at Dien Bien Phu and the Geneva Accords of 1954, which divided the country into two zones, about a million Vietnamese (most of them Catholics) moved south. In the North, the Communists imprisoned priests and closed seminaries as part of a campaign against superstition and "feudalism." When the country was reunited in 1975, they did the same in the South and imprisoned the saintly bishop of Saigon, François-Xavier Nguyen Van Thuan for thirteen years – apparently for no other reason than being the nephew of the US "puppet" President Diem of the 1960s. Before they could be confiscated, the Catholic hierarchy handed over its schools, universities, hospitals, and other social services to the state, but declared that it would continue to "live out the Gospel at the heart of the nation" and contribute to the country's reconstruction.[12] Catholic nuns were especially adaptable, continuing to run schools and clinics and winning the support of the local community. But the bishops' Social Action Commission, which had cared for war victims on both sides of the Geneva demarcation line since 1965, was shut down, as the Communists felt it had helped too many members of the former South Vietnamese army.

Following the collapse of the Soviet Union, the Vietnamese introduced their own process of *perestroika* and lifted some restrictions on religious bodies, but it was not until 2008 that the government allowed them to perform social work again. As a result, the Church's charitable work remains quite small (about $750,000 a year) and, like the state, it prides itself on raising most of its own resources. "How much money do you receive from Rome?" I asked the secretary-general of the newly formed Justice and Peace Commission, Anthony Nguyen Ngoc Son. His eyes wrinkled into a smile. "None," he said. "Except for small amounts for cyclone relief from Caritas-Germany, Caritas-France, and Secours Catholique [France], all our funds come from our own parishes." The program is rooted in social realities. If there is a striking number of abortions in the Philippines (600,000 a year), the figure is four times higher in Vietnam (2.4 million a year) – undoubtedly because of the country's coercive birth control policy. (The salaries of state workers are cut if they have more than two children.) The Church trains priests and nuns to promote natural family planning methods; it runs shelters for young women (many of them students) who have fallen pregnant accidentally; and it arranges adoptions, if necessary. And, in a violation of medical confidentiality that would raise eyebrows in the West, Catholic social workers visit hospitals and doctors' offices to track down mothers who have had abortions. They do this not to reprimand, but to comfort them. "Many women suffer serious depression and nervous breakdowns afterwards," Nguyen told me. "Many did not want an abortion, but had no choice economically. We offer them counseling and lodging for up to three months, until they have had a chance to recover."[13]

In Thailand, not only are Catholics in an extreme minority, but few of them are native Thais, which puts them even further out on the margins of national society. (Most are Vietnamese, Chinese, Cambodian, or

Karen – the descendants of an indigenous hill people in Burma.) Catholic schools are renowned throughout the country, but they are so expensive that very few Catholics can afford to send their children there. Do they make a positive contribution to the development of the national elite? "I'm not sure we challenge the students enough," David Townsend, a Jesuit retreat leader outside Chiang Mai, told me. "In fact, on the whole, the Church has not been very active politically, refusing even tacit support to the 'Red Shirts' who pressed for democratic reforms and a fairer distribution of income in 2009–10."[14] "Even our charitable work is paternalistic rather than empowering," observed another Jesuit, Vinai Boonlue.

> We should be much more involved in pressing for human rights and opening up economic opportunities. It is quite amazing how we separate the spiritual and social spheres. The Thai Church excels in the celebration of the liturgy. We are a church of piety, chanting, and meditation, but there is little outreach to the poor; in fact, religion stops at the church door. Last Christmas, we had a magnificent choir for Midnight Mass made up mainly of poor people and undocumented immigrants. After the service, we sent them home empty-handed, without even a coffee or a sandwich. Like Christ in the manger.[15]

Elsewhere in Asia, even in a very large country, a determined minority can have a giant effect. In India, with only 2 percent of the population, the Catholic Church is the second-largest source of health and education services (after the government).[16] It serves two and a half times its numbers in about 30,000 schools and colleges, 4,000 hospitals and dispensaries, and numerous orphanages, crèches, old people's homes, and hostels. Its primary schools, most of them in the rural areas, have more students (3.2 million) than any other Catholic school system in the world, and more than in the whole of North and Central America; the same is true of secondary schools (another 3.2 million students).[17]

The Indian bishops did not comment on issues of social justice until 1971, when they told clergy to live more simply, admit more poor people to their schools, participate in civic debates, and train young people as agents of social change.[18] But not everyone was happy about the Church's role. Some insisted that lay people should have more of a part to play, that the Church was treating only the symptoms of poverty, and that it was too dependent on foreign funds, compromising its reputation as a legitimate national force for change.[19] But the Church's positive impact is hard to deny. Although Hindu nationalists might contest the notion, Catholic charity appears to have pushed other faiths to be less resigned and more engaged in social outreach. For example, when Mother Teresa began her work in Calcutta, she encountered stiff resistance from Hindu priests, who resented the fact that she had set up one of her first homes in an abandoned temple of Kali. The police commissioner refused to expel her. "Listen to me," he told the grumblers. "I shall not get her out of this temple until you get your mothers and sisters to do the work these nuns are doing. In the temple you have a Goddess in stone; here you have a living Goddess."[20]

The Church's clearest impact is in Kerala, one of the most literate (94 percent) and least corrupt of India's twenty-eight states. Its per capita annual income is less than $300, but it has a life expectancy of seventy-two, equivalent to that of Lithuania, a member of the European Union.[21] Undoubtedly, one of the reasons for the high literacy rate is that by 1979 there were almost a million students in Catholic institutions of learning (out of a population of 33 million), including a third of all college students.[22] But this is not just a Catholic success story. Just as important was the priority assigned to basic health and education by successive state governments, most of which were Marxist, suggesting an unofficial "partnership" between Catholicism and Communism. Local Church leaders acknowledge that they have been pulling in the same direction, even if they deny that it was a formal arrangement or a model. Kerala has also had an impact on the rest of the country, as three-quarters of all nuns (50,000) come from the state.[23]

The first things a foreign visitor notices about Trivandrum, the state capital, are the rubbish, the broken sidewalks, the diesel-belching "rick-shaws," and some of the skinniest dogs on earth. A spice trading center since 3,000 BC, it also has tangy food and a remarkable archbishop. "Are you a priest?" he asked, as I sat down in his office at the end of a long white-pillared gallery that must once have been serene. Now the evening traffic outside forced me to raise my voice. "No, just a layman." (Apparently, the priest requesting the appointment had rattled off the names of so many clerics who had recommended me – from Rome to New Delhi to here – that he thought I was one of them.) Soosai Pakiam is the son of a local fisherman and the only member of his family to have gone to school. "Coastal families were despised and looked down upon. Not quite the lowest of the low, but almost. My family never had a proper house. The roof leaked and we were close to starving many times. But my parents worked hard and made certain I was educated." The area is intensely Catholic. "When the Portuguese missionaries came in the sixteenth century, whole villages converted and are 100 percent Catholic to this day. The idea that there was a single God and that we were all equal, as brothers and sisters, was refreshing to us. It brought us back our dignity." Ninety percent of his diocese still depends on the sea, but times are better. "We can't attribute this to the Church. We have benefited from the general rise in the standard of living across India." But he has played his part since becoming bishop in 1990, the same year the central government began removing some of the legal and bureaucratic shackles on the economy.

I asked him what he was most proud of in his more than two decades in office.

We were a feudal Church for a long time. The rules were basically "Pray, pay, and obey," and we told our people to accept their lot, lower their heads, and look forward to rewards in the next life. I knew this had to change. So we empowered our laity, created parish councils and a diocesan governing body, and promoted small Christian communities in all our parishes, where thirty or forty families discuss and decide for themselves how the Gospel applies to their lives.

He has also established ten training institutions in twenty years – junior colleges, a teachers' training institute, a nursing school, an information technology center, and a "center of excellence," where 100 boys and 100 girls from deprived or troubled families live, train, and are given career advice at the diocese's expense. "We could have put them into an orphanage, but we thought this would be better for their self-esteem," the bishop told me. "Besides, there is keen competition for the limited number of places, and the winners are proud to be selected." He has also established a medical referral center, which has developed into a proper hospital. "It's not the best one in town, but it is improving, and at least our people now have somewhere to go." Altogether, about 30,000 young people are studying in institutions he has set up. "Where did the money come from?" I asked. "Surprisingly, I had no responses at all to my requests for foreign help, so we raised it locally, much of it from the sale of land we owned and interest-free loans from wealthy people in the community. We have state help, of course [the government covers the teachers' salaries], but otherwise the colleges pay for themselves and we have no debt. We cover the bursaries for the center of excellence from diocesan funds."[24]

Over the years, his relations with the communist chief minister have been excellent (although the Marxists were voted out of office shortly after we met). "We are friends, but we know each other's limits. When the Church oversteps its mandate, the government lets us know. But it works the other way, too. If the state interferes with private belief and Church programs, we blow the whistle." This is no idle talk. In the late 1950s, there was violence when the newly elected government threatened to take over Buddhist, Muslim, and Catholic schools. The faith communities, led by the Church, won that fight. More recently, in the run-up to the 2011 legislative elections, the Latin Catholic Association organized a rally of 100,000 people (including eleven bishops) to demand more political representation and government jobs, social development programs for fishermen, and greater attention for disadvantaged groups like the Dalits or Untouchables. The Church has also campaigned against the production of alcohol on the coast. "The government was surprised by our success," the bishop told me. "There is still too much drinking, but at least the villages that were selling liquor have now gone back to fishing."

The diocese is one of the few in India to involve lay people in the running of Church structures, and 30 percent of those positions are reserved for women. The diocese is also pragmatic about family planning. "Most of our people use artificial methods," one pastor told me. "Some even confess it . . ." Fortunately for the Indian Church (and unlike Latin America in the 1970s and 1980s), the country has always been a democracy, so the moral issues that Catholic leaders have faced have been largely local. But the Church is conscious of its position and influence. "Our role is certainly out of all proportion to our numbers," admits Bishop Soosai, "but it would be hard for any government to erase it." Others think the Church too intrusive, complaining about "pastoral diktats" being read out in churches during past election campaigns – until the Electoral Commission stepped in.[25]

By comparison with the number of Catholics in India (20 million), the Church in Bangladesh is puny (barely 300,000 in a country of 170 million). Yet its impact is arguably even more impressive than in India – especially given its small size and the special constraints of an overwhelmingly Muslim environment. Half of the Catholic community is of tribal origin, regarded as outcasts by the rest of society. Since Bangladesh was created in 1971, Church–state relations have been generally good but, like a classical ballet, subject to agreed steps. The US-based Catholic Relief Services was denied the right to establish an office in Dhaka because of the "Catholic" in its name. Yet, thanks mainly to the Congregation of the Holy Cross, which has been working in what was then East Bengal since 1853, the Church runs more than thirty secondary schools (one for every seven state institutions), including some of the best in the country. St Gabriel's School in Dhaka, founded in 1882, has trained a large number of the political, military, and business elite, as well as the Indian Nobel Laureate in Economics, Amartya Sen, who studied there before the partition of India in 1947. Only fifty of its 2,600 students are Catholic.

In such an environment, the role of individuals is paramount. Take the example of Dick Timm, an American living in Bangladesh since 1952, who was still rebellious when I met him at the age of eighty-eight. The first thing I spotted in his office was a large painting of Brother André, the founder of St Joseph's Oratory in Montreal, the largest shrine of its kind in the world. Timm and the Canadian saint have three things in common: both were members of the Congregation of the Holy Cross, both lived at Notre Dame College (one in Montreal, the other in Dhaka), and neither knew when to give up. Brother André devoted himself to raising money for his shrine; Timm specialized in raising hell. A thorn in the side of the Church and the government the whole of his career, Timm was given a five-year residence visa for the first time in 2011, fifty-nine years after arriving; before that, he was kept on a one-year leash.

He entered religious life as a "secure refuge from a wicked world" and was more concerned about saving his soul than serving others. As a seminarian, he hated theology, except for the writings of a number of French theologians who were forerunners of the Second Vatican Council. A biologist and specialist in nematodes (roundworms), he described fifty new genera and 250 species in seventy publications; but he had his feet on the ground. At the newly founded Notre Dame College in Dhaka, he established a science department that soon became the foremost in the country, and prepared a college biology textbook, based on local flora and fauna, that would become the standard text for the next twenty years. He researched one particular parasite that was threatening the jute industry (the country's largest export industry at the time), as well as another that was affecting rice yields.

Although he was in his element dealing with such concrete issues, he was also able to step back and look at the larger picture. Fighting poverty, he wrote, was "less a work of benevolent giving and more a work of making people aware of their rights, a work of participation with people who are struggling for a genuine human existence ... Islam [and] all the major religions have been passive supporters of traditional exploitative structures and policies."[26] At the same time, he resisted pat answers to Bangladesh's problems. As early as 1981, he questioned the value of food aid (except in emergencies), even to a country that was a symbol of world poverty, because it helped Western farmers more than Asia's poor, and actually complicated local efforts to increase food production.[27] When a UN conference in Paris proposed quadrupling aid to the least developed countries, Timm published an article saying "the news from Bangladesh may be discouraging to those who believe that money can solve all problems."[28]

In November 1970, he was principal of Notre Dame College when a massive cyclone and tidal surge hit the country, killing more than 250,000 people and displacing thousands more. He spent most of the next year coordinating relief efforts on Manpura Island in the middle of the most devastated area, and also publicizing Muslim attacks on Hindu residents: "Thousands of Hindus came to Catholic missions begging to become Christians. The Catholic policy was to enroll them 'in the community,' give them a cross to wear, and tell them that when things settled down they could make up their minds about accepting baptism and becoming Christians. (I don't know of any who did.)" For a time, government officials kept their distance, doubting that the Church would help non-Catholics, until Caritas Bangladesh earned a reputation for getting things done by mounting the largest relief effort in its history ($50 million). Senior officials then invited Timm (now the Caritas director) to accompany them to devastated areas. But his patience was constantly tested: "On every trip to the countryside I would encounter at least one instance of corruption or flagrant injustice to the poor and the powerless."[29]

Not surprisingly, he was impatient with bureaucracies – even exalted ones. In February 1975, he was invited to a conference on hunger at the Vatican:

Most of the [first] day was taken up with a power struggle between Caritas Internationalis and Cor Unum over emergency preparedness and who was "top dog" in the field. Two days later, we were still not coming to grips with the hunger issue, so it was proposed that the gathering hear something from the affected countries themselves. I gave a 25-minute presentation on Bangladesh.

But it did not go well, as he raised the population issue. In the 1970s, as director of Caritas Bangladesh and inspired by the writings of the Brazilian educator Paulo Freire, he helped set up 17,000 "social awareness" groups, in partnership with the Bangladesh Rural Advancement Committee, which is now one of the largest self-help organizations in the developing world. "This was the most important thing to happen here," Timm told me, "as it made the subsequent microcredit revolution possible. Many of the members of these groups were women, eager to improve their knowledge and opportunities. Some, especially the Muslims, wanted adult education classes seven days a week." Eighty percent of the women participating in the Caritas-funded family planning program were Muslim, until the sponsor (Caritas Germany) objected.

In 1974, Timm was named head of the Church's new Justice and Peace Commission in Bangladesh, and the local hierarchy must have regretted its decision immediately. The first thing he did was to investigate abuses within the Church itself. Eighty years after Leo XIII had put the subject on the institution's social agenda, Timm recommended a living wage for the Church's own employees, including teachers, who were among the lowest paid. "It wasn't very complicated. We looked at the price of a bag of rice in different parts of the country and judged that monthly salaries should cover at least that." But the hierarchy was slow to react. "How can we put the Church at risk," grumbled one bishop, "for the sake of a single person [meaning Timm]?"

He also studied the Church's excessive land ownership in the northwest and how it could be managed better to serve the local population. He investigated the situation of female domestic workers, including the sexual abuse of women employed in Catholic homes. He looked into the working conditions of a thousand women in over fifty garment factories. And he exposed some of the worst cases of child labor. He publicized the army's forced sterilization of tribal women (which had led to eight deaths) and ended the program in its tracks by informing the principal funder, USAID. In 1979, he helped found the "Asia Hotline" – a Catholic version of Human Rights Watch – based in Hong Kong, to coordinate the efforts of Church people fighting abuses across the region. And in 1986, he became the first president of the Coordinating Council for Human Rights in Bangladesh.

Unfortunately, his energy and idealism did not permeate the national hierarchy. When I asked if there had been progress on human rights within the Bangladesh Church as a whole, he frowned. Vested interests, prudence, and even apathy, he suggested, were preventing it from following the example of Catholic activists in South Korea and the Philippines in the 1980s. The bishops did not even issue a statement on economic and social issues until 1995, and before that, their main publication had been a Letter defending *Humanae Vitae*, Paul VI's encyclical on contraception. "They're not even funding the Hotline any longer, and we're the only Justice and Peace Commission in all of Asia to drop out."

Timm was in Bangladesh for good: the day before we talked, he had chosen his burial plot. When I left him, he was about to finish off an article denouncing police street killings of suspected criminals that was destined for a human rights newsletter that he helps publish. He also still teaches social analysis at the university. He had said at the outset of our conversation that he taught universal human values (justice, love, and equality), and so I should have known better than to ask if he regarded himself as a Catholic, a Christian, or simply a humanitarian. I saw a flash of impatience in his eyes: "I don't use those categories. I'm just a person who is here and can help."[30]

One question I did not ask Timm was how Catholic schools in countries as diverse as India, Pakistan, and Nepal differ from those in the public system, and whether they were part of the Church's contribution to society or just an aspect of its wealth. I had raised that issue in Thailand with the director of a Catholic residential secondary school at Mae Sot, a scrubby remote northern town on the Burmese border. "It's good business," he told me with a broad, self-deprecating grin, in his far-from-Spartan office. "But what do you do with the profits?" I asked him. "We use them to fund scholarships for the best graduates of our primary schools (which serve the tribal people up in the hills). They account for about a sixth of our student body. For us, that is reason enough for having this school at all." I wanted to believe that, but I suspected the school was also funding other diocesan expenses. And how was Catholic education different, given that all schools used the state curriculum, and even religious instruction had to be done in the faith the students had grown up with? "We teach from the heart rather than just a sense of duty," he answered."[31]

The director of St Gabriel's School in Dhaka added another dimension. "Discipline," he said. "State schools often go through the motions and do not administer examinations properly. Teachers are absent, especially late in the day, earning extra money at home giving extra lessons to better-off students. Here, it is only the Brothers and Sisters who are around all day, supervising student sports, for example." I quoted the teacher in Thailand about working out of love rather than duty. "Here, unfortunately, many state teachers are not even doing their duty."[32] The ultimate test of Catholic education is the market one. Right across Asia, well-to-do families send their children to such schools, confident of their professionalism and focus. Countless business leaders, politicians, and senior civil servants can trace their intellectual start in life to a Catholic primary or secondary school. And while the direct contribution of these schools to the lives of poor people is harder to measure, the critical skills and values they inculcate have influenced policy and decisions at all levels.

But the other side of the coin is distressing to some, like Nithiya Sagayam, a Franciscan priest who runs the human development programs of the Federation of Asian Bishops' Conferences:

Here in India in the past ten years, hardly a single Catholic school has been built for rural people, even though they still make up 70 percent of our population. Originally, our educational and medical apostolate was inspired by a spirit of compassion and service. Now it is driven by a business model. There is a heavy competition to mint money by all means. Even Church ministries have become money-centered. Priests long to be in city parishes where more money will pour into the collection plate. There is hardly any value attached to the vow of poverty anymore or even voluntary self-denial. These elements are not just new to India. It has now become a contagious disease among Catholic institutions in most countries. The result is that, at private matriculation schools run by Catholics here, it is the creamy layers – the Brahmins, high-caste people, Hindu fundamentalists, businessmen and women, top officials – whose children are educated. Our educational ministry to the poor of India – including the Dalits (Untouchables) and tribal people who make up most of the Catholic population – has been forgotten.[33]

Education and health are not the only areas in which Catholics have been active. Individuals have also contributed to social progress in Asia through the development of community savings and lending systems. In Korea, a Maryknoll Sister named Mary Gabriella pioneered the first credit union in 1960, aimed at women in the garment industry who were at the mercy of moneylenders with their extortionate rates. By 1988, the movement was so large that South Korea led the way in encouraging credit unions throughout Asia. Just as importantly, the cooperative movement proved a training ground for future leaders of democratic political movements, universities, and labor unions.[34]

The wider implications of such initiatives were not lost on a Jesuit priest I met in northern Thailand, who had moved to a remote village to be closer to the poor. At first, Manat Supalak was reluctant to see me and so secretive that I actually did wonder if he was making weapons in his spare time. But his eyes brightened when I asked if "liberation theology" meant anything in Thailand four decades after its heyday in Latin America. "Definitely!" he answered. "But we prefer to talk of cultural rather than political liberation here." Since the 1970s, he and others had been working on a Thai version of the "preferential option for the poor." There were three ways to fight poverty, he thought. One was to stick to charitable works, which did not change very much; another was to overthrow society altogether ("but if we did that, there would be no Church or pope!"); and the third was to correct flaws in society that perpetuated poverty. As I suspected, he had been making weapons: economic ones. Concerned by the cost of credit, he had helped local farmers set up microcredit schemes, drawing initially on interest-free loans from friends. "All the schemes are flourishing now, the farmers can buy improved seed, fertilizers, and pesticides, and half the assets belong to them." Then he circled around to the subject of culture again: "Many members asked whether they should be baptized, and I told them: 'Not yet. You have already demonstrated love, self-discipline, and sharing to make the credit systems work and that is already a lot.' "[35]

Another promoter of credit unions was Charles Young in Bangladesh, a Holy Cross priest who arrived in the country in 1933. He spent a year in the 1950s learning cooperative development at the Coady Institute of St Francis Xavier University in Antigonish, Nova Scotia. The Christian Credit Union that Young founded on his return to Bangladesh grew slowly, from about 200 members in 1959 to about 900 in 1969; but by 2008 it had swelled to 30,000. About sixty other parish-based credit unions have been formed since then. Young's reasoning was simple. He was not interested in welfare work, youth recreation programs, and other traditional parish activities. Instead, according to his biographer (the omnipresent Dick Timm), he "had learned early in life that the poor must be taught self-reliance above all and that Christian charity means lifting a person up even more than feeding him when he is down."[36]

Such individual efforts have been much more important for economic and social progress in Asia than the initiatives of the Catholic hierarchy; but the institutional Church has also played its part. The Federation of

Asian Bishops' Conferences, set up in 1970 during a visit by Paul VI, stressed from the very beginning the importance of being "the Church of the poor" and has criticized development approaches that seem biased towards the elite and widen income differences.[37]

Catholic bishops have had to be careful about expressing "Christian" views on business, politics, human rights, and corruption, so as not to create a backlash, especially in Muslim countries. But even where they have been cautious at a national level (as in Bangladesh, Thailand, and Vietnam), as a group the Asian bishops have formally denounced human rights violations, defended pro-democracy movements, and promoted community building among peoples of different faiths. In particular instances, Church leaders have gone further and been identified with mass movements for change. In one famous incident in Seoul in June 1987, Korea's Cardinal Stephen Kim told the country's military government, incensed that rebellious students were taking refuge in the Catholic cathedral: "If the police come to arrest these students, they will meet me first. And then there will be the priests staging sit-in protests, then nuns. The students you want are behind the nuns. If you want to arrest them, then please go ahead, but you'll have to trample over me, the priests and the nuns."[38] Years later, he was to reflect: "I stood, unintended, at the center of human rights and social justice. Some might have assumed that I was personally interested in politics. Looking back, however, it was an era of oppression, a dark era. We had no other choice but to wait for the truth to free us. How could a priest, as a delegate of Christ, remain silent at such a time?"[39]

On the island of Negros Occidental in the Philippines in 1969, a Maryknoll Sister named Mary Grenough joined forces with the new bishop of her diocese, Antonio Fortich, on an ambitious social action program. Grenough was frustrated to be working in a hospital providing free care to sugar-company employees, while the children of the poorer field workers were dying of preventable illnesses like tetanus and diphtheria. Like Óscar Romero in El Salvador, Fortich (who was the son of local landowners) was at first welcomed by the wealthy as one of their own and was given a Mercedes when he took up his post. But later on, a hand grenade would be thrown at him, his residence would be burnt, and he would be denounced as a Communist by those selfsame landowners. His "mistake" was to press for better working conditions for the sugar workers and for their right to join a union. After a year-long strike, the workers were awarded a large settlement, which a decade later had still not been paid. Sister Mary stayed on, offering legal help to expropriated farmers and refugees, and documenting human rights abuses.[40]

It is impossible to put a value on this wide range of interventions, and it is certainly true that in the countries that have made the greatest progress in reducing absolute poverty – China and India – the Christian contribution has hardly been significant. But outside China, the Church's provision of basic social services, its steadying presence in difficult political times, and the inspiration of moral leaders like Soosai Pakiam in India, Manat Supalak in Thailand, Dick Timm in Bangladesh, and hundreds like them have added richly to national and local development in a number of countries and have had profound effects well beyond the boundaries of the Catholic community.

If Africa exemplifies the Church's role as educator, and Asia its importance in providing basic services to the poor, then Latin America has given the Church a unique opportunity to promote political stability and reform – a critical and often overlooked condition of economic and social development. This role was only possible because the region is the only "Catholic" one on earth and the Church has been present there for more than 500 years. Part of the very fabric of Latin American culture and society, the Church has had the chance to exert an influence more profound than that of any other outside actor in the political arena. The results have been controversial, impressive, and disappointing.

CHAPTER 7

Latin America: From Las Casas to Romero

ACCORDING to contemporary accounts, it was a priest who instigated the bloodshed. On 16 November 1532, two hundred Spanish soldiers waded into an army of 80,000 Inca warriors, slaughtering 7,000 of them with their superior weapons. The Spanish commander, Francisco Pizarro, had asked the priest to address the Inca Emperor Atahualpa. The priest obliged by handing him a copy of the Bible. Having never held a book in his hands before, the Emperor had trouble opening it and, apparently irritated, threw it to the ground. Furious at this supposed act of sacrilege, the priest urged Pizarro to punish the "heathens." Pizarro kept Atahualpa alive as a hostage for eight months, in exchange for an immense ransom. Then he executed him.[1]

In the shadow of such outrages, one may wonder why the Catholic Church had any moral standing at all in the centuries that followed. But the gruesomeness of that day was not emblematic. Pizarro was not acting on specific orders or a general understanding of his rights as a conqueror, for even in his own day he was regarded as a ruthless renegade. Nor were all priests blind allies of the sword. Twenty years before, in 1511, a Dominican friar, Antonio de Montesinos, gave a sermon in Santo Domingo using words similar to those that Shakespeare would put into Shylock's mouth nearly a century later: "Tell me, by what right or justice do you keep these Indians in such cruel and horrible servitude? Are these not men?"[2] The Spanish authorities demanded that Montesinos be recalled to Spain, but the head of the Dominicans replied that the friar had preached not just for himself, but for the whole order.[3] One of the people listening to him that day, Bartolomé de las Casas (1484–1566), a former colonial official and plantation owner in Cuba, was so stirred by the sermon that he became a Dominican priest himself and spent the next fifty years defending the rights of the indigenous peoples of the Americas. Las Casas crossed the ocean fourteen times to argue his case, while in New Spain (the future Mexico) Bishop Vasco de Quiroga of Michoacán (1470–1565) protested constantly against the inhuman conduct of the viceroys, the Spanish aristocracy, and the military.

Their campaigns coincided with the arguments of another Dominican, Francisco de Vitoria (1483–1546), a professor at the University of Salamanca, who founded a tradition of moral theology known as the School of Salamanca. Adapting Thomas Aquinas's teaching on human equality to contemporary circumstances, Vitoria questioned Spain's right to conquer overseas territories, suggesting that its only "right" was to preach Christianity.[4] Impressed by the Dominicans' arguments, the Spanish Crown introduced its New Laws (1542) on the treatment of the native people; although these were highly enlightened on paper, they were difficult to enforce at a distance. In 1550, Emperor Charles V organized an inconclusive debate on the morality of colonization at the imperial capital of Valladolid. Las Casas participated in that discussion. Unfortunately, in an inconsistency which seems inconceivable nowadays, his vision of humanity did not embrace all races, and at one point he suggested that Indian labor should be replaced by African slaves; he later regretted this bitterly, considering it the worst sin of his life ("I was not sure that my ignorance and good faith would excuse me in the eyes of God"). But it was too late.[5]

In addition to defending Indian rights, some Church leaders tried to care for the material and cultural well-being of local peoples. Wracked by war and disease, Indians were resettled into carefully structured communities, the best-known of which were Bishop Quiroga's Pueblo-Hospitals of Santa Fe, set up in Mexico in 1532–38. Modeled on Thomas More's *Utopia* (1516), they promoted communal agriculture, new crops, tools and techniques, health and education, and a degree of self-government. Missionaries also built aqueducts and irrigation systems. To insulate the indigenous population from the "bad" habits of the settlers, and to preserve traditions that were regarded as consistent with Christian values, missionaries discouraged the Indians from learning Spanish, produced Indian grammars and dictionaries, and studied local history and customs. This led to an intertwining of Catholic and Indian religious practices that seeded deep popular loyalty to the Church in the centuries that followed, even at times of political upheaval. In the words of a modern historian of Latin America, the Church adopted a "consistent stance in favor of the humane treatment of the American Indians: it worked to relieve their suffering, and promoted a life of dignity for them where it could."[6]

Church views, however, made no lasting impression on the Spanish American ruling class, which continued to treat Indians as inferiors, and the Church itself became part of that elite, mired in protecting its own material interests and nurturing its close ties to the military, large landowners, and emerging business class. By the eighteenth century, thanks to bequests from the rich, tithes from the general population, and the Mexican Inquisition (which confiscated the assets of condemned heretics), the Church was almost as rich as the Crown. In 1790, more than half the houses in Mexico City belonged to the Church.[7] Some of this wealth was spent on education, health, and relief for the poor, but most was devoted to building churches and convents, commissioning religious art, and supporting Catholic universities, the first of which were established in Santo Domingo (1538), Mexico City (1553), and Lima (1551). Not surprisingly, such wealth infected the Church with a sense of power, privilege, and arrogance.[8]

Inevitably, Church domination sparked a reaction; and nowhere was this sharper than in Mexico. In 1857, a liberal government confiscated Church assets, closed all monasteries, abolished religious holidays, and even regulated the ringing of church bells. The 1917 constitution went further, preventing the Church from owning real estate, soliciting funds, and expressing political opinions. Priests were not even allowed to vote. During the revolution of 1911–20, the Church was treated as a class enemy, leading to numerous atrocities; but soon after, it started to recover lost ground. According to one observer in western Mexico, the church bells started ringing so early in the morning that "you might imagine yourself in Ecuador or Peru."[9] The Church had also begun to reopen its schools, to the relief of parents disappointed by the quality of the state system. But the war of words – and weapons – continued into the 1920s and 1930s, with one side denouncing Mexican "persecution" of the Church and the other "exposing" Church efforts to overthrow a legitimate government. Graham Greene set one of his most moving novels, *The Power and the Glory*, about an underground priest, in this period of turmoil. Yet there was violence on all sides. In one ugly episode on 27 April 1927, a group of Catholic rebels called the "Cristeros," behaving like latter-day Islamist jihadists, attacked the Guadalajara–Mexico train and killed fifty-four passengers, including women and children, crying "Long live Christ the King." Three priests reportedly led the attack.[10]

From the early nineteenth century, tensions between Church and state were common across the continent, as countries became independent and as the values of the European Enlightenment spread from sitting rooms to legislative chambers. Although they were prepared to allow the Church some social role, most governments wanted to take the lead in health and education. Liberalism and Catholicism were largely anathema to each other. Tensions at the top of the national pyramid, however, were offset at the grassroots by the intricate embroidering of Christianity and popular traditions that occurred in the early missionary years. At the base of society, the Church remained a source of direction, solace, and support, defying the political storms that swirled around it and offering continuity and stability. As late as 1970, 96 percent of Mexicans still regarded themselves as Catholic, and even their own government was stunned by the turnout for the first visit of John Paul II in 1979.

For the Latin American Church, the watershed event had occurred eleven years before. The Medellín Conference of the continent's bishops in August–September 1968, attended by Paul VI, raised the volume of the Second Vatican Council's social message to such a pitch that it galvanized hundreds of thousands of Catholic activists for the next twenty years and infuriated many in power. The bishops described poverty on the continent as "an injustice which cries to the heavens," spoke of "frustrated hopes" and "a climate of collective anguish" in every sector of society, and called for "structural change." "The lack of political consciousness in our countries," the bishops said, "makes the educational activity of the Church absolutely essential." Political action was "a matter of conscience" and an expression of "charity in its most noble and meaningful sense." One means of engagement would be to set up small Christian communities to study Scripture and Catholic social teaching, apply them to local circumstances, and act as a countervailing force to the "minority groups" in power. "The Church – the People of God – will lend its support to the downtrodden of every social class so that they might come to know their rights and how to make use of them."[11] Summarizing what happened next is like putting a roomful of steam back into a kettle.

Some of the bishops at Medellín gritted their teeth and kept their own counsels, reluctant to step in front of a leftist locomotive. As one country after another succumbed to coups d'états and military rule, the Church was being torn in different directions. Some, like Valencia Cano, "the red bishop" of Colombia, continued to defend human rights; others kept their heads low and focused on social service; elsewhere, the hierarchy was friendly to dictators or simply muddled. In Haiti, the bishops were so divided that they never spoke up, even in Rome. Like Paul VI and John Paul II, most Church leaders tried to steer a middle course; but there were extremists, stragglers, and hypocrites, too. After being made a cardinal in 1985, Nicaragua's archbishop, Miguel Obando y Bravo, made a point of stopping off in Miami on the way back from Rome to say mass for leaders of the "contras," who were fighting to overthrow their country's Marxist government. "I do not object to being identified with the people who have taken up arms," he said afterwards. Back home, he pleaded ignorance of alleged brutalities committed by the contras. "Tell him to come to my parish and help me bury the dead," retorted one priest.[12]

As bishops equivocated, the lower clergy and religious communities were keen defenders of people's rights against dictatorship and reckless development. Priests, nuns, and brothers joined radical organizations like the Golconda in Colombia, the National Office of Social Investigations in Peru, and Priests for the Third World in Argentina. Military governments claimed that they were defending "Christian civilization" against Communism; but liberation theologians regarded merciless police tactics and the oppression of workers and farmers as the real danger. In the last two years of his papacy, Paul VI (1963–78) pressed for moderation. In 1977, he berated Argentina's new ambassador to the Vatican about his government's human rights record; but Argentina's bishops kept mum on the subject for several months. In contrast, when the Pope expressed similar concerns about Brazil the next year, the country's bishops promptly took up the cause, belittling military talk about "order" and saying that the Church's idea of political calm was not "the peace of cemeteries."[13]

In fact, from the early 1970s onward, the Church in Brazil – which is the largest Catholic country in the world (130 million believers) – was the most progressive in Latin America. Although it had supported all previous governments, including the modernizing dictatorship of Getúlio Vargas (1930–45), the hierarchy resisted the military governments of 1964–85 and, during the most repressive period (1968–74), was often the only body with sufficient political autonomy to criticize the regime and defend human rights.[14] Inspired by Vatican II, the Medellín

Conference, and liberation theology, the Church supported basic education and literacy programs for the poor, set up pastoral "commissions" for farmers, Indians, and workers, and encouraged the formation of "base communities." (By the late 1980s, more than 100,000 of these were operating across the country.) In some areas, priests were jailed and tortured for organizing resistance to "development" companies and large landowners.[15] The Church became the military's most powerful critic, publicizing army atrocities, pressing for political reform, supporting opposition labor unions and political parties, and fostering a new generation of leaders from the lower ranks of Brazilian society: the rural poor, favela dwellers, Africans, Indians, and women.

Luiz Inácio Lula da Silva, the politician who made the greatest single contribution to reducing poverty in Brazil as president in 2003–10, was a product of one of those Catholic trade unions. In the words of one scholar, "the Liberationist Catholic Church may have been the most significant contributor to Brazil's key democratic events of the 1980s: the return to civilian rule in 1985, the adoption of a new constitution in 1988, and the election by universal suffrage of a president in 1989."[16] The Church's political role tapered off after that, under pressure from Rome (which resented the use of Christ as a "revolutionary" figure), as well as from many Brazilians who found some "liberationist" language and tactics extreme. The Church now worked in a lower key, focusing on issues like the safety of missionaries in the Brazilian interior, the government's economic plans for the Amazon, and landowner violence against rural workers. But public opinion remained supportive. In a 2001 telephone survey, 58 percent of Brazilians said they had "a lot" of confidence in the Church, compared with 30 percent for the armed forces and 15 percent for the president.[17]

But perhaps the most dramatic test of the Church's moral values was the overthrow of President Salvador Allende of Chile on 11 September 1973. Since his election in 1970, the Church had tried to maintain good relations with the first democratically elected Marxist government in Latin American history. Three weeks after the election, in the face of rumors that US President Richard Nixon was urging the military to prevent Allende from taking office, Chile's bishops supported the democratic process. Later, the country's senior churchman, Cardinal Raúl Silva Henríquez (1907–99), backed Allende's decision to nationalize the copper industry without compensation, and lobbied hard to protect the country's relations with the World Bank. Returning the favor, the Central Labor Confederation invited Silva to the 1971 May Day parade for the first time, and when Fidel Castro visited Chile in November, the program included a meeting with the Cardinal. That same month in Santiago, Latin American bishops organized a course on Marxism with the Chilean Communist Party, by then the largest on the continent outside Cuba.[18] At a moment of transition and uncertainty, the Church was playing an important stabilizing role.

But a group called Christians for Socialism (CpS), representing about 5 percent of the country's priests and other religious people, kept pressing the Church to support the government more actively. Even Allende encouraged the CpS to tone down its positions, but passions were running high. Radical priests described the hierarchy as "bourgeois" for trying to preserve a "false unity" in the face of class conflict, while the bishops warned against fanning tensions in the name of "freedom."[19] The President and Church leaders were walking the same tightrope, pleasing almost no one. Committed to constitutional methods, Allende appeared too slow to his supporters and too radical to his opponents. The Catholic Left criticized the bishops for not officially endorsing the government, while the Right reproached them for being too cordial. In August 1973, Silva mediated between Allende and the opposition over the control of arms in private hands. But the initiative came too late to prevent the violent coup a month later.

A handful of bishops thanked the military almost immediately for putting an end to economic upheaval and ideological warfare, but the Church as a whole reserved its position, neither recognizing nor denouncing the coup. Some were disappointed that Cardinal Silva went ahead with the traditional High Mass on Independence Day; others noted that he avoided shaking hands with the junta afterwards. When Paul VI denounced "the violent acts of repression in Chile," Silva at first downplayed the issue, apparently worried about retaliation against the Church: 60 percent of Chile's priests were foreign-born and subject to deportation, and state funding for Catholic schools was also at risk. For six months, the bishops continued to waver. In April 1974, they complained about "arbitrary or prolonged detentions" and an "increase in unemployment." "We understand that particular circumstances can justify short-term suspension of the exercise of some civil rights. But there are rights which pertain to the very dignity of the human person, and those are absolute and inviolable."[20] This statement angered some junta members and bishops, who regarded it as "Marxist," so no new statement was issued for a year and half.

Cardinal Silva, however, became more outspoken. He was one of the first to call publicly for the restoration of political freedoms, and he strongly opposed the military's takeover of the Catholic University of Chile. With Jewish and Lutheran leaders, he set up the Cooperative Committee for Peace in Chile (COPACHI), which established cooperatives, credit programs, health clinics, feeding programs for the elderly and children, and other social service projects for victims of the regime. The junta was furious, accusing Silva of supporting the country's enemies and promoting international sanctions against the regime. It even tried to persuade the Vatican to reassign him. When the government shut down COPACHI, Silva set up the Vicariate of Solidarity as an official ministry of the archdiocese of Santiago, less subject to government pressure.

Situated on the second floor of the cathedral, with a small entrance that allowed people to visit it without walking through the church, the Vicariate "was where your parents or your wife or your children went after you didn't come home from work or school," according to Ricardo Lagos, the future socialist president of Chile (2000–06). "It was where [those who had] disappeared were mourned and their cases finally investigated. It was the last refuge for a society with no safety nets."[21] Almost singlehandedly, Silva built the Vicariate into the most important human rights organization in Chile, raising funds from as far afield as Belgium and Germany, opening it to everyone (not just Catholics), and helping families in distress. Across the country, churches became centers of public organization, the one place where independent voices knew they could turn; Catholic radio, too, was one of the rare outlets for opposition views. "When I traveled the country," Lagos later recalled, "most of my meetings took place with the help of bishops, priests, and monsignors. Although a non-believer myself, I knew the Catholic Church was saving Chile's soul."[22] The Vicariate became important again years later, when successive elected governments tried to determine what had happened to the 2,000 Chileans who disappeared between 1973 and 1988. Vicariate records were crucial to the process of national reconciliation and healing, and they had remained intact thanks to Church stubbornness. At one point, John Paul II sent a personal representative to Chile to back the Vicariate's refusal to hand over its files to the regime.

Silva's successor in 1983 toned down the Church's public statements, but could hardly ignore Catholic social teaching. The Pope's visit in April 1987 proved crucial, as he met with opposition representatives, including the Communist Party, giving them public respectability that the regime was trying to deny them. Ironically, it was Pinochet himself who united the bishops against him by treating them as an adversary, allowing security forces to harass pastoral workers, removing funding from Catholic schools, and expelling foreign priests. The Church was a prominent promoter of voter registration for the October 1988 plebiscite that ended military rule. As turnout was crucial to the final result, some regime hardliners accused the Church of siding with the opposition.[23]

In Peru, the Church was weaker and the political situation more confused than in Chile or Brazil. Because of piecemeal pastoral efforts and a shortage of priests, most Peruvians by the early 1950s were Catholic only in name. But the situation began to change with the appointment of Juan Landázuri Ricketts as archbishop of Lima (1955–88) and the assignment of hundreds of foreign missionaries to the shantytowns that were sprouting up around the capital. In just ten years, the new recruits created more than fifty parishes among the poor and "rediscovered" the Church's social mission ahead of Vatican II. Another key actor, inspiring the new recruits from overseas, was a professor at the Catholic University, Gustavo Gutiérrez, who would publish the first major work of "liberation theology" in 1971. During the 1960s, US missionaries played a central role by providing food aid and promoting literacy, health, and hygiene in the poorest communities at a time of rapid change, almost certainly keeping a lid on political tempers.

The Peruvian government took advantage of these programs to improve its own contacts with remote highland communities, the urban middle classes, and recent migrants to the towns. At the same time, the US government used channels like Catholic Relief Services to deliver food aid, and the recently established Inter-American Development Bank (a regional version of the World Bank) channeled money through Catholic housing and credit cooperatives. In this way, US assistance, which might have been resented at a time of rising nationalism on the continent, was disguised as help from the Church.[24] During the 1970s, the Peruvian hierarchy began distancing itself from an increasingly authoritarian government, but Landázuri (now a cardinal) was outnumbered by more tight-lipped prelates, who generally opposed taking public positions on national issues. As a result, apart from isolated statements (often disowned or contradicted by other bishops), the Church hierarchy was largely passive during the 1980s and 1990s, even in the face of runaway inflation, high unemployment, collapsing living standards, and political violence on a scale matched only in Colombia and Guatemala.

"You need to put yourself in their shoes," suggests Elías Szczytnicki, the Jewish representative for Latin America of the global organization Religions for Peace.

The Cuban Revolution was still fresh in people's minds and there were guerrilla uprisings across the continent. We are all democracies now and the tone of public debates is moderate. That was not so, then. On top of that, in Peru we had seen it all. Progressive military governments that introduced land reform. Elected right-wing governments who promised to fight inflation and didn't. Populist governments that pledged to resist the IMF and World Bank, then jumped into bed with them after taking office. The Church backed the left-wing military regime of 1968–75 and, after that, could hardly oppose elected governments. Like everyone else, the bishops were in the dark about what the right answers were.[25]

If the Church's political role was strong in Brazil, balanced in Chile, and largely passive in Peru, to many observers it was simply scandalous in Argentina. In Buenos Aires, I asked Carlos Ferré, the head of a Catholic think tank, whether the Church had contributed to political stability in Latin America since the 1960s:

Not at all, unless by "stability" you mean dictatorship! In this country, the Church was among the first to shake the hands of the new generals in power. In the 1970s, the papal nuncio used to play tennis with the head of the navy, and everyone knew it. He also refused to act on a large number of documented "disappearances" of suspected opponents of the regime, submitted to him by distressed relatives.[26]

Ferré was not surprised to hear that international critics put Argentina and Rwanda into the same basket as examples of the Church's moral failures. The Argentinian hierarchy of the time deserved that criticism.

It is hardly surprising that the bishops were largely complicit with the generals in Argentina, as Church and state had much closer relations there than in most other Latin American countries. In particular, there had never been the violent conflicts between the two that had occurred elsewhere on the continent. As late as 1990, the constitution – which had been largely unchanged since 1853 – required the government to support the Catholic faith and stipulated that the president be Catholic. Bishops, and even seminarians, were given state salaries, blurring the distinction between the secular and religious spheres and causing confusion and scandal when the hierarchy seemed literally in the pocket of military governments.[27] Perhaps because of this incestuous relationship, never in the country's history – including long periods of dictatorship in the nineteenth century – did the Argentinian bishops oppose a government in power, except on specific points related to the Church's own interests (such as the teaching of religion in schools and divorce).[28]

In Central America, civil war and US support for right-wing military regimes spread terror in several countries in the 1970s and 1980s, and the Church itself became a martyr in El Salvador. Archbishop Óscar Romero (1917–80) was not the only victim. About twenty priests, including six Jesuits (among them the rector of the Catholic University), and four American women missionaries were brutally murdered for their defense of human rights. Romero was actually uncomfortable with the Medellín "option for the poor" and other modernizing trends in the Church. As a result, he was shifted from his position as auxiliary bishop in the capital to the small rural diocese of Santa María. There, his eyes began to open. In 1975, he presided at the funeral of five peasants who had been murdered by the rural police, and he wrote to the country's military dictator about the local situation. President Arturo Molina had just proposed the first agrarian reform in Salvadoran history, but withdrew it in October 1976 under pressure from the large landowners. As peasant organizations were formally banned, farmers lobbied against this decision through their small Christian communities. When the archbishop of San Salvador stepped down, the country's powerful families pressed for the appointment of Romero, whom they saw as an ally, and to general astonishment he was named to the see in February 1977. Romero accepted the position reluctantly.

Just a month later, a good friend of his, the parish priest Rutilio Grande, was ambushed and murdered by the security forces. Romero closed all Catholic schools for three days, canceled Sunday masses across the archdiocese, and invited people to join him for the funeral mass in the Cathedral Square. It was the largest religious event in the history of the country. From then on, Romero was in constant conflict with the government, the military, and most of his fellow bishops. In July 1977, to protest against political violence, he stayed away from the inauguration of a new president. The next year, he was recalled to Rome for "consultations." During a long private meeting, Paul VI held his hand and (according to Romero) said: "[Your] work can be misunderstood; it requires a great deal of patience and a great deal of strength."[29] The Pope urged him to promote unity and peace, not violence.

But violence was already spiraling out of control, and the brutality of the military government was intensifying. Three months after Romero returned from Rome, the National Guard abducted Justo Mejía, a devout Catholic and co-founder of a peasants' union, broke his arms, gouged out his eyes, and decapitated him before dumping his body on a mountainside. At his funeral, National Guardsmen asked individual mourners whether they had known him personally and, terrified, all denied any personal connection.[30] The Salvadoran civil war, which was to last until 1992 and claim 70,000 lives, was about to erupt. On 6 August 1978 – International Peace Day – Romero and his deputy suggested that all political prisoners be amnestied; but three weeks later, the rest of the country's bishops issued a separate letter saying the Church should stay out of politics. The country's hostilities had now spread to the institution itself. As Romero's involvement in daily events intensified, so too did his international reputation. In December 1978, more than a hundred British members of parliament nominated him for the Nobel Peace Prize. But he had only fifteen months to live. On Sunday, 23 March 1980, Romero asked soldiers at his early morning mass to obey a "higher authority" and refrain from killing their fellow citizens. Senior officers saw this as encouragement to mutiny, and later that day he was shot as he celebrated mass at the Chapel of the Divine Providence Hospital. He died shortly afterwards in the hospital's emergency room.

Across Latin America, with greater or lesser intensity and internal divisions reflecting the range of Catholic views more generally, the Church played a role that was inconceivable in Asia and would be echoed only belatedly in Africa. Inevitably, given the passions of the time, opinions vary about the impact of the Church's political positions, with some suggesting that the hierarchy was most effective when it was least "prophetic." It was Cardinal Silva's cautious successor in Chile who helped put an end to military rule through a concerted voter registration drive, and it was Archbishop Romero's faithful deputy who was an effective mediator during the Salvadoran civil war.[31]

Even the Argentinian bishops did more behind the scenes than they are given credit for – according to an unlikely source. Now over eighty years of age, the Jesuit Juan Carlos Scannone was one of the fathers of Argentinian liberation theology. "Of course, as a group, I wish our bishops had been more courageous, like those in Chile. But, as you know, they weren't all apologists for the government. Some were killed in mysterious circumstances, while others discreetly saved people from torture and execution. Even the papal nuncio called in favors from his tennis partners."[32]

Shortly before he left office in 2001, the stodgy archbishop of Rio de Janeiro, who wanted the city's world-famous carnival abolished for its "immorality," claimed to have saved 5,000 political dissidents between 1976 and 1982, lodging them in diocesan-owned apartments or securing them safe passage abroad. Cardinal Eugênio de Araújo Sales credited his good relations with the Brazilian military for being able to do this: "They would pretend not to know anything. I would let them know everything. I would use the red telephone and say: 'Hello, [General Silvio] Frota, if anyone tells you that I am protecting Communists, know that it's true and I'm responsible.'"[33] But it was the "prophets" – Câmara, Silva, Romero, Gutiérrez – who instilled hope and purpose in the hundreds of thousands of Catholic activists who resisted dictatorship and oppression, and it was foreign priests, many of them intellectuals, who helped to revive militant spirits when they faltered.

Pere Negre ("Pere" is Catalan for "Pedro") now lives with his wife in a small apartment in the Barcelona suburb of Sant Joan Despí. Hoping to be a missionary in Asia, he joined the Society of Jesus in 1954 at the age of sixteen, and a few months later was crossing the South Atlantic on the *Andrea Doria* bound for Bolivia. He spent the first year studying only Latin and Greek, until he asked to study Quechua, the Inca language, as well; the next year, he was at the Catholic University in Quito, Ecuador and his blood began to boil. Radicalized by his year in Bolivia, where a revolutionary government had come to power in 1952, nationalizing the tin mines, abolishing the army and replacing it with an Indian force, and, most important of all, redistributing agricultural land, Pere was shocked that a feudal system still existed in Ecuador and that the Jesuits were running their own estates along the same lines. He and a few companions wrote a "secret" letter to the head of the order in Rome, denouncing this injustice; they never received a reply. Instead, the small band of rebels was dispersed and Pere spent the next three years at a Jesuit house in Indiana. Later, he completed a PhD in sociology at the Sorbonne in Paris and was ordained a priest in Barcelona, returning to Bolivia in August 1968. He was still a misfit. He worked with a social research institute run by American Dominicans, taught sociology at the University of La Paz, and met Luís Espinal, a Spanish Jesuit who was setting up a journalism department at the new Catholic university. They roomed together in a poor neighborhood and became close friends. Espinal was to be tortured and murdered by a military government twelve years later for trying to expose the dictator's connections with major drug cartels – thousands of people would pour into the streets to attend his funeral – but at this stage he kept his head down.

Pere was more vocal, joining a radical ecumenical movement called Iglesia y Sociedad en América Latina (Church and Society in Latin America), supported by the World Council of Churches. In 1969, he denounced the killing of student rebels who had been cornered by soldiers in their forest hideout. The army insisted that they had been given a "Christian" burial, and Pere speculated in an anonymous editorial in a leading newspaper that they had also been killed in a "Christian" manner. Then he helped organize a national hunger strike on behalf of the parents, who wanted to recover the bodies. The government relented, and the autopsies showed that all had been shot in the back of the head.

A few months later, Pere was hauled out of bed by police and shoved into a helicopter. He thought his time was up. Instead, he was brought to an abandoned railway station near the Argentinian border and kept there overnight. The next day, he was handed over to officials on the other side of the border and delivered to a Jesuit community under strict orders to keep him out of trouble. Espinal got word to him that he could "shelter" him if he slipped back into Bolivia, which apparently meant joining resistance fighters in the bush. But Pere was a scholar, activist, and priest, not a revolutionary, and he turned the offer down; apparently, Espinal never forgave him for "turning his back on the struggle." For the next eight years, Pere did teaching and research in Ecuador, Chile (until Salvador Allende was overthrown), and Argentina (until General Videla took power). Then he packed his bags and returned reluctantly to Spain. He wanted to continue his ministry, but was told that there was really no place for him, so he married in 1972.

Throughout our conversation, Pere referred several times to the "errors" of his youth. I asked him what he meant.

> Well, I was angry at everyone, the government, the landowners, even the Church, but it was a difficult time and I should have recognized that the choices people were facing were not all that plain. The Bolivian Church meant no harm. It was just trying to serve its people as simply as it could. I wanted it to be more vocal on social justice, and saw it sitting on the fence protecting its prerogatives. I realize now that that was better than supporting the government.

He is philosophical now. "We drive through life with our low beams on. Back then I wanted to change the world. Now I'm just trying to prevent the world from changing me."[34]

Like Pere, the Church has adjusted its sights and moved on to new challenges. According to Pamela Cox, formerly the World Bank's vice president for Latin America and the Caribbean, "Outside Central America, the Church's public role is no longer very important. People are still religious, but they don't expect the Church to take public positions on policy. Poverty is dropping, but disparities in income remain very worrying. So where are the Jesuits and the liberation theologians now that we need them?"[35] But the Church is still politically active.

As if to redeem itself from its apparent aloofness during the "dirty war" of the 1970s, the Church played a key role in Argentina's 2001–02 economic crisis. With five changes of president in a single week, a massive devaluation, unemployment at 40 percent, supermarkets being ransacked, and the middle class made poor overnight, the Church joined the government and the United Nations Development Programme in consulting more than 2,000 opinion leaders over a period of 3–4 months on issues of justice, education, employment, housing, security, and health. According to Maria Lia Zervino, a director of the national Justice and Peace Commission, this "Argentinian Dialogue" almost certainly prevented a civil war. In addition to laying the groundwork for economic and social recovery, the dialogue attended to urgent humanitarian needs. With World Bank financing, vaccine distribution was arranged through Caritas and the Red Cross. There were cash transfers to households. And structural and legal reforms were initiated, including new measures to fight corruption, change the way Supreme Court justices were appointed, and abolish long prison terms without trial. A decade later, the Justice and Peace Commission was perpetuating the process on a smaller scale.

The Commission is now composed entirely of lay people and is chaired by an engineer, not a theologian or priest. It promotes policies of social inclusion through dialogue with twenty national organizations (including the employers' federation and trade union congress) which gather four or five times a year. Every Monday afternoon, a core group meets with commission staff at the office of the national Bishops' Conference in central Buenos Aires to discuss specific issues like youth unemployment, anti-drug education in the schools, formalizing the informal sector, raising the quality of schooling for the poor, increasing the stock of social housing, caring for the elderly, and training illiterate mothers in the proper nutrition of their children.[36]

Peru's Comisión Episcopal de Acción Social (Episcopal Social Action Commission, CEAS) was founded in 1965 and has a budget of only $500,000. Originally focused on rural welfare, land reform, and labor union rights, from 1980 to 2000 it became concerned with human rights more generally because of the government's war against two separate rebel groups, the Sendero Luminoso (Shining Path) and the Túpac Amaru Revolutionary Movement (MRTA). The government and the two rebel groups all laid waste to entire communities as a way of controlling territory; they killed 50,000 people and displaced hundreds of thousands of others. Drug violence added to the horror, as the army and rebels competed to control the market. According to Humberto Ortiz, CEAS secretary-general, "In this nightmare, the Church was one of the few voices of protest, defiance, and hope. We also inspired the creation of many other civil society organizations."[37] In 2000, CEAS helped prepare the ground for a national Truth and Reparations Commission, supported the international jubilee debt relief campaign, and pressed for the establishment of a national human rights commission. It now sustains a network of "ecological solidarity" in the countryside that promotes more prudent uses of natural resources and runs leadership courses for community organizers; some CEAS graduates have gone on to important roles in government. Such activities may seem tame in the homeland of Gustavo Gutiérrez, the father of liberation theology, but they are an adaptation to experience, new priorities, and a more open and peaceful political system.

In smaller countries, and particularly Central America, the Church's political influence remains strong. Over lunch at the San Salvador Golf Club on a hill high above the city, the very symbol of upper-class detachment, I asked a prominent businessman if El Salvador was still an oligarchy. He shifted in his seat slightly, looked around and lowered his voice, as if he was about to betray his class:

Yes, but things are changing. You have to remember how relatively recent Western concern about the poor is and how deep the cultural gap was in Central America. When the Spaniards arrived, the peoples they encountered had had no contact with the outside world in thousands of years. Even the Incas had no written language, or hard metals, and they did not use the wheel (except in toys). This is not racist. It's simply a fact. The gap in culture, technology, and initiative had permanent effects on relative income. The decision to begin to narrow that gap through education came very late, in the 1960s, and the Church was a driving force behind this.

He is not a religious believer. "I went to a state university in Spain and it was the best decision in my life." But he thought the positive role of the Church in modern Salvadoran history was hard to deny.[38]

In Honduras, until he blotted his copybook by appearing to support the overthrow of an elected leftist president in 2010, Óscar Rodríguez Maradiaga was the most respected figure in the country. In 1980, the week Archbishop Romero was killed, 20,000 Salvadorans tried fleeing the country by crossing the river separating it from Honduras. The Salvadoran army fired on them, massacring men, women, and children, while Honduran troops stood idly by on the opposite shore. Rodríguez organized refugee camps for the survivors, and was regarded as a revolutionary by the Honduran military. In 1993, he founded the Catholic University of Honduras, and the same year was asked to chair a commission on police reform. (When the process was complete, the Honduran parliament appointed him as head of the new force, but he had to decline – presumably with a smile.) He also chaired his country's Anti-Corruption Bureau until the courts refused to prosecute anyone and he realized the government was using it as a screen for continued misconduct. When he was named cardinal in 2001, the celebrations were so intense that some likened it to the country winning the soccer World Cup. As secretary-general and later head of the Latin American Episcopal Conference, he was already a global figure, attending the Davos Economic Forum in

Switzerland and presenting a debt relief petition with 17 million signatures to the G–8 summit in Cologne in 1999. In 2006, he was elected president of Caritas Internationalis, the Vatican body that coordinates the Church's charitable and development activities in the world.

Politically, he is hard to categorize. Tough on "neo-liberal" reforms – feeling they have brought modest improvements at the price of much upheaval and hardship – he is also suspicious of economic populism. Economic policy, he argues, should adapt tools to specific circumstances, not erect ideas into idols: "The Church is not opposed to the market system. But if the market creates social injustice and poverty, we must change the rules. Otherwise, we will destroy society so as to allow the market to survive." He has a knack for sound bites ("I believe in the globalization of human rights and dignity, not just money, technology and power") and a view of the world that is a little outdated, suggesting that a pope from the developing world would be able to influence "North–South negotiations." But, in his own way, he is an heir of liberation theology: "I remember in 1979, when I was a young bishop, that it was extremely difficult to speak of the social doctrine of the Church. Even the phrase 'social doctrine' provoked suspicion. Now it is understood to be one of the Church's best ways of promoting development." The day John Paul II died in 2005, Rodríguez was in El Salvador to mark the twenty-fifth anniversary of Óscar Romero's assassination.

As president of Caritas Internationalis and, in some people's eyes, a future pope, Rodríguez thinks hard about the public role of the Church: "Even the clergy are not fully aware of how much the Catholic Church is a moral authority in the world. It's good that this authority should be used for just causes." The Sunday after Hurricane Mitch (1998), Rodríguez expected almost no one to attend mass. But he was wrong: "Never before had I seen so many people there." Two days later, the Honduran president asked the Church to manage the reconstruction program, conscious of a previous natural disaster when a military government had stolen much of the aid received. Even then, bad habits resurfaced. A woman member of parliament jumped the queue at one distribution center and demanded food and clothing for her family. She was turned away.[39]

One needs to be self-assured to send a politician packing. But more than any other institution on earth and certainly more than on any other continent, the Church has had a special opportunity to set its stamp on social and political developments in Latin America. Indeed, since the Second Vatican Council and the adoption of the "option for the poor," the Church's advocacy, charitable works, development activities, political mediation, and moral leadership have probably marked the lives of Latin Americans as profoundly outside church as within. The Church was so aligned with progressive forces that, especially in Central America, Catholic meant being "subversive" and a possible target of death squads; in some people's eyes, it was safer to be a Protestant.[40] Liberation theology also drew attention to Catholicism in intellectual circles previously cool towards it.[41]

Undoubtedly, the Church could have done more to confront military regimes in Latin America in the 1970s and 1980s and to promote the emergence of open societies. From Constantine to Hitler, the institution has always shown realism – even cynicism – in dealing with harsh rulers. But it may be argued that Church leaders in Latin America should be held to a higher standard. It is unclear how Pope Pius XII (1939–58) could have stopped Hitler or saved more Jews where the Western powers had failed; but the Church's potential role in Latin America was at least as large as the influence that a Polish pope would wield against totalitarian regimes in Eastern Europe in the 1980s. However, what the Church did achieve was remarkable. Popes and thousands of Catholics on the front line were ardent defenders of human rights, even where the bishops in between were indifferent, partisan, or even polarizing figures. Some had blood on their hands, while others died defending the weak. They were reading the same Gospels, but not always in the same way as John XXIII.

A major example of the Church's political influence was John Paul II's mediation (1978–84) in the conflict between Argentina and Chile over disputed islands in the Beagle Channel. A previous effort at arbitration under Queen Elizabeth II had failed, with Argentina rejecting the outcome; but apparently it could not say "no" to the Pope. People on both sides of the border believe that a war between two military governments and economies of roughly similar size could have lasted as long as the Iraq–Iran War (1980–88) and set back the development of both countries by decades. The mediation was so important that in 2009 the Argentinian and Chilean presidents, both women, marked the thirtieth anniversary of the event by attending masses on both sides of the border and paying a joint visit to Benedict XVI in Rome. In another example of the Church's special relationship, John Paul II made an unscheduled visit to Buenos Aires in June 1982, three days before Argentina surrendered to British forces in the Falkland Islands. If only the Church had been able to do the same in Rwanda . . .

CHAPTER 8

◆ ◆ ◆ ◆ ◆ ◆ ◆ ◆

Horror in Rwanda

NOWHERE has the Church's role been questioned more than in Rwanda, the most Christian country in Africa, where priests, nuns, and lay Catholics participated in the 1994 genocide. Church leaders did little to prevent the butchery, and some even seemed to encourage it.

Rwanda has rebounded impressively from that ghastly experience and has become an example for other countries to follow. Like Singapore in the 1960s and 1970s, it prides itself on hard work, discipline, self-help, and using the firm hand of the law. In the image of Singapore's old "schoolmaster" Lee Kwan Yew, Rwandan President Paul Kagame brooks no nonsense; some regard him as too authoritarian and accuse him of assassinating political opponents, even overseas. But it seems plain that the country needed a strong sense of direction after the genocide. The capital, Kigali, is one of the most orderly cities in Africa. There is little crime and corruption. There are more women in positions of authority than in any other African country. Foreign investment is pouring in. And the president has an "office" rather than a "palace." Kagame shocked onlookers in 2008 by saying that "the world does not owe Rwanda a thing," meaning that he did not take aid for granted. Of course, it will never be as rich as Singapore – only eighteen countries are poorer than Rwanda – but there is progress and hope for the future.

That progress should not disguise the fact that the country is still struggling with the trauma of 1994. The genocide had many causes, including misguided colonial policy, population pressures, and, in the view of many Rwandans, the callousness of the international community and inaction by the UN. But, in most analyses, the Catholic Church – with half the population under its wing – stands out as a principal actor, fomenting the horror in crucial ways. Rwanda was originally part of the German colony of Ruanda-Urundi (together with what is now Burundi), but after the First World War it was ceded to Belgium as a "trust" territory by the League of Nations. Almost immediately, the new rulers began distinguishing between the minority Tutsis (who, the Belgians claimed, were a people of the Nile, exposed to the sophisticated civilizations of Egypt, Nubia, and Ethiopia) and the supposedly backward Hutus, a Bantu people from the south. But this was specious. There were no real differences between the two communities: they shared the same language and customs and were intermarried. Rwandan historians now accuse Belgium of inventing or exacerbating minor jealousies so as to divide and rule. The colonial power issued identity cards classifying everyone by their "racial" origins: Tutsi, Hutu, and Twa – the pygmy-like people that accounted for about 2 percent of the population.

To make things worse, the Church focused its early educational efforts on the children of the Tutsi chiefs, deliberately creating a ruling class that eventually dominated the nation's institutions. Resentment naturally built up among the Hutus, but it was not until the 1950s that their politicians insisted on a change of course. In the run-up to independence, Belgium – and the Church – conceded the legitimacy of the majority's complaints. By then, Hutu nationalism had become corrosive, ideological, even maniacal, and hundreds of thousands of Tutsis fled to neighboring countries as killings and house burnings began. There were more massacres in the early 1990s. Then, on the night of 5–6 April 1994, a clinically prepared extermination of Tutsis began. The trigger was the shooting down of the plane carrying Rwanda's president back from peace talks with the Rwandan Patriotic Front (RPF), the army of former Tutsi exiles that was rapidly taking over the country. The degree to which thousands of Hutus obeyed the order to kill has been traced to the discipline, obedience, and deference to authority that were instilled in Catholic schools. This is probably one criticism too far. By then there was dry tinder everywhere, and the spark was enough. Evil example, social pressure, and sheer terror did the rest.

The Anglican bishop John Rucyahana heads the country's National Unity and Reconciliation Commission and spends every working day thinking of ways of healing the nation's wounds:

There is a local saying that, when people start throwing stones, the man with the biggest head gets the most blows. Because of its size, its influence, and – let us be plain – its involvement, the Roman Catholic Church attracted the most criticism. But no religion in Rwanda distinguished itself during the genocide. We refused to look through our own lenses. We saw what the government told us to see. There were heroic individuals, who refused to kill others and were often killed themselves. But, as organizations, all the churches failed in their prophetic mission in the face of political pressure. Now, we must build the future drawing on the moral example of those few individuals who responded to what was best in them.

"Can institutions, as distinct from individuals, really be brave?" I asked him.

Perhaps not. But they can give people the means and direction, or the inspiration, to be brave. Institutions don't evangelize either. But they provide materials and support to those who do. In the

Catholic Church's case, leaders actually gave people ammunition for hatred and division. How can we deny that their words helped lead to the burnings of houses and the forced resettlement of thousands of people, even before the genocide?[1]

His colleague, the retired Anglican archbishop of Kigali, Emmanuel Kolini, agrees that the blame is widespread:

> There were no differences between the churches. Not one priest or bishop died defending others. So how can we talk of moral leadership? One of my predecessors, the army chaplain, was described as the "errand boy" of the regime. He traveled widely around the world to represent them. Afterwards, I asked myself why people still went to church. Were they stupid? I concluded that it was their way of dealing with their grief. They went right past the failed church leaders and put themselves directly in the hands of God.

The damage was so deep, he said, that the Christian churches were not yet in a position to play a prominent political role again: "We need to redeem ourselves first. And we have to be careful not to repeat the mistakes of the past. But we remain a watchman, striking a proper balance. If we get too close to politics, we burn; if we get too far, we fail our members."[2]

Although it reached its grisly climax in April–July 1994, the Rwandan genocide unfolded over a period of thirty years, with peaks of violence in the mid–1960s, mid–1970s, and 1990, when a Tutsi rebel army invaded the country from the north. The role of the Catholic Church in these events took several forms. According to one priest, "There was a gap between word and deed. The Rwandan Church always talked social justice, but everyone knows that (until 1959) it favored a particular ethnic group, the Tutsi, to the detriment of the others. From the pulpit, it preached the equality and dignity of all the children of God, but in practice it affirmed the superiority of the Tutsi."[3] The first Church leader to use incendiary language was the Swiss White Father, André Perraudin, a bishop for more than thirty years (1955–89). In 1959, in a Lenten episcopal letter on the importance of charity, no less, he talked about the country's "well-defined" racial groups and the fact that one of them (everyone knew he meant the Tutsis) had acquired too much power. This was not "healthy," he said, and posed "delicate and unavoidable" problems for the government. He also blessed the creation of ethnic associations. In an accompanying circular to priests, he acknowledged that he was playing with fire: "The issues I raised are sensitive, but we cannot in good conscience avoid them."[4] Shortly after, the first wave of house burnings and forced expulsions of Tutsis began. The bishops condemned the violence, but it was too late.

In 1994, during the hundred days of barbarism, Perraudin was in Switzerland undergoing heart treatment. He was fortunate. Two other Catholic bishops reaped what they had sown. The first, Vincent Nsengiyumva, archbishop of Kigali, was a member of the central committee of the ruling party until John Paul II ordered him to resign his position as a condition of the 1990 papal visit. On 17 April 1994, eleven days after the president's plane had been shot down, he claimed on Rwanda Radio that "a government that does not avenge its own is like a nitwit."[5] The other clergyman, Phocas Nikwigize, bishop of Ruhengeri, told a Belgian journalist: "What happened was quite human. In such a situation, you forget you are Christian. You are first and foremost a human being. The Tutsis were in touch with the rebels. They had to be eliminated so as not to betray us. They are clever and deceitful by nature."[6] Nsengiyumva was killed by rogue elements of the RPF army in June; Nikwigize was reported missing in the Congo, where he fled with other Hutus, and is presumed dead. Despite the hateful words, there was more than a grain of truth in what Nikwigize said. A hundred years of evangelization had apparently left a layer of moral values so thin that the worst elements of human nature were able to come to the fore. What is more difficult to understand is why a genocide so carefully planned – rather than the product of sudden passion or injury – was not denounced by anyone in a senior religious position. Hatred seems to have hardened the hearts of the hierarchy as well.

Even after the killings began, the Rwandan Church was slow to react – referring to a "civil war" rather than a systematic pogrom – although, on 27 April 1994, John Paul II was the first world leader to denounce the "genocide." Even twenty years later, some Church leaders try to explain away the cruelty. "We can't all be martyrs," one priest told me, referring to the small number of people who defended the victims. "There were more errors of omission than commission." Théotime Gatete, secretary-general of the National Episcopal Conference, tries to salvage some light from the darkness. "It is not true that no priest or nun died trying to save others," he told me.[7] On the third day of the genocide, Ananie Rugasire (nephew of the notorious archbishop of Kigali) perished trying to prevent militiamen from entering a junior seminary where Tutsis had taken shelter. At about the same time, Félicité Niyitegeka, a member of the Auxiliaries of the Apostolate, was to have been taken to safety by order of her brother, an army colonel; but she refused to leave, died alongside others from the community, and was later named a National Hero. But there were priests and nuns among the murderers, with one pastor reportedly bulldozing his own church that was sheltering 2,000 people. The only bishop accused of direct involvement, Augustin Misago, was acquitted in June 2000 after spending eighteen months in prison.

Although it has come close, the Rwandan Church has never apologized for its role in the genocide, choosing instead to rebuild its reputation by promoting reconciliation through its Justice and Peace Commission and supporting the work of the community courts that tried more than 120,000 people. Many people, including Catholics, resent the Church's failure to acknowledge its role and to seek forgiveness.

Two places of worship south of Kigali still show traces of the horror. The young guide at the Ntamara church explained that, shortly after taking power in the 1950s, the Hutu government moved Tutsis to the area, at the time still a forest teeming with wild animals and tsetse flies, hoping the settlers would succumb to those dangers. Whether this was history or hearsay, there was little doubt about what happened in 1994. For the first few days, the Tutsis resisted the militias, hiding in the hills and ambushing their attackers when they could; then the army was called in to conduct the massacre on an industrial scale. In just two days (15–16 April), more than 25,000 people were murdered in and around the two churches. The clothes of the victims are still strewn over the pews, and there are bloodstains on the altar cloth and ceiling, caused by grenades. At the Ntamara church, in the room where children once studied their catechism, there are traces on the wall where the brains of infants were dashed out on the bricks. I asked the guide, a Catholic, whether he still went to church. "Definitely," he said. What did he think of the Church's role? "It is difficult to incriminate the Church. After all, it was individuals rather than the institution that participated in the genocide." Yet he still wanted an apology. Why? "Because, if your son has robbed the neighbors, the least you can do is to go next door and ask forgiveness." Mainstream Christians are not the only ones grappling with the heritage of the genocide. The Pentecostal churches are still trying to overcome internal divisions; and, while most Muslims deny killing anyone, others claim they spared fellow Muslims but went to neighboring villages to participate in the murders.

Bishop Servilien Nzakamwita, head of the Catholic Justice and Peace Commission, is at the heart of the Church's efforts to confront and cauterize the past. His diocese is an hour's drive to the north of the capital, past irrigated rice paddies and terraced hillsides more typical of Asia than Africa. Apart from its altitude (8,000 feet), gum trees, tin roofs, and potholes, Byumba could be an Italian hill town, sitting confidently on top of the world. The bishop's waiting room is simple: a row of wooden chairs and a bench set against a bare white wall stained with the hair grease of some of the 750,000 souls under his wing. When a nun led me into his office, he introduced me to the seamy side of Rwandan order. A young priest had recently been imprisoned for denouncing the government's burning of straw houses in his parish (intended to force the poor inhabitants to build more salubrious dwellings). The bishop tried to convince the priest to apologize for his public statements, but the young man was adamant. It was hard to choose between the bishop's realism and the stubbornness of the priest, just three years out of seminary, who saw social justice as central to his service and who was prepared to stay in jail to defend his right to speak up for the poor.

The bishop himself is a model of reconciliation. In the first days of the genocide, he took shelter in the seminary in Kigali, then came north to Byumba. His brother and sister, and their children, were murdered in 1990, their bodies thrown into a latrine. He recovered their corpses and arranged a proper burial. "Even now, I don't know how I overcame my hatred and rage," he says. Although a Tutsi, he tries to put the Church's mistakes into perspective. Even Bishop Perraudin's political stances have to be seen in the context of the time, he says: "In the 1950s, those pressing for political independence were seeking help from the Eastern Bloc and there was great fear of Communism in the Church." Later, different fears arose: "When my predecessor was murdered in June 1994, the Pope denounced it. But he was in Rome." Since becoming a bishop in 1996, Servilien has been helping people replace memories of hatred with acts of reconstruction. In his first few months, he organized summer camps for more than 300 children of returning Tutsi and Hutu refugees, so that they could learn to live side by side. Despite resistance, he arranged for land to be given back to the refugees, or at least shared with them, even though some of them had been away for decades. "Three sets of people have come together. Killers are living side by side with the survivors of their victims or with the families of people still in prison. Pastors have brought them together, sometimes with the simple message: You are all suffering. Recognize that."[8] The community has also contributed to the healing, with representatives of all three groups bringing food to people in prison *together* and one parish building three houses – one for a member of each group. When the bishop blessed the completed structures, one of the intended occupants (a convicted killer and young bachelor) gave his new house away to a family of survivors living nearby in a makeshift hut.

One priest's experience is a proxy for what the Church did – and failed to do – during the genocide. Gabriel Maindron arrived in Rwanda in September 1959, convinced that he was turning his back forever on his native France. He was determined not to be a missionary of the old school, preferring to complete his studies for the priesthood there and to serve a Church run by Africans. But the first thing he noticed was how wealthy the Church was. In every village, there was a church, school, dispensary, or community hall run by Catholics and, apart from government buildings, they were the only ones in brick. (Later, he learned that the Church was the largest employer and landowner in the country, and that the parish often had more power than the local mayor.) Arriving at the seminary in Nyakibanda, he was transfixed by how solid it was, calculating that 800,000 bricks had been used in its construction, while most of the local population were living in huts.

At the seminary, almost everyone was from a well-to-do family, intent on social status rather than social service. Discouraged by the academic tone of the lectures, he talked longingly about the preparations for the Vatican Council in Rome and the example of worker-priests in France. But many of his fellow seminarians had different values. "You're talking about a Church on the cheap," they muttered. "Priests need to protect their prestige." For them, a priest was a chief before being a pastor.

In June 1962, Gabriel was one of the first white priests ordained in Africa, assigned to help thirty-three "base communities" with small development projects, including a carpentry workshop for boys and dressmaking classes for girls. In his spare time, he relaxed in his vegetable garden and cared for five cows and a prize bull (given by Swiss aid), which local villagers could use to improve their own stock. Later, Gabriel was transferred to a parish in the west of the country, on the Congo–Nile watershed, the most densely populated place he had seen in his life. Ignoring Catholic teaching, he told parishioners from the pulpit: "If you really like children, try not having too many. Remember, you will have to feed them." His bishop later countermanded him. "Children are our problem, not yours," he told Gabriel. "Family planning is a White idea."

In 1990, after the Tutsi-led Rwandan Patriotic Front army crossed into the country from Uganda, Gabriel tried to calm spirits and helped rebuild Tutsi houses burnt down by Hutus. But he felt like a helpless country priest. In June 1991, he wrote an article in a national Catholic paper, accusing the Church of "total silence in the face of an absurd war." "Praying and making nice declarations about peace are close to hypocrisy when not backed up by courageous acts." The first telephone call came from the Catholic primate, the archbishop of Kigali: "So, Gabriel, are you accusing me?" He was right to feel targeted. A close friend of the Hutu president, the Archbishop had enjoyed the status of a government minister and was driven around in an official car; in June 1994, he would be murdered with two other bishops.

On 9 April 1994, the third night of the genocide, with about 200 Tutsi sheltering on grass mats in the corridors of the presbytery, Gabriel received a call from a friend in France: "I imagine you have been praying?" "Not for three days," he answered – he had been too busy. Several times over the next few days, he had to leave the presbytery and face down armed gangs wanting to enter. When one group grew insistent, he was tempted to insult them in their own language; instead, he knelt in front of them and said: "Well, begin with me." They moved away. Eventually, the local authorities sent buses to pick up the refugees and transport them to a nearby school; but Gabriel had been duped. The following Sunday, they were moved again to a football stadium, where they were slaughtered with thousands of others.

When he learned this, his nerve failed him. Knowing they would be killed anyway, he saw no point in protecting more Tutsis. At dawn on 14 April, a small group knocked on the door; Gabriel told them they were crazy to come out during the day, as they would be spotted by the militias, endangering both themselves and the five or six refugees that Gabriel was still sheltering in the presbytery. He raised his hands in a sign of helplessness and closed the door. But the six adults and seven children were exhausted, so they stayed outside waiting to be killed. At about nine in the morning, men arrived to take them a short way up the road. In his study, Gabriel closed his eyes and began reciting his rosary, hearing the clubs coming down on the skulls of those outside, the women screaming, the children dying in silence. He dropped to his knees, spread out his arms in the form of a cross, imagining Christ's passion and his mother's suffering. Later, he wished he had died trying to save them and understood the mistake he had made. Burying the bodies with the help of volunteers from town, he resolved to help others again.

But there were fewer and fewer Tutsis to save. Many had fled to the Congo or had already been killed. When French forces arrived on 30 June, Gabriel spread the word to Tutsis still hiding to come to the presbytery at midnight so that they could be taken to safety. The French troops admired Gabriel's devotion – he was one of the few foreigners who had decided to stay in the country – but he was bitter with himself and the world. A few days later, when he met the Pope's envoy, Cardinal Etchegaray, he thanked him for coming – "at last." As his parish emptied, first of Tutsis and then of Hutus fleeing the victorious RPF forces, Gabriel tried to understand how the most Christian country in Africa could have descended into such barbarism. In the confessional, he heard stories so perplexing and painful that he told several parishioners to come back in a few days, as he was unable to give them absolution. Others confided gruesome stories of how they had dealt with the horror. A Hutu man tried hiding his Tutsi fiancée in his house, but she was spotted, and a gang threatened to burn the house down. Out of her wits at the thought of an agonizing death, the woman persuaded him to bury her alive: "You will save me from something worse." They prayed calmly as he shoveled the earth on top of her, and she died, apparently peacefully. "Who am I to condemn their decision?" asked Gabriel.

With no one to minister to, he decided reluctantly to return to France in mid-July. There he was besieged by journalists. He tried to draw attention to the many acts of selflessness that had occurred in the middle of the savagery. One young journalist was almost insolent: "After all you have lived through, are you saying that the spirit of love won out over hatred? The heroism of a few Catholics can't wipe out the failure of the Church. You, the Church, have been in Rwanda for over a century and were apparently all-powerful, yet you were unable to prevent one of the greatest tragedies of the century!" The Rwandan Church had its faults, Gabriel admitted, but it had its own victims: more than 200 bishops, priests, and nuns. The journalist was intransigent: "We're talking about your efforts to spread the Gospel. You spent thirty-five years there, and what do you have to show for it? Isn't it a failure?" Gabriel hesitated. "Everything collapsed, not just the Church. It was a failure for everyone: the state, civil society, the international community." "Of course it was a failure for everyone," the journalist persisted. "But it's the failure of the Church that matters most. Why can't it show more courage in the face of great tragedies?" Gabriel was pensive. "You're right," he conceded. "Even I lacked courage . . ."[9]

CHAPTER 9

Tilting at Condoms

IF Rwanda was a piercing challenge to the Church's moral conscience, population growth and the spread of HIV/AIDS, especially in Africa, have been regarded by some as another shocking case of Catholic indifference. In October 2010, the University of Oxford Current Affairs Society invited me to debate the issue of contraception in Africa with the UK spokesman for the Catholic movement Opus Dei. My debating partner exuded the joy and confidence of a born-again Christian who tries to speak and live by the truth without adopting holy airs along the way. A month before, during the pope's visit to Britain to beatify the great nineteenth-century cleric John Henry Newman, my partner in the debate had been put in the awkward position of defending Newman against suspicions of homosexuality. There was a time, he had told the media ruefully, when men and women could have close friendships with people of their own sex without being accused of expressing it physically.

But there was steel beneath my opponent's geniality. During our debate he plied so close to Church teaching on sexual matters that it almost became a caricature. "The population issue is grossly exaggerated," he suggested. "You could squeeze the world's entire population into the United Kingdom and everyone would still have 35 square feet to move around in." (So much for long country walks, I thought to myself.) He was just as categorical about the fight against HIV/AIDS: "The Church is not telling prostitutes in Africa not to use contraceptives. It's simply telling them to stop being prostitutes." "Not everyone with HIV/AIDS is a prostitute," I countered. "Many women have died simply by sleeping with their husbands." But there was no budging him, and the small audience of mainly Catholic students, some of whom had taken the train up from London to cheer him on, was just as resolute. I felt like raising my voice: "Obviously, none of you has ever seen a person die from AIDS." But this was Oxford and I wanted to respect the rules.

At the opposite end of the Catholic spectrum is the US-based organization Catholics for Choice. Although the US hierarchy has not excommunicated its members, the bishops have repeatedly reminded people that it is not an official "Catholic" organization. Like the Opus Dei spokesman, the president of the group, a former Irish journalist named Jon O'Brien, does not lie awake at night worrying about world population numbers: "People in the West want to control other people's birth rates, ignoring the fact that our consumption of world resources is the issue." A photograph in the organization's magazine *Conscience* illustrated this point humorously. A young demonstrator holds up a placard: "Save the Environment. Kill Yourself." Nor does the organization promote abortion. What O'Brien is worried about is saving women from ravaging their bodies with multiple pregnancies. "We are also concerned about religious freedom," he told me. "The same religious freedom the Church stood up for in the Soviet Union and Eastern Europe and now defends in the Middle East. Most Catholics ignore Church advice on contraception and we defend their right to do so."[1]

These two sets of opinions reflect the broad diversity of thought within the Catholic Church on what specialists call reproductive health. They also suggest the high emotions and confusion that Vatican stubbornness has sparked. But in examining this subject more closely, it is important to separate principles, biases, and facts.

Many people believe the Catholic Church has been obsessed with sex for 2,000 years. John Allen, the Vatican correspondent for the *National Catholic Reporter*, takes a different view – that it is Western culture that has been fixated on the subject, and only for the past fifty years.[2] Until the latter part of the twentieth century, very little of what the Christian churches taught was controversial. It is Western practice that has raced ahead of the Church's ability to change its positions. Jews and Muslims, not just Christians, believe in the "sanctity" of marriage, encourage sexual abstinence outside the marital state, and insist that the primary purpose of sex is to produce children. One of the few issues that divide them is whether births can be spaced, using artificial methods.

To be fair, Catholic teaching was controversial long before the sexual revolution of the 1960s. Joseph McCabe (1867–1955), a British Franciscan and philosophy professor, left the Church in 1895, and fifty years later was still steaming about its "stupid, futile and insolent" sexual ethic. But he put things into perspective: "The average Catholic takes no more notice of the refinements of his church's sex-ethic than he did in the Middle Ages ... The Catholic girl and youth kiss as ardently and lingeringly as others do ... Broadly, Catholics learn more from their non-Catholic neighbors as to the practical and sensible code of life than they do from theologians."[3]

The details of birth control are a relatively recent feature of Catholic teaching. In fact, until the biological discoveries of the late nineteenth century, no one realized that births could be controlled *naturally*, by avoiding intercourse during a woman's brief periods of fertility. And it was not until 1930 that a major Christian denomination, the Anglican Church, approved any form of birth control. Even then, it was subject to strict conditions. Abstinence was still considered better than contraception; there had to be "a clearly felt moral obligation" to limit or avoid parenthood; and the reasons could not include "selfishness, luxury or mere convenience."[4]

Shaken by this decision, and before the year was out, Pope Pius XI issued the encyclical *Casti Connubii* (On Chaste Marriage), which reaffirmed the Roman Catholic position that any sexual intercourse "deprived of its natural power of procreating life" was a "grave sin." But, reflecting new developments in Catholic theology, the Pope made two important concessions. He opened the door to using the "rhythm method" for controlling the size of families, and he recognized that there were other ("secondary") reasons for having sex, such as "cultivating mutual love" and quieting "concupiscence," the ancient Christian word for sensual desire.[5] Pius XII diluted the Catholic position further in 1951. While still opposing artificial methods, he decreed that couples could be excused the duty of procreation for "serious reasons." Three years later, in 1954, addressing the World Population Conference in Rome, he said that he hoped the rhythm method could contribute to limiting the expansion of the world's population. Thereafter, Church teaching hit a brick wall and stayed there for more than half a century.

With the advent of the pill (which some Catholics described as "helping nature along"), several participants at the Second Vatican Council (1962–65), including the prominent Belgian Cardinal Leo Jozef Suenens, wanted birth control added to the Council's agenda. Instead, John XXIII (1958–63) and then Paul VI (1963–78) reserved that issue, along with clerical celibacy, to their own judgment. The original commission set up to study the matter consisted of thirteen men, but in 1965 Paul VI expanded it to fifty-eight, including five laywomen.

An American couple named Crowley, active in the international Christian Family Movement, was especially influential. They surveyed 3,000 devout Catholics, 63 percent of whom thought the rhythm method had harmed their marriage; 65 percent also said that it had not prevented pregnancies. One husband lamented:

Rhythm destroys the meaning of the sex act; it turns it from a spontaneous expression of spiritual and physical love into a mere bodily sexual relief; it makes me obsessed with sex throughout the month . . . I have watched a magnificent spiritual and physical union dissipate and, due to rhythm, turn into a tense and mutually damaging relationship.

His wife echoed his feelings: "I find myself sullen and resentful of my husband when the time of sexual relations finally arrives. I resent his necessarily guarded affection during the month, and I find I cannot respond suddenly."[6] Doctors reminded the commission that nature gives women their greatest sexual desire at just the moment that rhythm prevented them from making love.

When the theologians on the commission convened for a vote, the result was 12–7 for changing Church teaching. Stunned by this outcome, the Vatican demoted the commissioners to the rank of "advisers" and replaced them with sixteen bishops. The tactic didn't work. In June 1965, with a few abstaining, the bishops voted 9–3 for change. The votes in the other groups were even wider, with fifteen of the nineteen theologians and thirty of the thirty-five other members urging a retreat from the Church's untenable position. The majority agreed that the main purpose of marriage was to raise children, but they saw nothing inherently evil in artificial birth control and wanted the Church to be concerned about the well-being of married couples in general rather than about individual acts in the privacy of those couples' own homes.[7] The bishops had agreed that there would be only one report, but the American Jesuit John Ford drafted a so-called minority report and submitted it to the Pope. Shortly after, the commission report was leaked to the press.

Instead of acting, the Pope sat on the report for three years. Press reports and encouraging statements by Western bishops fuelled a general expectation that the Church would soon loosen its position. So the Pope's 1968 encyclical letter *Humanae Vitae* (Of Human Life) – half of which was reportedly written by Polish Cardinal Karol Wojtyła (the future John Paul II) – came as an utter surprise. The Pope admitted that he was asking for a "heroic effort" on the part of Catholic couples, but he gave no strong reason for overruling his own commission, apart from referring vaguely to their lack of consensus on the "moral norms" to be applied. He certainly did not explain why natural methods for tricking the reproductive cycle were more acceptable than artificial ones, or how they were still "open to the transmission of life." In an apparent hint of desperation, he appealed to priests to speak "with one voice" on the subject and "implored" bishops to safeguard "the holiness of marriage."[8]

His appeal fell on deaf ears, and there was immediate public opposition, even from within the Church. The Dutch bishops thought the encyclical's total rejection of contraceptive methods was "not convincing." The Belgians advised Catholics to come to their own "personal" judgment after "serious examination before God." The Swiss suggested there could be exceptions to the rule, and the Scandinavians said bluntly that no one should be considered a "bad Catholic" for disagreeing.[9] The US hierarchy advised the faithful that "the norms of licit dissent" came into play. And the Jesuit John Ford, who issued the minority report and helped draw up the encyclical, found his moral theology classes back in the US boycotted by his students. His teaching career – like the moral authority of the Church – was severely shaken.[10]

Ironically, the main reason for holding the line was to protect the Church's moral authority. How, insiders asked, could the Church alter its position on something as "central" as birth control and still be trusted to be steadfast in other areas? For many Catholics in Europe and North America, the encyclical had exactly the opposite effect, deeply damaging the credibility of the institution. How, they wondered, could the Vatican be so distant from the daily realities of millions of Catholics and so insensitive to the potential harm that its stubbornness would cause to poor, uneducated families in Africa, Asia, and Latin America?

Many Catholics had simply been ignoring the Church's quaint instructions; now many decided to leave the Church altogether. Others, who stayed, were outraged. Andrew Greeley, an American priest, sociologist, and novelist, thought the Church's leaders were all the more "arrogant and ignorant" because they "had no personal involvement in the experiences about which they were making judgments."[11] Denis Hurley, archbishop of Durban, South Africa, complained on the front page of the Catholic weekly *Southern Cross* about the lack of consultation. The encyclical was "the most painful experience of my life as a bishop. I have never felt so torn in half."[12]

Shortly before *Humanae Vitae*, two-thirds of US Catholic priests said they would forgive anyone confessing to birth control; five years later, the number had shot up to 87 percent.[13] In fact, few priests understood the Vatican's position. Some would have signed off on a condemnation of a contraceptive "mentality" – having small families purely for the sake of affluence – but few could share Rome's preoccupation with sexual mechanics. A French Canadian priest working among the Muong people of Laos was as amazed as anyone by the encyclical. The Muong used a concoction of local herbs to control menstruation. "I had nothing to say to them. Their methods were certainly natural."[14] Paul VI never recovered from the shock. Two years after the encyclical, he confided to an associate: "If I'd known the reaction it would cause, I would never have issued it."[15] A gentle, scholarly man, committed to Church reform in so many areas, but weighed down by the responsibility of his office, he served as pope for ten more years, but never wrote another encyclical.

A senior canon lawyer in the Church summarized this sorry episode differently:

> The major mistake was to appoint a commission in the first place, as it set in motion a whole series of unreasonable expectations. Approving the use of the pill or condoms would have removed the single brick holding up the entire edifice of the Church's doctrine on sex and marriage. This teaching is certainly not as important as the Church's belief in the Trinity or the Incarnation, but it does cover a large part of human life and ethics. The basic doctrine of the Church has never changed. Even *Casti Connubii* [the 1930 encyclical] was mere "squeaking" compared with the bedrock teaching, which is that all sex is bad, except performed by married people intending to produce children, and that even within marriage "unnatural" practices are frowned upon.

The second mistake was made by the bishops who publicly opposed the Pope's decision. They ensured that the Vatican would dig in its heels and make the topic, to this day, the "third rail" of Church teaching. As for the logic of birth control, the Church's suggested methods do not interfere with Nature; they simply cooperate with it. If I am in the habit of gesticulating with two hands and one of them is broken and in a cast, I will gesticulate with only one. But cutting off a hand to do that would be sinful.[16]

Most Catholics did not understand such fine distinctions and had clearer concerns, emotions, and desires to deal with. But Paul VI's successor, John Paul II, was not the kind of man to flinch in the face of opposition. His obstinacy came to a head at the 1994 International Conference on Population and Development in Cairo. In the run-up to the conference, a number of organizations petitioned unsuccessfully to have the Vatican's permanent observer status withdrawn, on the grounds that it was not a state, but the governing arm of a religious institution. The petitioners included the International Women's Health Coalition, the Women's Global Network for Reproductive Rights, and, more surprisingly, the National Coalition of American Nuns. Asked why the Church should have a voice at the UN, when Muslims, Protestants, and Jews did not, the Holy See's observer to the UN replied: "Our diplomacy is the oldest in the world ... [We have] been a diplomatic force for centuries, before even most of the states of the world existed."[17]

Feminists considered the preparatory documents for the conference a great improvement over those for Bucharest (1974) and Mexico (1984), as they covered a wider range of issues, including sexuality, reproductive rights, empowerment of women, male responsibility in women's health, and the needs of adolescents and young adults. "If approved," one participant said, "it would suggest a dramatic shift in attention and resources away from reducing numbers of people as rapidly as possible to investing in the entire well-being of people, especially women."[18]

But the Vatican started fighting the new approach immediately, objecting to language as anodyne as "safe motherhood" and "unwanted pregnancies." At a preparatory meeting in New York, a Vatican official told the *New York Times* that the conference was basically "about a type of libertine, individualistic lifestyle, and it would be the first time the United Nations would endorse this lifestyle." Another papal official, Diarmuid Martin, added: "When talking about lifestyles in the future of the society, we have a lot to say." The Vatican's ambassador to the UN declared that anyone opposing the Church's position lacked ethical principles. Fred Sai, an eminent Ghanaian physician, a former population adviser at the World Bank, and the chairman of the drafting committee, objected to this bullying; the Vatican, he said, was not the only one with moral views on population issues. Diarmuid Martin's assessment was bleak: "There was much talk of gender equity and equality, of reproductive rights and of individual choices, but two words were completely absent: marriage and love."[19]

On 19 March 1994, John Paul II wrote to world leaders expressing concern about the "individualistic" tone of the draft UN text and the implication that marriage was now outmoded. "It was an eloquent and elegant letter," said one Filipino activist, "done with such finesse that one could not simply ignore it. Straightforward yet gentle, almost poetic, the letter stirred something in me, a certain sadness perhaps, as I realized how much I disagreed with the Pope."[20] On 25 March, he met all 120 ambassadors accredited to the Holy See, and on 24 April (just after the New York preparatory meeting had ended) he beatified two women as "models of Christian perfection:" Gianna Beretta Molla, an Italian pediatrician who had suffered from uterine cancer and had refused an abortion to save her own life, and Elisabetta Canori Mora, who had remained married to an abusive man until he finally abandoned her and their children.

The Pope received strong support from the Muslim world. The Al Azhar University in Cairo said that the draft document condoned extramarital sex, easy abortion, homosexuality, and possibly prostitution, undermined parental authority, and incited adolescents "to follow their instincts."[21] Saudi Arabia, Iraq, and Lebanon boycotted the conference in September, and Sudan's official press called it "a meeting of homosexuals and Jews." Even Pakistan's Benazir Bhutto, who spoke not just as prime minister, but also "as a woman, a mother, and a wife," mentioned "serious flaws" in the document.[22]

Throughout the conference, the Vatican acted as a spoiler of compromise. After one protracted discussion on "safe abortions," in which the language was watered down to virtual insignificance, the Vatican still objected, provoking boos from other delegates. The Egyptian population minister was exasperated: "Does the Vatican rule the world? We respect the Pope, but if they're not going to negotiate, why did they come?"[23] In the end, apparently to mend fences, the Vatican gave "partial" endorsement to the final document. Having rejected the conclusions of the two earlier population conferences, this was progress.

Seventeen years later, I asked Diarmuid Martin, now archbishop of Dublin, whether he would moderate his public position if he were attending the Cairo Conference today.[24] He has a modern sense of outreach, not mincing his words or worrying about being quoted. He can also swim against the tide. Shortly before I met him, the redoubtable *New York Times* columnist Maureen Dowd had canonized him as one of the few Church leaders to take the child abuse issue seriously. (Her June 2011 article was entitled "An Archbishop Burns While Rome Fiddles.") "You cannot sound bite your way out of a catastrophe," he had told another reporter. "The scandal is not an invention of the media."[25]

During our conversation, Martin did not recant any of his 1994 statements, but explained the background. As on previous occasions, John Paul II had urged Martin to speak up for what was positive in the UN conference document (particularly the sections on migration and education), but to oppose what was objectionable "noisily" (*clamorosamente*), if necessary. "It would be very easy to accept a draft UN statement in its entirety, or snipe at every part of it, but it would be wrong," the Pope had told him. Martin's job was to speak the truth, and, yes, to seek common ground; but not to be popular. The starting point for the conference was very different from the one in Mexico ten years before. In 1984, the Reagan administration had objected to anything that smacked of support for abortion; in 1994, the Clinton administration was intent on expanding women's "rights" in the opposite direction. One form of stridency begat another.

Was he not embarrassed about the odd company that the Vatican kept at the conference? "It was wrong to lump us together on the basis of apparently similar positions," Martin told me, "although of course it helped journalists describe the debate more colorfully. It was not the labels that concerned us. Rather, it was what the drafters were trying to slip through, under apparently innocuous headings." And there were differences in emphasis. In the final hours of the conference, Iran managed to obtain fifty-seven deletions of references to "sexual rights" in the document. "They had a particular concern about homosexuality," Martin said. Back at the Vatican, the delegation was being sniped at from "Left" and "Right," with extreme conservatives briefly persuading the Pope that the delegation was betraying the agreed position and misleading him on developments.[26]

As the Church held its ground, Catholics around the world simply ignored its teaching. By January 2011, 98 percent of sexually active US Catholics were using some form of artificial contraception, and 73 percent believed that Catholic hospitals should provide condoms to prevent HIV/AIDS. Reflecting the loss of credibility of the Church's hierarchy, only 8 percent thought the opinions of their bishops were "very important" in their decision on how to vote.[27]

While most of the world's Catholics followed their own consciences or simple common sense, Church teaching still prevailed in the largest Catholic country in Asia four decades after *Humanae Vitae*. In 2006, the Catholic Bishops' Conference of the Philippines blocked a trial sex education program in public schools on the grounds that this was the responsibility of parents rather than "strangers." Yet "strangers" were already filling the gap. Surveys showed that two-thirds of young people preferred not to discuss sex with their parents, and more than half were using pornographic materials.[28] At the same time, the government blocked legislation that would have expanded access to condoms. Funds for contraception were given to a group called Couples for Christ, to teach natural family planning methods. While Filipinos are highly religious (83 percent of them are Catholic), surveys suggest that they are no more beholden to Church teaching on contraception than are North Americans or Europeans. But the damage caused by government policy and the absence of family planning services, particularly among the poor, runs deep – especially in efforts to prevent the spread of HIV/AIDS.[29] Barely 50 percent of Filipinos practice any kind of contraception, and only 30 percent use modern methods. The other 20 percent fall back on natural methods, including simple withdrawal.

As it happens, not every Filipino president has kowtowed to the Church. The dictator Ferdinand Marcos (1965–86) started a major family planning program in the 1970s, and one of his successors, Fidel Ramos (1992–98), a Protestant, expanded state support for contraception in the 1990s. But most heads of state have been too weak politically, or too faithful to Church teaching, to stand up for common sense, including – ironically – its two women presidents, Corazon Aquino (1986–92) and Gloria Macapagal Arroyo (2001–10). Aquino owed her presidency to the strong support of Cardinal Sin during the People's Revolution of 1986.

While population growth does not rival African rates (it was about 2 percent in 2010), it is the highest in Asia. More tellingly, there are an estimated 600,000 abortions per year – a shocking level, even for a nation of 100 million people. In poor neighborhoods, distraught women leave plastic bags at church altars in the hope that the priest will give their fetuses a decent burial. Local "practitioners" line up outside church doors to offer pregnant women watered-down potions of belladonna; sometimes they are not dilute enough, and the mother dies as well. Many economists see this as a sign of unsatisfied demand for family planning; some moralists regard it as yet another boomerang effect of the Church's commitment to "life." All these abortions are illegal and furtive; if they survive, many women carry the scars of their desperation for the rest of their lives.

"The Church's official position," I was told by Aniceto Orbeta, of the Philippine Institute of Development Studies, "is that corruption, not population, is the cause of poverty here. But it's a smokescreen. They're entitled to their moral positions; but not to distorting the truth. Time and again, our studies show that family size and poverty are directly connected, and corruption is not a factor at the household level. The Church claims to believe in life, but their teaching is condemning future generations to continued poverty."[30] Furthermore, the Church's advocacy efforts do not match its own analysis. "If the bishops spent half their time fighting corruption rather than contraception, this country would be a much better place," another economist told me.[31]

John Russell is a Jesuit priest with long experience on the subject, having sat on President Marcos's 1970 Population Commission as president of the national sociological association (the Church was also invited to nominate a representative, but it pulled out shortly after). Apart from a decade teaching at the Gregorian University in Rome, he has worked in the Philippines since 1946. He is a social scientist, but not just a theorist. For twenty-two years, he said mass every Sunday near the dumpsite at Payatas, where hundreds of families support themselves by scrounging through the rubbish; in 2000, some 400 people died when torrential rains caused some of the huge mounds to collapse, burying the victims in their ramshackle shelters. One of his chapels was used as a morgue. While there, he introduced poor families to the principles of natural family planning. Aged eighty-seven when I met him in 2011, he was bent over and used a cane; but his positions were clear and upright. He regarded the last forty years as a "tragedy," with the Church expending 90 percent of its energy in opposing government proposals, and almost none in promoting its own approach to family planning. He was not aware of any other country where the Church had been so passionate on the issue and so successful in blocking comprehensive population programs. He was also worried that the Church's bull-headed approach to a Reproductive Health Bill under discussion would leave it with virtually no allies in any future fight on legalizing abortions.

I asked him to explain the moral difference between artificial and natural methods.[32] His answer was elegant but oblique: "Some people argue that natural methods are cheaper, have no side effects, and respect the woman's body, but those arguments are secondary to the Church's main consideration. The best way I can express it is this: respect for the most sacred act two human beings are capable of, bringing into the world another person with a soul and destiny that should lead the person back to God." Father John has seen the perpetuation of poverty that accompanies unbridled population growth: "At the food program we have here at the university, many of the people who come are the daughters of women we helped earlier." He supports the use of contraceptives in the fight against HIV/AIDS.

After all these years, even he cannot explain the depth of Church opposition to family planning in the Philippines. The Vatican certainly supports the bishops' stance, but is not dictating it: "The bishops have shown that they can be independent. In 1986, Rome told them to tone down their public opposition to Marcos, so they asked themselves whether this was an instruction or 'fraternal advice.' Citing recent papal statements giving bishops the responsibility to resolve local issues, they decided to ignore it."

Others insist that there is outside pressure to keep the country a model of Catholic obedience, and that, in any case, Church leaders have little contact with the poor. "The only large families those 'perfumed priests' see," one critic told me, "have well-to-do parents (many of them members of Opus Dei) with all the resources they need to keep their children healthy and happy." Still others point to the Church's strategic interest in expanding its numbers in a region where there are few Christians and a fast-expanding Muslim population. Philip Medalla, an economist at the University of the Philippines, once sat next to the formidable Cardinal Sin at an official dinner. "How's the economy doing?" the prelate asked. "It's growing more slowly than population," Medalla replied drily. "But," the cardinal intoned, "think of all those new Catholics . . ."[33]

As a young man, Medalla had two teachers at opposite ends of the debate. One was an irreverent Belgian priest, who pointed out that sex was one of the few free pleasures the poor had left: "Why should we complicate it?" The other was Bernardo Villegas, now professor emeritus of economics at the University of Asia and the Pacific. A member of Opus Dei, a layman, and a bachelor, Villegas has strong views about what other people should do in bed. "There is no relationship whatever between population and poverty," he told me. "We are poor because we followed once-fashionable import substitution policies to promote industry and neglected agriculture. We need people. Look at Thailand. They had an aggressive family planning program and now they are going to be the first country in history to grow old before they grow rich." Nor does he accept the link between the lack of family planning services and abortions: "The United States has wide-open access to contraceptives; yet, there are two million abortions a year."[34]

Villegas believes that the Philippines may have a special calling to export workers – including priests – to other countries; already, their remittances back to their families make an important contribution to the Filipino economy. Mainstream economists disagree, seeing this as a sad and circuitous way of building a prosperous society. It may be difficult to prove that population growth has slowed the country's development, but in other respects the statistical evidence is undeniable: large families have strained public services to breaking point and have imposed a terrible burden on Filipinos at the bottom end of the income scale. Surveys suggest that even rural couples – who once wanted large families to help on the farm and provide a safety net for old age – would now prefer three or four children, but are having an average of six. Those "unwanted" children are testament to a failed population policy.

The Philippines, however, is almost unique. Fortunately for the rest of the developing world, including most of Latin America, friction between the Church and governments about family planning ebbed into insignificance decades ago, and attention turned instead to how to prevent the spread of HIV/AIDS, especially in Africa. In that respect, common sense appears to have won out over supposed dogma. In Bangladesh, Catholic community organizations offer all the necessary information and training on contraception, but not the condoms themselves. In Côte d'Ivoire, in the early 1990s, I met Italian nuns who went further by handing out contraceptives to young girls who, they knew, would be forced to sleep with their uncle, their teacher, or even their priest. At about the same time, in Niamey, the capital of Niger, the wife of the World Bank representative encountered an even greater example of moral leadership. Asked whether she would be willing to provide sex education to local women, she showed up at a large hall, where two French nuns were demonstrating to about 200 women how to put a condom on a wooden phallus. When a few of them objected that their husbands would probably not allow them to use contraceptives, the nuns showed them an old prostitute's trick: how to slip them on discreetly with their mouths. The visitor was dumbfounded. "How can you justify this?" she asked the sisters. "Oh, you mean the Pope? We respect him. In fact, we love him. But [pointing to the women] this is the reality. If we don't do this, a large number of them will die."[35]

Many Church leaders in the developing world have also been pragmatic rather than dogmatic. As early as 1960, on the occasion of their country's independence, Nigeria's bishops issued a pastoral letter saying that there was "nothing in Christian doctrine to suggest that Catholics are bound to have as many children as ... physically possible."[36] Fifty years later, I asked the retired bishop of Moshi in northern Tanzania whether he had ever preached against contraception from the pulpit. "No," he replied with a wry smile. "It wouldn't have served any purpose. Half the congregation would feel falsely accused, and the other half wouldn't care what I said because they were already doing it. So we tried to promote natural methods in low-key ways, referring interested families to the right people in the diocese." Another African bishop told me: "The only forms of 'family planning' we oppose strongly here are sterilization and abortion.

For the rest, we try to educate young people's consciences before God and, if you will, society that it's wrong to do just anything sexually."

Réal Corriveau, who was a priest in Cuba (1957–68) and the bishop of Choluteca in Honduras for thirty-five years (1973–2008), cannot even remember where he was or how he reacted when *Humanae Vitae* was issued. Contraception was a "mere detail" in his day-to-day life as a priest. He never preached about it, and if someone wanted advice he would refer the person to specialists. The only cleric I met who admitted to talking about contraception from the pulpit was an Opus Dei bishop in Lima, Peru. "But not every day," he added with a smile, apparently acknowledging that it was an unusual subject to broach in church.

Occasionally, there have even been tacit understandings between Catholics on the front line and those in authority. I asked Sister Karoline Mayer, a German nun who runs two large clinics in northern Santiago, Chile, about family planning.[37] "We offer women the full range of contraception services," she told me. And she got away with it? "Well," she reflected, with wryness building at the corner of her lips, "our parish priest told me that we were sinning and he stopped saying mass for us for a while. But I told him it was a matter of conscience and mine was as good as his, so I didn't need his absolution. We were preventing unnecessary births, as well as AIDS and syphilis." Then, to appease her pastor, she went to see the cardinal for advice:

We talked for an hour and he was full of questions about our work. (He visited our clinics and colleges twice.) But suddenly our time was up – there was an insistent knock at the door – and I had not got around to raising the issue that interested me. "Make another appointment," he told me. The next time I saw him, the same thing happened. He was curious, enthusiastic, talkative, supportive, and before I knew it, there was that knock-knock again. I protested that I had something important to raise with him. Later, I tried making another appointment four or five times, and it was no use. I got the message. He didn't want to say yes or no to what I was doing.

And, what about abortions? "No one has ever asked for one, but we organize a lot of adoptions. And if women ask for comfort and counseling after they have aborted, we do everything we can for them. We have no choice. We are Christians."

The most prominent opponent of Church extremism on contraception is Kevin Dowling, the Catholic bishop of Rustenburg in South Africa, who has been fighting the spread of HIV/AIDS at the community level for more than twenty years. Starting his prevention efforts with women sex workers who were fighting for economic survival on the outskirts of mining settlements, he saw the distribution of condoms as pro-life: "If you're going to have sex anyway, and break the Sixth Commandment (Thou Shall Not Commit Adultery), it makes no sense to say 'Go ahead now and break the Fifth (Thou Shall Not Kill)' because it's illicit to use a condom to prevent the transmission of a death-giving virus."[38] (As we will see, Pope Benedict XVI eventually agreed with him.)

Of course, other Church leaders stick to traditional positions, sometimes in the extreme. At the African Synod of Bishops in Rome in 2010, Ghanaian Archbishop Charles Palmer-Buckle suggested that Western volunteers involved in condom education "hang around boys in order to introduce them to homosexual relationships."[39] But, overall, the picture is encouraging. According to Kevin Osborne, the senior AIDS adviser for the International Planned Parenthood Federation, it is wrong to tar all religious groups with the same brush: "There are a lot of good – Catholic in particular – groups doing amazing work in a very progressive manner. At the coalface, people are saying we have to provide condoms, not moralize, and treat everyone who comes in – gay men, people using drugs – because that's what our role is."[40]

So what has been the impact of the Church's sexual teaching in the developing world? Let us separate population growth and the fight against HIV/AIDS. To begin with, there is no way of measuring what would have happened to world population if Paul VI had refrained from issuing *Humanae Vitae* in 1968. The largest countries (China and India) were certainly not affected by the views of the Roman Curia, and they proceeded to introduce large-scale programs of family planning within a decade of the encyclical. It would also be very hard to demonstrate that Latin Americans and Africans had large families in the 1970s and 1980s simply to please the Church or soothe their consciences; in fact, strong cultural and economic factors were driving family size in those regions. At the same time, Catholics have been as eager as anyone else to resort to family planning services – when they are available.

Priests, of course, have interfered with parental decisions, sometimes crudely. The mother-in-law of an American newspaper columnist was told by her confessor that she was "no better than a whore on the street" when she admitted to using birth control.[41] I owe my own existence to a priest telling my mother that it was wrong to start using contraceptives after having only four children. But even if Church teaching had some effect on family size in isolated cases, how could we measure the damage? Theories about population and development have come almost full circle in the last thirty years. The passion that many economists, particularly Americans, brought to the issue in the 1960s and 1970s has now largely dissipated in the face of evidence that prosperity itself, rather than official family planning programs, is the best "contraceptive." So long as there is economic growth, some specialists argue, reasonable population increases can be accommodated. "Why will there be a chapter in your book on contraception?" the head of a Catholic think tank in Buenos Aires asked me. A 68-year-old former parliamentarian, he was not being facetious or naïve. "What does that have to do with development?" he wondered.

Others have seen demography as a senseless distraction. Peter Bauer, the British scholar whom we saw earlier questioning the notion of "developing countries," the value of foreign aid, and even the morality of papal encyclicals, also had strong views on this subject: "Poverty in the Third World is not caused by population growth or pressure. Economic achievement and progress depend on people's conduct. Not on their numbers . . . The crisis is invented. The central issue of policy is whether the number of children should be determined by the parents or by agents of the state."[42] He also pointed to the oddities of national statistical methods: "Ironically, the birth of a child is registered as a reduction in national income per head, while the birth of a calf shows up as an improvement."[43] If families and societies were threatened by population growth, he argued, reproductive habits would change automatically.

The trouble with this theory is that it assumes families have access to the necessary knowledge and services to space births if they want to. Africa – where most of the world's poorest countries are concentrated – still bears the scars of runaway population growth during its three decades of economic decline (1970–2000) in the form of overcrowded schools and hospitals, low levels of public services, and widespread youth unemployment. Yet fertility rates there are still among the highest in the world, and efforts to expand family planning services remain mired in political and cultural inertia. The obvious synergy between birth control and disease prevention makes this slow progress all the more tragic. But religion is not the major reason.

Paolo Marandola is a urologist at the University of Pavia in northern Italy. He has the astonishing ambition of promoting sex education among children in Africa, starting at the age of two. It would begin with what he calls "life values" (respect for others, friendship, personal restraint, and hygiene) and build up gradually to more explicit topics when children reached puberty. Anything less, he believes, will fail to dent a situation in which up to 80 percent of African adults suffer from chronic sexual disease. Marandola has been working in Africa for thirty-five years and has been the personal physician of several African presidents, including Idi Amin of Uganda, who boasted of being "the world's greatest lover" and was also his country's minister of health. Over coffee on a hotel roof terrace overlooking Rome's cavernous railway station, I asked Marandola whether Catholic teaching had had any impact on individual behavior in Zambia, the country where he had worked most recently. "Not at all," he sighed. "In fact, when I visited a Catholic school to talk to adolescents recently, the teacher interrupted me in front of the class: 'Just reassure us that you don't want to deprive us of our sexual pleasure.' "[44]

But Catholic teaching has complicated an already difficult situation. "The so-called 'civilized' countries," said one cleric in Guinea in 2000, "fear the rise of the 'colored' people in the face of their own failing numbers."[45] When pressed, defenders of the Church's position – even in the Vatican – will point out that "our people" are already being flexible where it counts. But the official Church remains adamant and vocal, putting so-called "life" issues at the very start of the 2010 social encyclical *Caritas in Veritate* (Charity in Truth) and never missing an opportunity to assert its position, even abrasively, in international forums. Cardinal Peter Turkson, who heads the Pontifical Council for Justice and Peace, told the September 2010 summit of heads of state and government on the Millennium Development Goals that the "Goals should be used to fight poverty and not to eliminate the poor!" "Controlling one's passions," he continued, "and overcoming hedonistic impulses constitute the starting point for building a harmonious society."[46] "I don't like to question people's sincerity," he told me in December 2011, "but, to some of us, there has always been a whiff of racism in Western calls for birth control."[47]

The impact of Church teaching on the fight against HIV/AIDS is just as difficult to measure, but it has probably been far greater than in the case of population growth – though it falls far short of the direct link that many observers draw between Catholic opposition to condoms and the death of millions of people in Africa. Perspectives on the subject vary radically between those who believe that contraceptives are the only sure method of preventing the spread of the HIV virus and those who think that abstinence and fidelity are the best way of containing the disease. Some in the latter group suggest that condoms encourage irresponsible behavior, hence worsening the problem.

Nowhere has that debate been fought more furiously than in Uganda, the first African country to take the HIV/AIDS catastrophe seriously and actually reduce infection levels. Shortly after seizing power in 1986, President Yoweri Museveni spoke openly about the disease and assumed personal leadership of the national information and prevention program.

For a long time, he was the only African head of state to take such a stance. Some traced his commitment to personal sentiment, especially his camaraderie with fellow soldiers who were dying of the disease. The truth was more compelling. He had sent thousands of his troops to Cuba for training and had received a telephone call from Fidel Castro. "Half the trainees are dying," he told Museveni. "You're going to lose your army."[48] And the army was still his power base at the time. At first, condoms played a leading role in the national campaign, but abstinence and fidelity assumed increasing importance as Museveni came under the influence of Protestant Evangelical opinion, including that of his wife. As a result of government efforts, Uganda reduced its HIV rate from 15 percent to 5 percent of adults between 1991 and 2001.[49] But progress has stalled since then, and the factors contributing to early success were more complex than a simple choice between condoms and fidelity.

Faith leaders, including Catholic bishops, have played an important role in raising awareness in Uganda, promoting changes in behavior, fighting stigmatization, and providing medical care, including tests and medicines. But political commitment has waned. After a prolonged involvement by politicians, the churches, the traditional kings, and the media, complacency has begun to set in. Infection rates are inching up again, apparently because older men now feel more secure sleeping with young women, knowing that the disease can be treated. (People in their forties are still petrified by what they saw when they were growing up.) Among specific groups like fishermen and sex workers, infection rates remain as high as 30 per cent. Field professionals without a religious axe to grind now agree that a comprehensive approach is needed: abstinence, fidelity, condoms, wider testing, male circumcision, and greater use of antiretroviral drugs (which protect against opportunistic infections, but also lower transmission risks). "Let's face it," the UNAIDS Country Coordinator for Uganda, a 58-year-old Muslim from northern Nigeria, told me. "What does abstinence or fidelity mean to an unmarried man of twenty-five? Even at our age, it's hard advice to follow. So condoms have to be part of the answer. But saying yes to condoms without some grounding in ethical principles is not enough." Faith leaders had a point, he thought.[50]

In November 2010, Pope Benedict threw the whole debate wide open again, and also appeared to blow the Church's theological position into smithereens, by allowing an exception in the use of condoms. Although it was a strange place on the slippery slope to make a stand, he suggested that male prostitutes would be acting morally in protecting their clients from possible infection. In the days that followed, Vatican officials scrambled to contain the damage, but were forced to admit that the Pope was only being illustrative; in other words, there could be other exceptions. Within hours, the World Health Organization (WHO) and the UN secretary-general welcomed the announcement. But in Africa, the epicenter of the pandemic, there was as much confusion as relief.

When I visited the general-secretary of the Tanzanian Episcopal Conference ten months later, the bulletin board outside his office still displayed the clarifications issued by the Sacred Congregation for the Doctrine of the Faith. "You should remember how conservative our social mores have been in Africa," Anthony Makunde told me.

> Some local cultures killed people for fornicating, not to mention homosexual sex. Our outlook is still very different from that of the West. After the Pope's statement, several young people told me they used condoms but preferred that the Church maintain its position, as they hoped to curb their sexual appetites one day, and it would not be helpful for the Church to condone what they were doing.[51]

The pastor of the oldest mission church in Tanzania, at Kilema on Mount Kilimanjaro, was also perplexed by the Pope's announcement. "What were we to recommend now?" wondered Damian Temere Mosha. "That couples where one partner was infected could now use them?" At the same time, his conscience had always been torn, seeing people engage in promiscuous activity, knowing they would kill five or six people before dying themselves. "In the circumstances, how could I condemn those who protected themselves and others?"[52]

Faith communities in general have trouble accepting the use of condoms. In August 2011, the secretary-general of Burundi's Islamic community, Haruna Nkunduwiga, said that condoms were a way of "calling people to sexual debauchery." A Catholic professor of philosophy in the same country, Emmanuel Gihutu, was shocked to be told that he should teach students to protect themselves by using contraceptives: "Do you believe that as spiritual people we can teach such things?"[53] The retired Anglican archbishop of Rwanda's capital, Kigali, explained the Christian quandary in a way no Roman Catholic priest could:

> The Anglican Church allows the use of contraceptives within the bounds of marriage and accepts that the state needs to encourage their use to prevent disease. But we still oppose them for "health" purposes, except where one of two married partners is HIV-positive. So don't expect the Christian churches to jump on a bandwagon and promote the wide use of contraceptives outside marriage. It would be like my wife putting a condom in my bags before I traveled. She would be giving me permission to be unfaithful. Sex is meant to express love, or bring new life in the world. Nothing else.[54]

But a theological discussion of contraception seems a feeble sideshow in the face of the facts. A straight-talking American nun in East Africa suggested to me that wives might put condoms into their husbands' bags simply to protect themselves from AIDS, because they knew their spouses would be unfaithful anyway. The Christian churches have complicated government efforts to offer the full range of options to those fighting the spread of HIV/AIDS. Some Evangelical Protestants have done even greater damage by persuading gullible believers to abandon their medications and trust in prayer. But, as a whole, Church teaching has had less to do with the spread of AIDS in Africa than have ignorance, irresponsible sexual practices, irresolute governments, a lack of respect for women, and poverty, which has forced many young people into prostitution to pay for their school fees and put food on their parents' tables. If governments had taken the issue seriously in the late 1980s, as Uganda's President Museveni did, no religious organization could have stood in the way.

Supporters of the Church's position have used weak arguments to defend it, including the suggestion that condoms are not 100 percent reliable or that they tend to rupture or leak after prolonged storage in the African sun. Skeptics from the other side will admit that abstinence and fidelity may work, *when practiced*. But while the gulf between the two remains wide, no one can debate that, overall, there has been real progress in reducing infections and treating those living with the disease. Faith communities have been a major part of the fight against the disease, and the Catholic Church is one of the largest sources of help to people affected by HIV/AIDS. Catholic Relief Services alone in the United States receives a billion dollars a year from USAID, most of it to support the President's Emergency Program for AIDS Relief (PEPFAR). Some estimates suggest that the Church is responsible for the distribution of a third of all the antiretroviral drugs currently being used in the world. In India in 2005, Catholics (who made up only 2 percent of the population) were the second-largest provider of health care for those with HIV/AIDS, after the government itself.[55] In a society where sexual issues are discussed less openly than in the West, the Indian Church's openness and leadership have been described as "impressive."[56] Other forms of care for those living with the disease are widespread. As early as the late 1980s, Mother Teresa was setting up hostels in the United States for people infected with HIV, suggesting that her entire career had been a preparation for helping the world deal with the disease.[57] Unlike some Evangelical Christians who suggested that the disease was divine "retribution" against homosexuals and drug users, the Catholic Church has generally taught respect and support for those unfortunate enough to contract the virus.

Overall, however, it would be wrong to let the Church's care for the sick blur the havoc it has caused. Although very few Catholics heed the Church's advice on sexual matters, it is wrong to say that it is irrelevant.

According to Jon O'Brien of Catholics for Choice, the Church had a profound effect on the design of PEPFAR – probably the single most important program for fighting HIV/AIDS – when it insisted on the removal of family planning advice from the program. His broader assessment is sobering:

> Although it is impossible to prove a negative: "What would have happened if *Humanae Vitae* had not been issued . . .?", the Church's opposition to birth control has almost certainly retarded progress on reproductive health in the world. Catholic practitioners have turned a blind eye to the rules and done a great deal of good; but Church officials have caused immeasurable damage in complicating the adoption of sound public policies worldwide.[58]

The New York-based Population Council agrees with O'Brien, suggesting that the Church has been an impediment, both locally and globally, to the implementation of high-quality family planning services around the world.[59]

The gap between official thinking and actual practice on contraception is now so great as to constitute a "silent schism" within the Church. Unfortunately, the majority of very poor people in the developing world probably do not have an opinion on the matter. Their lives are too pressing, their access to contraceptives too limited, the issue of choice (particularly among women) theoretical. And infant mortality is depressingly high.

Solving these problems is at the heart of development and requires action on several fronts. The Church's charitable network (known as Caritas) and thousands of individuals "as anonymous as the coral polyps which built up the Great Barrier Reef" have been working on them for decades.[60]

CHAPTER 10

· · · · · · · · ·

Catholic Charity: "A Network to Die For"

IN 1937, at the age of twenty-three, inspired by the works of traveler-writers like André Malraux and troubled by what he thought was a cultural crisis striking Europe, France's youngest doctor traded a potentially brilliant university career for a mud hut in Cameroon. Trying to serve 150,000 people from a small dispensary, Louis-Paul Aujoulat and his wife were regarded at first as eccentrics, even by the local missionaries. Like another Frenchman who had wiped out sleeping sickness in central Cameroon in the late 1920s, Aujoulat used large teams, tested entire villages where necessary, and trained nurses and midwives to practice "mass medicine" with a human touch. "We want to do more than just hand out medicines to A, B, and C. We want to treat body and soul together and respect everyone's individual dignity." Cut off from the rest of the world during the Second World War, he manufactured quinine and morphine substitutes from local plants and later became a member of parliament for Cameroon, a minister in the French government, and adviser to two popes – John XXIII and Paul VI.[1]

In 1992, another Frenchman, Dominique Lemay, set up a foundation in the Philippines to work with street children in Manila. Since then he has rescued 15,000 of them. One afternoon in 2011, he took me to a large square in the Chinese quarter, where one of his volunteers was teaching about sixty children and pointing out the dangers of inhaling solvents for fun. Men in yellow T-shirts from the neighborhood patrol looked on sullenly or stood behind, trying to learn something themselves. For a change, instead of expelling street families from their cardboard lodgings, policemen were taking pictures of the smiling children. I asked the trainer, a young woman from southern Brittany, whether she did this work as a Christian or a humanitarian. "Both, I suppose. Although I think I would do this even if I had no faith."

Aujoulat and Lemay are lay heirs of the missionary "awakening" of the late nineteenth century, which was inspired by the Romantic Movement as much as by religious convictions. Just as many modern-day students of international politics or development have a strong interest in living in developing countries, so the idea of helping the needy and creating "new" societies in faraway places appealed to those late-nineteenth-century Christians. The breadth of their ambition was also breathtaking. "Nothing that ministers to the well-being of these people, body, soul, and spirit, must be considered outside the scope of the Gospel," wrote one Presbyterian in southern Africa.[2] Thinking of Christ's miracles, the Scottish evangelist David Livingstone (1813–73) joked that "God had only one son, and He gave Him to be a medical missionary."[3] Their work was funded by a vast number of individual Christians across Europe, and, in the case of Catholics, performed largely by communities of nuns, many of which had been founded for that purpose. In France alone, after the closure of convents during the 1789 Revolution, the number of nuns grew from 12,000 in 1808 to 130,000 in 1901.[4] Through them and others, individual acts of mercy were combined with broader and more permanent improvements in people's lives, such as new crops, preventive health, and improved nutrition, long before the word "development" was popularized by economists.

The most striking feature of the Church's charitable effort is its size. This is hardly surprising, given the long history and reach of the institution. In medieval Europe, the Church ran the first hospitals and staffed them even after governments in the late sixteenth century began to take them over. Public health services developed slowly, so religious charity remained important right up to the beginning of the twentieth century. In France, the first nursing diploma was awarded in 1922, and lay nurses did not outnumber religious ones until 1939. So it was only natural that missionaries should take the lead in health care overseas. By 1987, French nuns and brothers were running more than 1,100 hospitals in the developing world, 90 percent of them in India and Brazil. Today, the Catholic humanitarian and development network Caritas spends about $3 billion a year and is the largest private charity in the world after the International Red Cross.

But to Catholics, the quality of the Church's work is just as important as its scale. Catholic charity is intended as an end in itself. This may surprise those who think of Christian generosity as a none-too-subtle device for converting people. Yet from Africa in the late nineteenth century to Rome in the early twenty-first, the opposite has been the ideal. In Algeria, the founder of the White Fathers, Charles Lavigerie (1825–92), expressly forbade preaching to the sick, calling it "a grave error which will delay and even prevent the rapprochement we want in the long term."[5] Out of respect for Muslim custom, women were to be treated by nuns wherever possible. This principle of gratuitousness was restated by Benedict XVI in his first encyclical *Deus Caritas Est* (God is Love) in 2005: "The Church cannot neglect the service of charity any more than it can neglect the Sacraments and the Word . . . [but] it cannot be used as a means of engaging in what nowadays is called proselytism. Love is free; it is not practiced as a way of achieving other ends."[6] The Pope was expressing a Christian, not just a Catholic, principle with very down-to-earth implications.

But not every Christian practices it. Franklin Graham, son of the renowned US Evangelical preacher Billy Graham, runs a relief and development organization called Samaritan's Purse. "I would never take advantage of [the world's poor] for personal gain," he has written. "But you better believe I will take advantage of each and every opportunity to reach them with the gospel message that can save them from the flames of hell." And, in fact, the head of the medical arm of Samaritan's Purse has admitted that doctors in the organization's African hospitals will treat patients differently if they are not Evangelical Christians, postponing operations if necessary until they have been given a chance to see the light. "The main thrust is on telling them about Jesus Christ, not getting the operation done," he explained to an American journalist.[7] This is an extreme example, says Peter Howard of the US-based Evangelical charity Food for the Hungry: "In Indonesia, the same charity [Samaritan's Purse] behaves very differently. All of us face the same challenge from the Book of Micah (6:8): 'To do justice, love kindness, and walk humbly with your God.' Some of us get the balance wrong at times and the 'humbly' is especially hard."[8]

The other aim of Catholic charity is to help everyone, not just Christians or Catholics. An employee at the US-based Catholic Relief Services expressed it succinctly: "We are called to help others not because they believe, or because they might someday believe, but because *we* believe."[9] Archbishop Diarmuid Martin of Dublin cites the parable of the Good Samaritan: "Perhaps its most important feature is that we are told absolutely nothing about the background of the victim, even though we are given the identities of others in the story. All that we know is he needed help."[10] Of course, the Church can sometimes play favorites. In East Bengal, a bank for poor people founded by the Holy Cross Fathers in 1916 charged 25 percent interest for Catholics and 50 percent for everyone else. (Village moneylenders were charging more than 100 percent.) But Caritas Bangladesh now advertises the Church's concern for everyone by siting its offices away from churches and missions. "This was a revolutionary idea in Bangladesh," said a former director.[11]

Admirable as this approach may appear, the Church often overstates the point by claiming that Christian charity is unique. Frédéric Ozanam (1813–53), founder of the St Vincent de Paul Society, was one of the early proponents of this Catholic exceptionalism. "Philanthropy," he suggested, "is haughty, looking at itself in the mirror and regarding good deeds as an ornament. Charity is a loving mother focused on the infant at her breast."[12] In *Rerum Novarum* (1891), Leo XIII picked up the same theme: "No human expedients will ever make up for the devotedness and self-sacrifice of Christian charity. Charity, as a virtue, pertains to the Church."[13] In 1999, the secretary of the Vatican's Pontifical Council for Justice and Peace expressed it differently: "A society built only on justice or the affirmation of personal rights would be inhumane. Compassion is an essential element in the building up of society."[14] Other Christians set themselves the same high standard. "It's easy to tell the difference between someone who has a contract and someone who has a calling," an American Evangelical aid manager told me. "If people see no difference between our approach and that of USAID or the UN, something is missing."[15] In the words of another Vatican official: "Charity requires justice, but goes beyond it. The leper has the right to be treated, but not to be kissed [as he was by St Francis]. If the scales are the symbol of justice, charity has no scale; it weighs no one."[16]

Michel Roy, the current head of Caritas Internationalis, the Vatican body that coordinates 165 national Catholic organizations around the world, tries to live up to that ideal:

We don't just want to give people handouts; we want to be at their side. If someone collects a bag of rice in the queue and we haven't been able to reach out to her as a person, we have failed. We want to serve others as equals or even from below. We can't engage in partisan politics or hold public office, but we must be the voice of ordinary people where necessary. We must be advocates of social justice, even if that makes people uncomfortable − including people in the Church.

A gentle Frenchman, Roy is the former head of France's Secours Catholique and the very model of subsidiarity. He wants to involve all Caritas members in decision-making and plays his own hand lightly.

"Our goal is to be the heart of a network rather than the top of a pyramid," he told me in his office on the Piazza San Callisto in Trastevere, one of the Vatican's extra pockets of territory in the city of Rome. He is particularly concerned that the hundred or so developing-country members feel fully part of a system that includes giant organizations like Catholic Relief Services (United States) and Caritas Germany: "Our mission is social service, but we also want to nurture our Catholic identity. What kind of society do we want for our children: one that is self-centered or one that is oriented to family and the community at large? How do we stop being absorbed by Facebook and open ourselves to a genuine connection with the rest of humanity?"[17]

The forerunner of Caritas was an international organization set up in 1921 by Benedict XV that became dormant during the Second World War and resumed its activity in 1951, under Pius XII. National Catholic charities existed before then – the first was established in Freiburg, Germany in 1897 – but Caritas was created to coordinate their activities, share knowledge and experience, and strengthen their "development" focus. While not conceived as such, the 1965 Vatican II document *Gaudium et Spes* (Joy and Hope) offered a kind of charter for Caritas, drawing a direct link between "the progress of the human person and the advance of society itself." Everyone, the document said, should have what was needed for a "truly human" life: food, clothing, shelter, education, employment, respect, information, privacy, and freedom of religion. As "citizens of two cities [of Man and of God]," Christians were to work with others to build a better world, and economic development was not to be left "to the judgment of a few men or groups . . . or certain more powerful nations."[18]

Caritas's international network allows it to respond to events in three-quarters of the planet, and the structures it works within – usually the local dioceses and parishes – give it an advantage over other humanitarian organizations. Its knowledge of local languages and customs and its deep roots in the community can cut through red tape and simplify the more complicated aspects of emergency relief, like distributing cash grants. And, because of the large numbers of volunteers and religious personnel involved, it can accomplish things at a fraction of the cost required by official agencies. A Catholic reconstruction program in Bangladesh following the 1971 war of independence built 180,000 homes in just a year, at an average cost of $35. The administrative portion of the budget was only 2 percent.[19] In Sri Lanka, following the December 2004 tsunami, Caritas involved 85 percent of the families they were helping in the construction of their own homes.[20]

Humanitarian and emergency relief, however, is only part of the Caritas mission; its main role is charity and development. Examples of both – a drug rehabilitation center and a technical training school – can be found an hour's drive west of Dhaka, the capital of Bangladesh. When I visited, the school was still under construction, but courses were already underway. "We didn't see why we should put off the training simply because the kitchen wasn't equipped," the Caritas director said. (Most official aid projects would have waited for the ribbon to be cut.) The drug rehabilitation center prided itself on a "holistic" approach. Government facilities released patients after fifteen days, but Caritas looked after them for up to six months. The results have been mixed – only half the patients have given up drugs; but the center allows them to return for a second, third, or fourth try. Eighty percent of the staff are former addicts, including one assistant director, whose long black hair and piercing eyes recalled the Archangel Michael battling Satan. In fact, until a few years before, the 30-year-old had been a different kind of warrior – a member of a street gang so violent that even the police avoided neighborhoods where the gang operated. Although a Muslim, he was passionate about giving back some of what he had received at the rehabilitation center. The director was a devout Catholic. "Otherwise, I would be working somewhere," he confided to me. A charismatic manager and acknowledged expert in his field, he could have been earning two or three times his salary at another establishment.

Although the Caritas network tries to be evenhanded, some members are more important than others: those in the rich countries that receive no aid themselves, but raise funds at home for projects overseas. In the Democratic Republic of Congo in 2005, a Catholic emergency relief and reconstruction program drew help from Caritas members in Belgium, Canada, England, France, Germany, Ireland, the Netherlands, and the United States.[21] The US contributor, Catholic Relief Services (CRS) (which, along with Caritas Germany, is the largest member of the network), was founded in 1943 to care for people displaced by the Second World War; it later branched out into funding development activities around the world. Then, out of the blue, the genocide in Rwanda sent it reeling. "Those 100 days in 1994 became a watershed event for us," said a former head of the organization.

> Our staff lost friends, colleagues, and family members. And we were forced to face – in very stark terms – what we already knew; it is not enough to do good development work. We knew and were known by every priest, nun, bishop, shoeshine boy, and government minister; CRS was part of the fabric of that country. And yet we were caught unprepared ... We had to stop and ask ourselves how this could happen.[22]

Belatedly, CRS immersed itself in the Church's social teaching, hoping that it would trigger new thinking on how to promote religious, ethnic, and economic cooperation. Rwanda also forced CRS to think again about the "Catholic" in its name; until then, staff had tended to mumble it when asked where they worked, fearing that "religious" implied second-rate.[23] In fact, most CRS staff were not Catholic at all. In New Delhi, for example, the country representative would be American, but most of the staff would be Hindu or Muslim. Promoting social justice, not just development, meant new involvements in community organizing, legal advocacy, land reform, conflict resolution, and other concrete applications of the Church's social doctrine. CRS's mission now moved beyond "relief and development" to the broader goal of "peace-building."[24] As CRS became more "Catholic," ironically, its funding became less so.

Three-quarters of its $800 million budget now comes from the US government, much of it from the President's Emergency Program for AIDS Relief. After emergency relief, HIV/AIDS was the single largest component of CRS spending in 2010 (20 percent).

On the receiving end, Caritas organizations in developing countries have their own priorities, which are usually down to earth. In Uganda, not surprisingly, the largest single item in the 2009–14 strategic plan was the prevention of HIV/AIDS and malaria, followed by food production, environmental information, and promoting "people's awareness of their rights and responsibilities."[25] In Kerala, India, the Trivandrum Social Service Society (the local Caritas) trains leaders of 1,200 self-help groups, supports fifty women's forums in combating alcoholism and domestic violence, lends money to 4,000 women fish vendors, helps workers set up unions, and offers scholarships to Dalit (Untouchable) children.[26] Some national organizations have also been quite inventive in diversifying their sources of funds. Caritas Peru now draws half of its funding from the "corporate social responsibility" budgets of private firms, including international mining companies.

How effective has the Caritas network been in promoting international development? To begin with, like other religious charities, it has been largely on the sidelines of decisions and investments affecting the overall prospects of individual countries. Christian charities do not have the money or inclination to invest in hydroelectric dams, revamping rural road systems, or making large transfers to government budgets to underwrite reforms in education or agricultural services. That is the role of the official development assistance agencies. Nor has the Church been active in the corridors of power, lobbying politicians or challenging proposals, except in very small countries or on "moral" issues like birth control. In the heyday of foreign aid in Africa in the 1980s and 1990s – when grants and interest-free loans were considered a richer prize than private investment – one was more likely to run across an impeccably dressed international arms dealer outside a finance minister's office than someone in a Roman collar.

But in its own limited sphere, some would argue that Caritas has touched more lives than most official agencies. That is because its focus is on structures and services that communities really need, and most of its projects are small enough to be managed carefully. Caritas certainly makes mistakes. Its workers hurtle around the capitals of poor countries in fancy four-wheel-drive vehicles that are just as shocking to real volunteers living on a shoestring budget as the conspicuous perks of "secular" aid agencies. In countries where the Catholic community is small, it can prove amateurish in recruiting expertise. In Myanmar (Burma) in 2008, the people it hired after Cyclone Nargis were found to have had very few qualifications except the ability to extract a visa from a reclusive military regime. On the other hand, the reconstruction program was supported by sixty-five different organizations (more than half of them from within the Caritas network), and 90 percent of the funds were spent within the country – a rare event in international assistance.[27] Does Caritas differ very much from other Christian aid organizations? "Not really," says Christine Allen, director of policy and public affairs at Christian Aid, the UK charity sponsored by forty-one Anglican and Protestant churches (their motto: "We believe in life before death"). "The big difference is governance. Our stakeholders are more diverse, whereas our Catholic equivalent, CAFOD, is an *agency* of the Catholic Bishops' Conference. That makes us less subject to the preoccupations of any one sponsor; but our professional ambitions, approach, and outcomes are broadly the same."[28]

Large as it is, the Caritas network is only part – and by no means the greatest part – of Catholic outreach to the poor and the distressed around the world. Most of it occurs off-stage, in hundreds of thousands of schools, clinics, community groups, and religious orders. Individual Catholics only loosely linked with the institutional Church are also engaged in work which outsiders would call Herculean, but which many of them regard as simply human. Sometimes their dedication can be amusing. The Irishman Diarmuid Martin, who traveled widely as secretary of the Pontifical Council for Justice and Peace, told me that each time he arrived in a country he asked to see the Irish nuns. But he always had trouble tracking them down, as if they were afraid of him. They were. Most worried that he wanted to order them back to Ireland.[29]

Jean Pruitt is not Irish, but she could stand in for thousands of other Catholic nuns just like her around the world. She is a self-proclaimed introvert who has been helping people for forty-three years. Born in Detroit, she wanted to live in Africa from the age of seven, when she discovered the continent in the pages of her grandfather's *National Geographic* and *Maryknoll* magazines. Her parents were poor, so Jean sold candles, tablemats, and other objects she made to the neighbors, embarking on a long career as artist, organizer, and fundraiser. In 1958, she entered the Maryknoll Sisters at Ossining, New York, where she attended teachers' college and felt like a fish out of water: "I wanted to be a teacher like I wanted to be a policeman." So she switched to a program in community development at the University of Buffalo. It was 1967–68 and a time of change. She started the year in a nun's habit and ended it in civvies, as her order had decided to blend more into the world. Waiting for an overseas assignment, she heard that she might be sent to Taiwan; but a few days later an insider tugged at her apron in the kitchen to let her know that she had got her way. Within a matter of months, she was looking out on Lake Victoria, learning Swahili, and feeling perfectly at home. "I think God intended me to be born here, and Detroit was just a mistake."

She is often asked about her attachment to Tanzania. "This country has its problems. But, in life, you get to choose your problems. Every country has them." More to the point, she has been finding solutions. First, she supervised the building of three secondary schools for girls that were later taken over by the government and are still operating today. Then she worked with Catholic Relief Services, keeping her eye open across the country for extraordinary craftsmen, materials, and motifs. In 1972, she set up an artists' cooperative called Nyumba ya Sanaa ("The House of Art") that at its height employed 180 people directly and drew on 600 artists and artisans. "This was not just a business," she explains. "I saw it as an act of social justice, aiming at self-reliance." It helped that she had a Midas touch. Her watchman became one of the most prominent artists in East Africa. She even raised five children. "You mean you adopted them on your own?" I asked, trying to picture a nun as a single mother. "I didn't have to," she explained. "They came from troubled households." One of them now works for the Public Service Commission of the District of Columbia; another is a filmmaker in Ohio. Later, she founded Dogodogo, an association that has helped 2,000 street children transform their lives, and recently created a program called Vipaji (Swahili for "talent") to help young artists turn a pastime into a career. This time, instead of approaching her usual donors (the Scandinavians), she called on the Tanzanian Cigarette Company, an enterprise eager to improve its image.

Now aged seventy-three, Jean is beginning to pace herself a bit. She swims in the ocean every morning to battle her incipient arthritis. She also suffers from bilharzia, the enervating disease caused by freshwater parasites. I was surprised that she had allowed herself to swim in African lakes or rivers. "I didn't," she assured me. "I assume I contracted it pushing my car out of the mud over the years." I asked her what she was proudest of in her life. "Nothing," she said crisply. "I can say what makes my juices flow, or gives me joy, but I don't look back. Of course, changing the lives of 2,000 children comes close . . ."[30]

Two continents away, on the west coast of South America, Karoline Mayer is just as energetic. She grew up in Germany. One day, when she was eleven years old, a beggar came to the door while her parents were out. As there was no money in the house, she decided to give him some apples from the kitchen table. Later, she regretted not giving him all of them. "Why didn't you?" her father asked afterwards, with a smile. "Ever since, I knew that I should always obey my heart when it tells me to do something."[31] Later, when she became a nun, he advised her: "Never let the order distort your character. Follow your own path, as you see it. Always stay true to yourself. And if your path doesn't match that of your order, follow it by yourself."[32]

She arrived in Chile in 1968 and stayed at first at a large convent in a comfortable residential neighborhood of Santiago, but soon afterwards insisted on living in a poor neighborhood in the north of the city. When Salvador Allende was overthrown five years later, her order called her back to Germany for her own safety – but also so as not to antagonize the generals, who regarded any foreigner living in the slums as a subversive. Perhaps mindful of her father's advice, she decided to stay and create her own religious congregation. (Forty years later, it has only twelve nuns serving the poor in Chile, Bolivia and Peru.) As economic hardship mounted and people threatened by the military government sought legal support, Karoline set up a foundation to fund nurseries, kindergartens, orphanages, clinics, community organizations, and training for women and the unemployed. With the return of democracy in 1990, the foundation was re-labeled Cristo Vive (Christ Lives). By 2012, nearly 800 children from poor families were being looked after in five nurseries and kindergartens. Another 850 young people were attending two technical colleges. Two clinics and a drug rehabilitation center were serving more than 22,000 people. And the foundation was providing legal services, supporting the unemployed, offering scholarships, and caring for widows and orphans.

Most of her funding now comes from government. The clinics are so well run that the city's medical schools send students there to observe the work. The government is also interested in adopting her approach to preventive medicine, which has staff visit families in their homes on a regular basis, so that they can be aware of the standards of hygiene, spot illnesses as early as possible, and look for signs of domestic abuse. As we toured the poor neighborhoods served by her foundation in her small white SUV, young bare-chested toughs – whom I would have avoided if I had been walking down the street – broke into smiles and cheered her as we passed by. At a nearby clinic run by the foundation, she stopped to kiss everyone she passed, doctors and nurses, but also patients and cleaning staff. At the age of sixty-eight, she was as motivated, focused, and stubborn as she must have been forty-four years before.

But how different are these two women – who happen to be Catholic nuns – from other men and women trying to make the world a better place? Katy Allen's grandfather was a Methodist missionary, and she did not take after him in any obvious way. Yet, as a tax lawyer in the City of London in the late 1980s, she felt a strong sense of disquiet: "People were making obscene salaries and complaining they were not earning enough." At the age of thirty-six, she climbed Mount Kilimanjaro and had a kind of vision, looking out at the dawn rising over the Maasai Plain. "What am I doing with my life?" she asked herself. She went home, quit her job, and decided to return to Tanzania. For seven years, she lived in a one-room house without water or electricity. She panicked during her first Swahili lesson, wondering whether she had made a mistake; but she persisted, helping to renovate primary schools and improve English teaching in the area. To fund this, at first, she used her own severance payments, small contributions from her mother's bridge partners and church, and the help of acquaintances from her London gym. Her annual budget is now over £150,000, much of it raised by charity climbs of Kilimanjaro, and she is engaged in preparing improved textbooks for the country's 40,000 English teachers. Had the quality of education improved in the seventeen years she had spent in the area? "No," she admits. "In fact, it has got worse. But we are not the government. There is only so much individuals can do." I asked about her motives. (She earns less than the UK minimum wage.) "I've always been skeptical about religious motives. I just want to do the right thing. And, as far as improving education is concerned, I suppose I want to prove a point."[33]

Kilimanjaro features prominently in another woman's story. In 1994, at home in Norway, Tone Ellefsrud was shaken by reports on the genocide in Rwanda. Turning to her husband, she voiced her relief that she didn't live there. A week later, the prime minister's office in Oslo asked her to join a team setting up a UN field hospital in Kigali, the Rwandan capital; that was Thursday and the team was leaving on Monday. "Given more time, I probably would have said no," she admits now. "I was stunned when I got off the plane. I was expecting Africa to be flat, dry, and brown; instead, there were green hills everywhere. Then a dog walked by with a human leg in its mouth, still wearing a shoe." She was shocked again when she went home six months later: "Everyone was working, working, working in order to buy, buy, buy." Africa had changed her life.[34]

In 2002, after climbing Kilimanjaro, she and her husband sold everything they had to improve the local hospitals. But they ran into immediate obstacles. At the large Lutheran hospital in Moshi, the bishop charged them $100 each for the privilege of being volunteers. With the help of hospitals in Norway, they arranged shipments of medical equipment, which started disappearing almost as soon as it arrived. Tone would report the guilty party to the hospital director, who would invite everyone to chapel to ask for forgiveness and pray that the person would not offend again. This went on for six years. Surgeons even offered patients the choice of having their operation performed using sterilized (for a fee) or unsterilized scalpels. "I was so stupid. I kept trying to stay positive, but I finally gave up." Now she spends $30,000 a year promoting environmental, HIV/AIDS, and human rights awareness among secondary-school students. She took thirty young men to attend a session of the International Tribunal at Arusha, which was investigating alleged leaders of the Rwandan genocide. Before the trip, she asked the students what they wanted to do in life. They were perplexed, never having thought they had a choice at all. Some of them expected to follow the example of their fathers and brothers and be porters for the climb up the mountain. But after the trip, three young men told her they wanted to become human-rights lawyers; so Tone lined up people in Norway to sponsor their studies.

These "un-Catholic" examples of charity bring us back to the issue of identity. In May 2010, Benedict XVI raised eyebrows at the annual meeting of Caritas heads in Rome, when he urged them to be "more Catholic." More than a third of those present were bishops. Chris Bain, the director of CAFOD, the Caritas organization for England and Wales, is quite relaxed about trying to be more Catholic: "Broadly, that means trying even harder to help our neighbor. Operationally, it means rooting our work in social justice and concern for the whole person, not just material progress, and drawing on the Church's parishes, missions, religious congregations, schools and clinics, justice and peace commissions, and so on. It's a network to die for." Most CAFOD staff – including those who are not Catholic – are reportedly comfortable with stressing rather than shirking the charity's identity. "Until recently," Bain said, "there wasn't even a crucifix on the wall. Now, staff selection criteria include a basic knowledge of Catholic social values, and we have five theologians on staff helping us to apply them in fresh ways. That does not mean erecting walls. Our Muslim staff (who use our prayer room on Fridays) also see Catholic values as important to our mission."[35]

Those values inspired the founding of the Lacor hospital in northern Uganda, which is quiet about its Catholic roots, but provides an epic story of what committed individuals can accomplish with support from Church structures. Lucille Teasdale and Piero Corti met at Montreal's Sainte-Justine Hospital in 1955. She was the only woman surgeon in the hospital. He had studied psychiatry and radiology in Italy and was now focusing on pediatrics. Between them, they were a general-hospital-in-the-making. When they fell in love, Piero's interest in working in Africa became a common goal. Her faith was not the kind to move mountains; but her humanism was, and Piero's undemonstrative but socially engaged Catholicism acted as an anchor for both of them. They may not have read any of the Church's social encyclicals, but they were to demonstrate the gigantic power of Christian conviction, as well as plain humanity.

The clinic they founded is now one of the largest referral hospitals in Eastern Africa. But its growth was long and bumpy. Raising funds and keeping the remote facility supplied – even now it is 4–6 hours north of the capital, depending on the weather, road, and driver – were only part of the challenge. Decades of civil war also kept throwing the hospital off balance. Long after peace had been re-established in the south, the Lord's Resistance Army would raid the premises in the 1990s, demanding drugs or money. The Cortis worked in the same spirit as the jack-of-all-trades who had picked them up at the airport back in 1957 – "one of those religious brothers from the Comboni order," they reminisced later, "who pray with a hammer in their hands." Piero was once asked why they stayed in Uganda, in the face of great personal risk: "For all of us, the question was not how to keep operating in such conditions, but how to refuse to do so. None of us wanted to blow out a candle that was beginning to grow brighter and brighter." They also had strong support from the local bishop. When Lucille and Piero had to make a rare trip abroad, they suggested that their heir-apparent Matthew Lukwiya run the hospital. "Is anyone else more competent for the job?" the bishop asked. "No," replied Piero. "But you know he's Protestant and some priests may not like him to be in charge of a Catholic hospital." "I know he's Protestant," the bishop said. "But are any of the other doctors more Christian?" "No," Piero answered with a smile.[36]

Matthew died in 1995, during an outbreak of Ebola fever. (WHO experts would later say that the hospital had been "too compassionate" in not isolating the victims.) Lucille was also dead by then, of HIV/AIDS, which she had presumably contracted during one of the thousands of operations she performed. And Piero died of pancreatic cancer in 1998. The management of the hospital is now entirely in Ugandan hands. It cares for 35,000 people a year and is free of charge for expectant mothers and young children. Patients cover only 20 percent of the budget; the rest comes from international donors (principally the Corti Foundation, run by the founders' daughter) and the Ugandan government. Now that the hospital has been fully incorporated into the national health system, I asked an Italian adviser in what sense it was still Catholic. "The bishop still heads the board of governors," Tommaso Molteni told me. "We keep our focus on reaching the poor rather than just those capable of paying the fees. And we apply 'Catholic' values in managing our personnel. We pay them the market rate so they don't have to suffer for serving the poor. Everyone, even casual workers, and their families get free care. We expect our personnel to work hard and we let people go if they are dishonest. We try balancing three aims: low-cost care, treating staff fairly, and respecting (while also challenging) local culture."[37]

Dominique Corti, who runs the foundation named after her parents, gives high marks to the local bishop. "Of the thirty-two Catholic hospitals in Uganda, Lacor is the only one legally constituted as a non-government organization headed by a bishop. He is a good delegator, but is not hands-off. He leads the board discussions and reviews the minutes carefully. He even drives himself to the meetings, which is dangerous at night, and is deeply committed to protecting the hospital's mission: its focus on the poor." She also explained how pragmatic the Italian Bishops' Conference had been in 1995–96, when the hospital served as a shelter from crazed members of the Lord's Resistance Army. "At night, we would have up to 10,000 people staying with us, so we had to redo the water treatment and sanitation facilities completely. This was not a very 'sexy' project, and the Italian bishops would have preferred to fund local schools. But we pointed out that the schools would close if dysentery broke out. So they agreed to help."[38] The hospital may continue to carry the fading imprint of the Church, but its greatest success is that two imaginative and dedicated individuals devoted their lives to creating it for their own humanitarian reasons, inspired by their faith but eager to pass it on intact to a new generation that would not be interested in religious labels.

How significant has Catholic aid been in fighting poverty? No one can put a monetary value on the total contribution of Catholic individuals and organizations to improving social and economic services around the world, given how widespread they are and how many are provided by volunteers and religious personnel. Estimates can also understate the range of impacts. The total annual spending of the Caritas network (about $3 billion) is no more than the World Bank lends to a single country like Brazil, Indonesia, or Turkey in a single year. Yet, except in a manner so indirect as to be meaningless, no official agency would claim to reach 100 million people (as Catholic Relief Services does) or be in a position to reach out to a billion people in the developing world. In that sense, the Church is in a category of its own. At the same time, like other development organizations, Catholic bodies try to design their programs carefully, to assess the outcome (even in the case of disaster relief, where there is usually pressure to do things quickly), and to apply the lessons that they and others have learned. Catholic projects have also pioneered best practices.

Atto Brown, a young Ghanaian engineer who has worked for the World Bank/United Nations Water and Sanitation Programme, tells the story of an American Franciscan brother in Ghana in the mid-1980s, who visited the US to raise money for six wells in the north-central region of the West African country. He was successful in finding donors, but they asked him why he wanted to contract out the work when he could buy a reconditioned drilling rig and do the work himself, more cheaply. Drawing on graduates from Catholic technical schools, he sank not six wells, but 600 over a few years, using six people on the rig (compared to an average of fifty on a government project). The Franciscan also set up inter-faith groups in each village to take responsibility for the wells, and insisted on a minimum contribution from the community to cover maintenance, five years before the government adopted the same practice. It was the Church, not the World Bank, which demonstrated that it was possible and perhaps even necessary for poor people to pay for part of an essential service. Now, whenever Brown visits a country for the first time, he tries to find out what the Catholics are doing.[39]

Church people have also remained important in pressing for the rights of poor people and in urging them to exercise those rights. Nithiya Sagayam, the executive secretary of the Indian bishops' Justice, Peace, and Development Commission for nine years (2001–10), helped organize seminars across the country on a "rights-based" approach to justice and peace, and took up the cause of the national Right to Food Campaign, in conjunction with lawyers, non-government organizations, government officials, interreligious leaders, and human rights advocates. Booklets, leaflets, and CDs were prepared for poor people in twelve regional languages. These contained ten "commandments" (do's and don'ts), publicized government programs, and proposed "peaceful but firm" strategies for obtaining access to public services. For a country so large, the results were modest – 40,000 people obtained their monthly food rations on a regular basis and another 40,000 received their "job cards" for a hundred days of state-subsidized labor – but the example was strong. In another remarkable initiative, moving on to work for the Asian Bishops' Conference, Sagayam brought bishops together for three days on the outskirts of Bangkok to meet HIV/AIDS patients, prostitutes, and victims of human trafficking and to hear their testimony at first hand, followed by another three days during which the bishops reflected on what they had learned and how to respond to it in the light of Catholic social teaching.[40]

Has the Church been successful in raising incomes? "I'd like to say yes," Ignatius Sabbas, the Caritas director in Kerala told me. "Some individuals have done well through our programs, but the major change for the community has come from young people finding low-skilled jobs in the Persian Gulf and sending money home to their families." As a secondary actor on the economic scene, the Church can help equip young people through its schools, and others through literacy and adult education programs, to seize opportunities created by good policy and private investment; but its role remains a supporting one. More importantly, it can educate people in their rights, encourage them to press for reforms that will make the market "work for the poor," and meet needs that otherwise would go unattended. It is sometimes less and sometimes more than standard definitions of development. But there is little doubt about what was important to the 10,000 people at the Lacor hospital sheltering at night from the cruelties of the Lord's Resistance Army. It is unclear who else would have created the hundreds of jobs Jean Pruitt did in Tanzania, selling a winning concept to foreign funders and using her energy and supervision to make it work. The private sector could not have made up for the extraordinary efforts of a single German nun in Chile. And some measures of success must remain relative. I asked Dominique Lemay in Manila how he reacts to suggestions that his work with street children is just a drop in the bucket compared with the overall development needs of the Philippines. He answered with the story of a man walking along a vast pebble beach and meeting a child who was throwing starfish back into the water. "You can spend your whole life doing this and never finish," he told the boy. The child kept working. "Two more saved while we were talking!" he exclaimed.[41]

CHAPTER 11

Looking Ahead: A Fading Social Mission?

IN Barcelona, in the sumptuous *art nouveau* auditorium of the Museum of Catalan Music, I made the mistake of smiling at him as he stood in the central aisle; so he edged into the row and sat next to me. Reeking of tobacco and too large for his seat, he grumbled throughout the interminable opening ceremony of the annual peace gathering of the Community of Sant'Egidio, a Catholic lay organization. After three hours, his buttocks and nicotine addiction were getting the better of him and he even scowled at the remarks of the two "princes" of the Church, including the cardinal from Barcelona, which surprised me, as my neighbor was Italian, worked for the Sacred Congregation for the Propagation of the Faith in the Vatican, and was wearing a Roman collar. Buddhist monks slept soundly in their seats (succumbing to jet lag), while the presidents of Cyprus and Montenegro rubbed shoulders with the head of the National Transitional Council of Guinea, an enchanting woman from a troubled West African country, who was draped from head to toe in powder blue. The Israeli and Palestinian ministers of religious affairs debated with each other on stage for half an hour, before shaking hands to general applause.

The Community of Sant'Egidio is one of the Church's many adaptations to the challenges facing an ancient institution – challenges that include striking a proper balance between identity and relevance. The first can lead in the extreme to fundamentalism, and the second to the institution slowly dissolving into the rest of society. "We are the children of Vatican II and 1968," the older members of Sant'Egidio like to say.

Founded in Rome in the late 1960s by a handful of left-wing students who wanted to remake the world "on the basis of the Gospels," the Community installed itself in a former convent in Trastevere, the bohemian-chic neighborhood west of the Tiber, on a small square from which it took its name; in 1986, the Vatican recognized it as an international lay movement. Since then, it has embraced the full range of Church activities, from a deeply spiritual prayer life centered every evening around the Church of Santa Maria in Trastevere, through soup kitchens for the poor and displaced in and around Rome, annual inter-faith meetings (like the one in Barcelona) modeled on John Paul II's gathering of world religious leaders in Assisi in 1986, an international campaign to end the death penalty, and political mediation.

Although the Community's only prominent success was in helping to end the Mozambique civil war (1977–92), which claimed more than a million lives (the peace agreement was signed at its offices in Trastevere), its ambitions have ranged widely, from Algeria and Lebanon to Guinea, and it has played a positive role in Burundi, Côte d'Ivoire, Guatemala, and Niger. "What made them successful in Mozambique," an American diplomat later reflected, "was that they were real outsiders, true mediators, above party factions, seriously dedicated to the cause of peace without any imaginable political or economic motives or interest in international prestige."[1]

Sant'Egidio does not fit into ideological boxes. While it was founded by "progressives" and puts service to the poor at the heart of its work, its daily prayer gatherings are remarkably traditional. Both John Paul II and Benedict XVI (neither of whom could be described as liberal) supported the Community's work, while the Italian Left frowned upon its attention to the marginalized, the gypsies, and immigrants, feeling the Italian poor deserved attention first. In the 1970s, some liberation theologians berated the Community for focusing on charity rather than "structural" justice. "Give the poor a fishing rod rather than fish," was their advice. The Community replied that the poor first had to be made strong enough to hold a fishing rod. The founder, Andrea Riccardi, is a very practical man – in 2011, he agreed to serve as Italy's minister of international cooperation in a transitional technocratic government – but he never strays very far from the spiritual, quoting a Russian theologian, Vladimir Soloviev (1853–1900): "Faith without works is dead, and the first work is prayer."[2]

Kishore Jayabalan would be the first to say that he is no Andrea Riccardi, both because he is very modest and because he has a very different mission. The product of Catholic schools in the American Midwest (where his parents moved from Kerala), he converted to Catholicism as a young man and worked with the Vatican delegation at the United Nations, and later the Pontifical Council for Justice and Peace in Rome. He now heads the Roman staff of the Acton Institute, named for the English historian, politician, and writer Lord Acton (1834–1902), which is based in Grand Rapids, Michigan and is dedicated to making Church leaders more comfortable with the market system. "We stand firmly on the ground of the Church's social teaching," Jayabalan told me, "but on the subject of reducing poverty we believe it does not go far enough. We need to promote free trade and enterprise, too."

Mainly an educational body, the institute trains future Church leaders to approach issues of poverty and development "with their heads as well as their hearts." In Jayabalan's words:

We're trying to get religiously minded people to overcome their often overly paternalistic attitude towards developing countries, which usually results in relying on foreign aid and philanthropy instead of business in the fight against poverty. In developing countries, our message is that if you promote free enterprise it will usually result in inclusive growth because young businesses have to look for workers and customers wherever they can. Western capital and technology are useful but not enough. Being marginalized and excluded, not exploited, is the more important problem in today's global economy, so we need to involve more and more people in a network of productivity and exchange. It is not a simple question of transferring wealth from the rich to the poor, but helping the poor become rich (or at least less poor) by using their talents in conjunction with God's Creation. There is dignity in producing instead of just receiving.

Focusing its efforts in Rome – where 95 percent of bishops have been trained and 15,000 students attend the pontifical universities – the institute offers scholarships and travel money to study economic issues. Up to 600 people at a time attend the "Acton University" in the US, a four-day workshop which is more ecumenical. But the approach is still very Catholic. "We do not believe in an unregulated market," Jayabalan assures me. "It is not a god, and individual men and women are not robots responding to the same signals. Each is unique in God's eyes."[3]

A story that might have featured at an Acton Institute seminar is that of a Chicago priest who decided to set up a soup kitchen in his church to cater to the poor and unemployed in his neighborhood. Shortly after, he dropped into a local café for a smoke and coffee and asked the owners, a middle-aged couple, how business was going. It had fallen off sharply, they told him. Realizing his mistake, the priest decided instead to distribute coupons, redeemable at the café. That way, he could help a local business, not just the down-and-out, save himself the trouble of buying groceries and preparing the food, and probably stretch his charity budget further as well.

The Community of Sant'Egidio and the Acton Institute are two expressions of a diverse institution that continues to expand and evolve. Other examples are Fe y Alegría, a Jesuit program in Latin America that tries to make school curricula more empowering for students from poor families, and the Focolare movement, which promotes inter-religious unity in more than 180 countries, as well as an "economy of communion," in which private enterprises invest a large part of their profits in improving the lives of their workers and the local community. They and other new lay groups, not to mention existing congregations of brothers and nuns, are trying to harness the lessons of the past to make the Church's evangelization and social mission more effective. They have a large task ahead of them.

Writing presciently in 1965, the French Catholic commentator Bernard Lecomte saw the contours of the development challenge already changing:

> Increasingly, the Church will be on the sidelines of the fight against poverty. It can only offer palliatives to relieve misery here and there. That is because the battle is no longer for redistribution, but for access to the very sources of wealth, i.e. knowledge, technology, capital, markets. Charity can only go so far. The poor will be saved only through their own efforts to promote development.[4]

Lecomte underestimated the capacity of the Church in the following decades to give a real development dimension to its "charitable" work. He also overlooked the fundamental and enduring contribution of the Church's educational activities. But his central point remains sound. Official aid agencies, like private ones, are now dwarfed by the volumes of market capital potentially available for improving the lives of the poor. And, where they are most effective, aid donors are only minor actors in a drama dominated by progressive governments and dynamic entrepreneurs.

Dick Timm, the indefatigable Holy Cross Father in Bangladesh, summed up his life experience in five powerful sentences:

> People must be the basis of development and the best way of involving [them] is through appropriate non-formal education. By coming together to understand their life situation and its causes and by organizing and working together the people also

enter into the decision-making process of the village. They can improve their financial position [through group savings and income-generating projects] and by united actions can gradually shift the balance of power, so that they are no longer completely at the mercy of the traditional forces arrayed against them. Without such organization at the base, no legislation to protect the rights of the poor can possibly be enforced, no matter how enlightened the attitude of government or how determined the political will. The forces of rural society are too strongly ranged against the interests of the poor.[5]

Timm's views were formed in the predominantly rural setting of Bangladesh, but they can also be applied to the hundreds of millions of people now living precariously in urban areas in the developing world. His summary features the three traditional thrusts of Church action: education, basic development services, and advocacy, with an important twist: it is people, not the Church, who must lead the process.

If this is so, how can the Church build on the experience it has amassed in the last fifty years of development work? It will need to tackle a number of related issues: its own concerns about identity, the apparent waning of its social mission, working with other faith communities and the private sector, and managing its wealth more effectively and understandably.

The issue of identity was highlighted by Benedict XVI in May 2010, when he asked the 165 Caritas directors meeting in Rome to be "more Catholic." This puzzled practitioners and observers alike, who assumed that this did not mean employing only Catholic staff or helping only fellow believers – as this would be a contradiction of Catholic tradition. Nor could it be a reference to shunning support for family planning programs, a long-standing prohibition that hardly justified a papal clarion call. Instead, it seems to have been another example of the odd and irritating Vatican-talk that suggests that Christian charity is better than other forms of kindness, less self-centered than philanthropy, more significant than alms-giving, and unique to the Church. This arrogance can be elegantly phrased; but it is arrogance all the same, seemingly blind to the fact that people of all faiths, little faith, and even no faith at all are capable of devoting themselves to the welfare of others, impelled by principle, reason, instinct, or pure humanity. It is even puzzling why the Church should try to parse the nature of generosity. Whatever the reason, such attempted distinctions come close to the scribe in the New Testament comparing his religious devotions favorably to those of the publican. And it is difficult to believe that the Vatican is really worried about the Church dissolving into society-at-large as a result of not asserting its core values, like a giraffe concerned about being lost in the high grass. To many onlookers, the beauty of the Catholic "identity" is that it is universal, but at the same time diverse and, where possible, self-effacing.

Issues of identity and outreach are closely linked to a lingering debate about the meaning of the Second Vatican Council itself. Quite amazingly, fifty years after a watershed event in Church history, theologians are still asking what actually happened there, with some clinging to the narrow "letter" of council documents, seeing them as an updating of long-standing positions, and with others celebrating the "spirit" not just of renewal, but also of transformation that most people saw at the time. This is not a simple debate. Some traditionalist theologians welcomed the Council's opening out to the world and its dropping of the Augustinian idea of the Church as "an island of grace in a world of sin." But they also felt that the Council did not reflect enough on what Catholics were to do in society (apart from performing good works) and what it meant specifically to be Christian, "representing it, radiating it, translating it believably in the world."[6] Most of the people interviewed for this book have been exemplars of the "spirit" of the Council, seeing no difference between service and being Christian, less interested in preaching than in solving urgent problems, and preferring example to outright evangelization. But a large number of today's younger clergy are attracted to a narrower cause, achieving personal sanctification and nurturing it in others. This is not to demean the importance of seeking personal "holiness," whether Christian, Muslim, Buddhist, or Hindu. But the "wages" of such seeking can be self-absorption.

This new accent on identity and evangelization is increasingly at odds with the strong social mission that inspired large numbers of Church people after Vatican II and had such a palpable impact on millions of people's lives. It also reinforces a trend in the West in the last twenty years to associate "Catholic" with a narrow range of moral issues, and even retrenchment, rather than with the openness and reforming zeal it stood for in the 1960s and 1970s. (Apparently to prevent such confusion, in 2005 the UK Catholic Institute for International Affairs changed its name to *Progressio*.)

Nor is the tension between faith and service restricted to theologians or even very new. In the early 1990s, the US-based Maryknoll order polled readers of its monthly magazine. One of them reported that "I first became exposed to the Maryknoll mission as a young soldier in the Far East during the Korean War. I respect what they do and feel that whatever small contribution I have made monthly will be used to help those less fortunate than myself." Another reader was feistier: "Maryknoll is unable to comprehend that people can love Christ simply through simple faith. Prayer, contemplation, meditation have no place in Maryknoll's work. Just social action, that's all!"[7]

In March 2011, Cardinal Robert Sarah, who heads the Pontifical Council *Cor Unum* (One Heart), which is responsible for overseeing the Church's charitable work in the world, told a group of seminarians that priests should focus on prayer and divine praise: "The priest is not a psychologist, sociologist, anthropologist, nuclear scientist, or politician. He is another Christ destined to open to the souls in his care the spiritual treasures they are sadly lacking today."[8] He was echoing the views of a Belgian theologian writing three years before Vatican II: "Christ was not a social reformer. The call of Jesus was to *conversion*, a *personal* matter. The Christian lives in society, and he will be guided in his social duties by his faith, but his true life as a Christian is a life in God."[9]

Fortunately, this rebalancing of Christian priorities – if that is what it is, rather than a new retreat from the world – is not yet the rule. Ghanaian Cardinal Peter Turkson, head of the Pontifical Council for Justice and Peace, whom many Vatican-watchers see as a future pope, acknowledges that young priests in the West are focusing more on liturgy, prayer, and immediate pastoral work than on their wider social mission. "It's an issue," he told me. He also acknowledged that the first draft documents prepared for an upcoming synod on evangelization had hardly referred to charity. "They were drafts intended for discussion and they will be fixed," he said, a little impatiently. But he was convinced that the Church's social mission should remain central, and not just for priests, brothers and nuns: "In a sense, it's the 'vocation' of the laity. If Christians don't promote social change, who will?"

Such a call presumes a pastoral spirit, which many see as sadly lacking in today's Vatican, preoccupied as it is with theological, moral, and narrowly spiritual matters. Even the new evangelization effort, insiders complain, has been put in the hands of people not renowned for their "common touch." The Church's social teaching also seems to have become less practical. Benedict XVI's 2010 encyclical *Caritas in Veritate* said a great deal about "life" issues like contraception and abortion, very little about education, and nothing at all about health and gender. The 2011 Justice and Peace publication calling for a "new international financial authority" was a commendable response to the crisis facing capitalism and analyzed its causes credibly enough, but it was widely challenged for not explaining how its proposed solution would improve on current arrangements.[10] And Catholic activists in the UK pressed their bishops for months to issue a pastoral statement on development, poverty, and the environment ahead of the UN Global Summit in Rio in February 2012. "We got nothing," one activist told me. "But the bishops organized a national petition within days of the government's announcement that it wanted to legalize same-sex marriage."

The Church may well be running up against the limits of promoting general principles and expecting decision-makers to apply them to specific situations. Some of its statements now seem vacuous. In a major statement on Africa in February 2012, Benedict XVI condemned "traditional practices which are contrary to the Gospel and oppressive to women in particular," but did not make plain that he was referring to female genital mutilation, which affects hundreds of thousands of women every year.[11] Certainly, many people in developing countries would like the Church to be more forceful in combating "structural sins" (like corruption) that affect their daily lives. It needs to keep reminding itself, as Uganda's bishops did in appealing for national electoral reform in November 2009, that "the promotion of human dignity and the equality of people's rights and participation is not interference in politics, as many politicians think, but an integral part of the mission of the Church."[12] The role of national justice and peace commissions remains central to Catholic outreach. In some countries, they appear to exist only in name; in others (like Argentina) they shine with purpose and imagination. Some are well funded (much of the Rwandan program is financed by the European Union), while others (like Tanzania's) operate on a shoestring. "Are we to be donor-driven or Gospel-driven?" asked an organizer in Dar es Salaam, refreshingly. But a reassessment of their role and a sharing of their experience across continents would probably be in order. And the Church needs a new focus for its moral instruction. As the shape of the world economy changes, distinctions between developed and developing countries become thinner, and attention begins to center on relative rather than absolute poverty, so faith communities will face a new challenge.

That challenge was summarized for me eloquently by the Peruvian Elías Szczytnicki, the Jewish representative for Latin America of the international organization Religions for Peace:

> The issue in Latin America is not poverty in the old sense. It is inequality. Our region will meet the UN's 2015 Millennium Development Goals on average but there are great pockets of misery in many countries. Even in Peru, we have the resources to look after the very poor. The obstacle is political will and determination. Young people have to feel they have an opportunity to

succeed. Maybe it is only illusory. After all, how many *mulatto* children from Hawaii can expect to go to Harvard like President Obama? But the possibility through education and effort of being one in a hundred is better than the grim future facing many of our young. Yet very few people in Latin America care anymore about such inequality, accepting it like many people in the West as an inevitable feature of the new economy. The faith communities have a special responsibility to fight public apathy, appeal to people's consciences, and promote good public policy.

In Szczytnicki's view, moral example will be stronger than any statement:

Some bishops have marched against mining companies that were poisoning people's water supplies. Others have been photographed in the tabloids hobnobbing with the mine owners. Fine, the Church is part of the establishment; but some religious leaders are prisoners of their upbringing and others are able to slip free of that noose and relate to other classes, including the poor. You don't need to put an ideological label on their foreheads. People recognize who they are.[13]

Keeping issues of identity under control and sharpening its social message will help the Church collaborate with a larger set of actors. Fortunately, on the ground, some Catholic organizations already have a wide range of partners. In Peru, for example, the largest Caritas program in Latin America works with World Vision, Lutherans, Anglicans, and Mormons, who channel some of their own assistance through Catholic programs. CAFOD, the Caritas organization for England and Wales, was a pioneer in working with international Islamic relief organizations. In Rwanda, however, the US Evangelical Rick Warren's Saddleback Church has been "begging" Catholics unsuccessfully to join it in a multi-faith effort. One reason may be that Saddleback's "holistic" approach seems like old hat to activists steeped in Catholic social teaching dating back to 1891. Saddleback's rhetoric is also overblown – it wants to make the Church the "center" of the community and the "hero" of development – but its approach is eminently down-to-earth. Using hundreds of volunteers, who act as community extension workers seven hours per month, it promotes preventive health care in villages and poor urban neighborhoods. Significantly, its only Catholic ally is the head of the country's Justice and Peace Commission, a bishop willing to sit down with rank newcomers if that will serve the cause of the poor.

In what many observers describe as a "winter" of ecumenism, it may not be surprising that some faith communities regard the Church as setting its own course in charity and development work. "The great believers in ecumenism have died," one insider told me, "and we have gone as far as we can with preparing the necessary texts. What is lacking is vision, energy, and purpose. It has become a bureaucratic exercise. Even the dialogue with Judaism has been put in the hands of people who have had little direct exposure to the subject." But fortunately, as in the case of family planning, Church people "on the ground" are generally more practical. Greater harmony at the institutional level may still be a long way off. In the words of the French Dominican theologian Yves Congar (1904–95), "you can only proceed through the gates of ecumenism humbly, on your knees."[14] But individual Catholics, like the Rwandan bishop, will lead the way.

The Church should also join forces with business people who see enterprise – or "making the market work for the poor" – as a key part of fighting poverty. A good example is the Valle Grande agricultural school in Peru, run by Opus Dei, a Catholic movement not usually associated with a "social mission." Originally an educational radio network for agricultural extension workers in the Andes, Valle Grande converted itself into an educational facility in 1990. Catering to about 150 children aged 16–19 from poor rural families, only a third of the college's costs are covered by fees; the rest comes from income obtained through agricultural consulting and corporate sponsors. Students alternate two weeks in residence at the college and two weeks as apprentices on commercial farms or in agricultural companies. A third of those admitted each year – the best performers on the entry exam – receive a full scholarship, while the families of all the others are charged a fraction of the costs. This is a canny, generous, and economical approach wedded to Opus Dei's broader aims. "We want to change these young people's lives, not just improve their job prospects," the college director told me. "We see ourselves injecting Christian values into the bloodstream of the entire society by producing capable and principled graduates who will set a good example."[15] Opus Dei has similar colleges in Argentina, Brazil, Chile, Colombia, Ecuador, and Mexico.

One private sector the Church is comfortable with is its own. In Uganda, it runs the largest development bank, founded in 1985, on the occasion of the hundredth anniversary of Catholic evangelization in the country. The Centenary Bank is currently managing a four-year line of credit from the World Bank to support small-scale enterprises. But by far the largest income-earning assets of the Church are its thousands of secondary schools across the developing world. Some critics have called on the Church to give up these "schools for rich children." In one purist's words, "Are these really necessary as an expression of the Gospel?"[16]

But it would be wasteful and self-defeating to do that. To begin with, children from privileged families deserve a good education, too, and given continued inequalities in human societies, the investment in their futures may have larger-than-average repercussions for society as a whole. Most of these establishments already devote a portion of their profits to scholarships for poorer students. However, more could be done to expand and formalize such practices and to make them known to the general public, which otherwise sees these institutions as part of the wealth rather than service of the Church. A minimum rule might be that all school earnings must be invested in improving the quality of teaching and increasing the proportion of students drawn from less-favored families. Only exceptionally would such income be used to subsidize other diocesan programs. In the management of its vast land holdings around the world, the Church should also ask itself the question that Paul VI implicitly posed to large landowners in Latin America in his 1967 encyclical *Populorum Progressio*: were they managing that wealth in the best way possible for the whole of society? If not, he said, it would be moral to confiscate it.

To those concerned about the blurring of priorities within the Catholic Church, the election of the first pope from the developing world in March 2013 was deeply encouraging. Sidestepping the choice between identity and relevance, Francis made it plain that the Church needed to be true both to itself and its mission. "We can build many things, but if we do not witness to Jesus Christ then it doesn't matter," he told the cardinals in the Sistine Chapel the day after his election. "We might become a philanthropic NGO but we wouldn't be the Church."[17] But his commitment to improving people's lives was also manifest. In 2007, he told a meeting of Latin Americans that "we live in the most unequal part of the world, which has grown the most but reduced misery the least." In an echo of the 1968 Medellín Conference, he called the unfair distribution of wealth a "social sin that cries out to Heaven."[18]

For all its accomplishments, experience, size, and prestige, the Church must continue to improve its outreach to the poor, while trying not to draw too much attention to itself. In the words of an activist Indian priest, "Amidst globalization, competition, and privatization, our faith must inspire us to really serve the poorest of the poor. In spite of all the criticism she received, Mother Teresa was a genius in recognizing this forgotten dimension and restoring dignity to the poor."[19] The Frenchman Bernard Lecomte's words in 1965 are also still appropriate:

> Respecting others means first of all not throwing our truth in their face, or letting our propaganda, universities, and research institutes turn in on themselves. The Christian is called to join others (including people without labels) in fighting poverty not as Crusaders, but as people of the present age pursuing scientific and technical progress, our hearts open to the Gospel, demonstrating our commitment to something greater than ourselves.[20]

CHAPTER 12

Conclusions: "Everyone Who Fights for Justice Upsets People"

One Saturday morning in June 1968, a young Peace Corps volunteer named Stephen Heyneman was buying vegetables at his neighborhood market in Malawi when he spotted about a thousand people outside the local police station. Women and children were huddled on the grass, seeking police protection from the Youth League, which had been beating up anyone who was not a member of the ruling party. Cycling home, Heyneman passed a group of red-eyed toughs carrying machetes and clubs. There was smoke on the horizon, indicating where men were killing villagers, most of them Seventh Day Adventists.

Heyneman rushed to a nearby Catholic church to find Father Timmermans, a Dutch priest who had lived in Africa for half a century. His teeth were stained from years of smoking cigars and his robes were often dirty, but he was a good administrator. Today, he drew a line: "I am here to save souls, not to do politics. These things happen in Africa. There is nothing we can do about it. Our church cannot survive here if we interfere." Heyneman then cycled over to appeal to the minister at the Scottish Presbyterian Church, who had also spent most of his life in Africa. "What can we do to stop the killing?" shouted Heyneman. "It's over," the clergyman told him. "I called the president this morning and told him that if the killing did not stop within an hour I would close this mission and return to Scotland, and so would the Church of Scotland. He is a deacon of our church, and he got the message."

Now a professor at Vanderbilt University in Nashville, Tennessee, Heyneman still tries to make sense of the experience. At first, friends told him that the incident showed the difference between Catholics and Protestants, with Catholics believing that the word of God comes first through the pope. "The pope," I was told, "passes it on to the Church and the Church passes it on to the people. For them, the institution of the Church must be protected at all costs. Protestants, I was told, think differently. To them, the most important issue is God's word, not the institution. It is the individual who must act." But Heyneman is no longer comfortable with that explanation: "I don't think there is a great difference among religions, with one protecting itself and the other not. Rather, the difference was that one man knew *when to act*. And the responsibility for doing the right thing comes from within."[1]

Most of the people described in this book have acted as individuals rather than as conscious representatives of an institution. Like the Protestants in Heyneman's account, they put the Gospel and simple humanity before everything else. Yet inevitably they were connected by deep Catholic traditions: the importance of Reason, the obligation to serve everyone (not just other Christians), and a body of social teaching that has gone further than any other religion in questioning the structures of capitalism and socialism alike. Nor have they just consisted of nuns, priests, and lay people working at the grassroots; they have included bishops, archbishops, cardinals, and popes.

What can we say about the Church's impact on development since the international community began to take world poverty seriously after the Second World War? To begin with, forces beyond the Church's control – globalization, free-trade policies (particularly in the United States), private investment, and the emergence of India and China – were much more important for the well-being of millions of people around the world than anything Catholics and other Christians may have done. In some areas, the Church's actions worked against those positive forces; in others, its contribution reinforced and broadened their effects.

The Church's views probably had no impact at all on the total volume of foreign aid in the world, as Catholic appeals to rich countries to meet long-standing UN targets were merely an echo of established liberal opinion on the subject. However, Church doubts about private enterprise and markets probably compromised the impact of aid in some countries and stifled private investment, a much more important contributor to growth and development. (Some would argue in the Church's defense that it was only trying to cushion the poor against the harsher aspects of economic reform.) The Church's position on birth control also complicated the efforts of national policymakers keen to offer their citizens informed choices on family size and to rein in the fraying effect of population growth on the quality of public services. Fortunately, Church people – including many bishops – were more pragmatic about contraception on the front line than were the theological hardliners in Rome. And, in the fight against HIV/AIDS, where contraceptives were at the heart of a bitter debate, Church leaders were prominent in raising awareness, fighting stigmatization, and providing care and treatment to people living with the disease. The Catholic Church is now one of the largest distributors of antiretroviral drugs in the world.

Such a prominent role is a reflection of the Church's commitment, facilities, and experience at the community level. Health networks set up during the heyday of missionary activity in the 1950s played a key role in the World Health Organization's enlarged programs of vaccination in the 1960s and 1970s, and were central to the historic drop in infant mortality across the developing world.[2] No one has yet bottled the formula for successful development in the world, but almost everyone agrees that basic health and education is key to spreading the benefits of economic growth. The Church has been a leader in education across the developing world, equipping elites, empowering poor people, and having a particularly positive effect on girls and women, especially in cultures where they were regarded as inferior to men.

Another key factor in fighting poverty has been political stability. Although the Church's actions varied across countries and rested once again on the insights and courage of individual men and women rather than some general plan in Rome, broadly speaking the Church has been a promoter of political balance, a champion of human rights (a role that would have been foreign to it before the Second World War), and a shock absorber for political frustration. Although some would have preferred it to be more militant, and others would have liked it to be less opinionated, in no country in the modern era has the Church been a cause of division, civil discord, or violence.

Inevitably, the Church's role has varied across continents. Although still complex, it is easier to describe in Africa, where it is relatively young, and in Asia, where it is generally in the minority, than in Latin America, where it is part of the very culture and personality of the region.

In Africa, where states continue to struggle to establish reliable networks of basic health and education, the Church remains a central actor in giving poor people the confidence, literacy, and physical strength to change their own lives. As public policy improves, markets are linked, and opportunities open up, Catholic schools and clinics will have given hundreds of thousands of people across the continent access to the modern economy they otherwise would not have had.

In Asia, the Church had almost no role in the greatest reduction of poverty in human history (in China and India), and bishops have had to be careful about expressing "political" opinions. But overall the Church has been a consistent defender of democracy, and in some cases (Cardinal Sin in the Philippines and Cardinal Kim in Korea) a front-line actor in changing the political system. Even where the Church is minute, it continues to have a remarkable influence. In Bangladesh, where there are only 300,000 Catholics in a population of 170 million, Catholic high schools are the ones that well-to-do parents most want their children to attend.

In Latin America, except for Brazil, Chile, El Salvador, and Guatemala, Church leaders generally failed to confront dictatorship and to speak up for the rights of those persecuted, imprisoned, or killed for their political beliefs. In Argentina, the Church's posture has been compared to its failure to head off the genocide in Rwanda, leading to resentment deep enough to ensnare a new Pope. But almost without exception, on the ground, right across Latin America, Church people – individual bishops, priests, religious, and lay activists – working in parishes and hundreds of thousands of small Christian communities, mobilized resistance and gave humble people a sense of their rights and the courage to press for change. Even in Chile, controversial as the conclusion may be, the Church's role in preventing a civil war during the Pinochet regime was a key contribution to one of the most impressive successes in poverty reduction since the Second World War.

Globally, the Church has played an important role as honest broker and political mediator. The most important example is John Paul II's successful intervention in the dispute between Chile and Argentina over some small islands in the Beagle Channel in 1978–84. Less dramatic – but locally just as important – was the Church's chairing of national conferences in African countries like Benin, Togo, and Zaire that led to the introduction of democracy. Catholics were also instrumental in ending the prolonged and devastating civil war in Mozambique.

In the international development debate, Catholics and other Christians have put pressure on international institutions to reform their approaches, sharpen their focus on poverty, and recognize the damaging effects of some of their policy advice and investments. It was Anglicans and Protestants who spearheaded the Jubilee 2000 campaign, which led to the thirty poorest countries having their total debt cut from over $100 billion to $40 billion by 2006; but the seed of that campaign was sown by John Paul II in 1994.

Overall, while it is difficult to prove by conventional methods, the circumstantial evidence is overwhelming. With the possible exception of the central ministry of education of the People's Republic of China (because of the sheer numbers involved), and despite its obtuseness on the role of the market and family planning, the Catholic Church has probably lifted more people out of poverty than any other organization in history.

That achievement will be difficult to repeat. The last fifty years have seen extraordinary geopolitical change and social and economic progress, despite the "lost decade" of the 1980s in Latin America and thirty years of decline in Africa. Fortunately enough, the spread of open political systems has narrowed the range of "prophetic" actions that Catholics and other Christians need to take to give substance to the messages of the Gospel. Perhaps the Church must now give greater emphasis to spiritual direction and solace. But the opportunities to help poor people around the world to transform their lives remain manifold – if only the Church can overcome its current preoccupations with identity. Pope Francis has said in the past that he prefers the risks of being "in the streets" to those of being self-centered and introspective.[3]

Henri de Lubac (1896–1991), a French theologian who was highly suspect in Rome before Vatican II but who played an important role during it, talked in 1969 about a new "crisis," in which many Catholics were turning their impatience with society against the Church itself, rejecting its authority, distorting its history, glossing over its positive achievements, and turning its "living" tradition into the "waste-products of a dead past." "I am amazed at the good conscience of so many of the church's children who, without ever having done anything great themselves, without having thought or suffered, without taking the time to reflect, each day make themselves, to the applause of the crowds outside, the accusers of their Mother and their brethren."[4] What would he have said now?

By its very nature, the Church is a conservative and sometimes repressive organization. New challenges have brought out some of its worst instincts. In moving up the ecclesiastical ladder, theological expertise, a certain line of thought, and media skills are now more important than a good pastoral record. Many Church leaders see themselves on the walls of a fortress rather than in the middle of a sheepfold. The notion that the Church is the "People of God" rather than a collection of structures and high offices has barely been murmured in the Vatican since 1985 (although here, again, the election of Pope Francis may change things). And the Vatican II generation is retiring or dying off. Yet the Church is not about to close its 140,000 schools, 18,000 clinics, and 5,500 hospitals. It still has work to do in its 37,000 centers of informal education, 16,000 homes for the elderly and handicapped, 12,000 nurseries, 10,000 orphanages, and 500 leprosaria. Church people in those institutions are still largely motivated by their faith and their sense of service rather than by the passing preoccupations of theologians. Their energy, example, and momentum will inspire others long after current debates have taken new turns.

What about the warning at the start of this book about not confusing "some upright abbot or bishop" with the Church as a whole? Wouldn't any organization as large and diverse as the Catholic Church inevitably throw up individuals who led exemplary lives of service? Certainly. But the consistency and breadth of their actions, the impact they have had, and the conscious support they received from Church leaders are impressive. So is their modesty. Julian Filochowski, who headed CAFOD for twenty years, told me that one could reach the same positive conclusion about any development organization "if you string together a series of good stories."[5] On a smaller canvas, I asked Paul Schindler, the priest who dug up the bodies of four American women missionaries murdered by the El Salvador National Guard in December 1980, how he measured his contribution to the country after decades of service. Like others I met, he answered simply: "I don't think in those terms. I've just tried to be helpful."[6] But the Church's record belies these efforts at self-effacement.

Although it believes it is divine, the Catholic Church is a highly scarred and pockmarked institution. Diverse and all too human in its internal organization, the Church has varied greatly in its responses to social challenges. Vagaries of character, pressures of circumstance, and instincts of self-preservation have sometimes won out over the eternal truths to which it is dedicated. As the English writer and statesman Lord Acton suggested, "The cause of the Church, which is the cause of truth, is mixed up with human elements, and is injured by a degrading alliance. In this way even piety may lead to immorality, and devotion to the Pope may lead away from God."[7] But the Church can only operate in this world rather than some ideal one. Certainly, it is individual men and women who have filled in the pockmarks and given a sometimes formidable institution its human face. But they have not been acting alone. They have been drawn together by the same Gospel, traditions, and fellowship that inspired many of their predecessors and been supported by the structures, resources, teaching, and worldwide presence of an organization without parallel in history. Their trials and successes have been common ones, not isolated efforts, and have formed part of a global undertaking on a scale few would have imagined when Leo XIII issued his momentous encyclical *Rerum Novarum* in 1891. Where the Church has put faith and service before self-interest – both as an organization and as a constellation of individuals – it has been a shining example of what is best in humanity.

Individuals like Dick Timm in Bangladesh, Karoline Mayer in Chile, Soosai Pakiam in India, and Jean Pruitt in Tanzania have been prophets – speakers of discomforting truths – not just servants of society. They share a faith that transcends the hardships and disappointments of this life, and an institution, with all its faults, that has sustained their hopes and purpose. Unfortunately, the Church is as uncomfortable with prophets as the people of the Old Testament were. I asked Roger Etchegaray, the long-time head of the Vatican's Pontifical Council for Justice and Peace, why Denis Hurley, archbishop of Durban for forty-five years, was never made a cardinal. "Was he a controversial figure in the Church?" Etchegaray's smile was enigmatic: "You know, everyone who fights for justice upsets people." Progress, he seemed to be saying, is never as straight as an arrow. Later, in Etchegaray's memoirs, I spotted a quote from Václav Havel that could give eager development economists and Catholic social activists some pause for thought:

> I wanted History to move more quickly, like a child pulling on a plant to make it grow faster. We can't fool a plant any more than we can fool History. But we can water it every day with understanding, humility, and love.[8]

Notes

Introduction

1. H. Rider Haggard, *King Solomon's Mines*, London, Cassell, 1933, p. 265.
2. John F. Chuchiak, "Writing as resistance: Maya graphic pluralism and indigenous elite strategies for survival in colonial Yucatan, 1550–1750," *Ethnohistory*, 57:1 (2010), pp. 88–90.
3. Wade Davis, *The Wayfinders: Why ancient wisdom matters in the modern world*, Toronto, House of Anansi Press, 2009, p. 101.
4. Author's direct experience.
5. Wangari Maathai, *The Challenge for Africa*, New York, Pantheon Books, 2009, p. 38.
6. Interview with Fr Damian Temere Mosha, 19 August 2011.
7. Interview of 11 February 2010.
8. *Evangelii Praecones* [On Promotion of Catholic Missions], 2 June 1951, para. 51.
9. Interview of 1 December 2011.
10. Joseph McCabe, *The Social Record of Christianity*, London, Watts & Co., 1935, pp. 97–8.

Chapter 1: Two Troublemakers

1. Hélder Câmara, *Church and Colonialism*, London, Sheed and Ward, 1969. pp. 4, 11–12, 21–2, 45 (translation from the Portuguese adapted by the author).
2. Quoted in Guy Aurenche, *Le souffle d'une vie*, Paris, Albin Michel, 2011, pp. 57–8 (author's translation).
3. Câmara, *Church and Colonialism*, pp. 31, 103 (translation adapted).
4. Quoted in Aurenche, *Le souffle d'une vie*, p. 56 (author's translation).
5. Obituary in *The Tablet*, September 1999.
6. Robin Nagle, *Claiming the Virgin: The broken promise of liberation theology in Brazil*, New York and London, Routledge, 1997, pp. 9, 46.
7. Câmara, *Church and Colonialism*, p. 56 (translation adapted).
8. John Dear, SJ, "Dom Helder Camara, Presente!" *National Catholic Reporter*, 28 April 2009.
9. Interview of 2 February 2012.

10. See chronology of events in Nagle, *Claiming the Virgin*.
11. Paddy Kearney, *Guardian of the Light: Denis Hurley – renewing the church, opposing apartheid*, New York and London, Continuum, 2009, p. 255.
12. ibid., p. 33.
13. Anthony M. Gamley (ed.), *Denis Hurley: A portrait by friends*, Pietermaritzburg, Cluster Publications, 2001, p. 4.
14. Kearney, *Guardian of the Light*, p. 212.
15. ibid., p. 192.
16. Ian Linden, *Global Catholicism: Diversity and change since Vatican II*, New York, Columbia University Press, 2009, p. 181.
17. Interview with Pierre Hurtubise, St Paul's University, Ottawa, 23 September 2011.
18. Kearney, *Guardian of the Light*, p. 135.
19. ibid., p. 142.
20. Fr Agathangelus, *The Catholic Church and Southern Africa*, Cape Town, Catholic Archdiocese of Cape Town, 1951, pp. 10–11.

Chapter 2: The Catholic Church: "Seven Inches of Condemnation and One of Praise"

1. Bertrand Russell, *Why I Am Not a Christian*, New York, Simon and Schuster, 1957, pp. 24, 34.
2. G.K. Chesterton, *Orthodoxy*, London, Hodder & Stoughton, 1999 (originally published 1908), p. 173.
3. Hans Küng, *The Catholic Church: A short history*, London, Weidenfeld and Nicolson, 2001, p. 15.
4. Francis X. Blouin, Jr., 'Introduction' in *Vatican Archives: An inventory and guide to historical documents of the Holy See*, New York and Oxford, Oxford University Press, 1998.
5. G.K. Chesterton, *Autobiography*, London, Hutchison, 1936, pp. 55–6.
6. Olga Hartley, *Women and the Catholic Church: Yesterday and today*, London, Burns Oates & Washbourne, 1935, p. 222.
7. Linden, *Global Catholicism*, p. 61.
8. ibid., p. 72.
9. Thomas Cahill, *Pope John XXIII: A life*, New York, Penguin, 2008, p. 183.
10. ibid., p. 198.
11. ibid., pp. 202–4.
12. John Webster and Ellen Webster (eds), *The Church and Women in the Third World*, Philadelphia, Westminster Press, 1985, pp. 59–73.
13. Benedict XVI, *Light of the World: A conversation with Peter Seewald*, San Francisco, Ignatius Press, 2010, p. 71.
14. Conor Cruise O'Brien, in Dermot Keogh (ed.), *Church and Politics in Latin America*, London, Macmillan, 1990, pp. 138–9.
15. ibid., p. 150.
16. Hartley, *Women and the Catholic Church*, p. 61.
17. Anne Soupa and Christine Pedotti, *Les Pieds dans le bénitier*, Paris, Presses de la Renaissance, 2010, p. 31.
18. Jean-Claude Djereke, *L'Engagement politique du clergé catholique en Afrique noire*, Paris, Karthala, 2001, pp. 180–1 (author's translation).
19. Roger Etchegaray, *J'ai senti battre le cœur du monde*, Paris, Fayard, 2007, p. 70 (author's translation).
20. Georges Cottier, *Église et pauvreté*, Paris, Les Éditions du Cerf, 1965, p. 199 (author's translation).
21. Henri Tincq, "I've two sick relatives: Burundi and the church," *Guardian Weekly*, 28 April 2006, p. 17.
22. John Paul II, *Entrez dans l'espérance*, Paris, Plon, 1994, pp. 55–61 (author's translation from the French).

23. G.G. Coulton, *Two Saints: St Bernard and St Francis*, Cambridge, Cambridge University Press, 1932, pp. 1–2.
24. Hendrik Kraemer, *The Christian Message in a Non-Christian World*, London, Edinburgh House Press, 1938, pp. 114–15.
25. Thomas Dixon, *Science and Religion: A very short introduction*, Oxford, Oxford University Press, 2009, p. 42.
26. ibid., and personal communication from Timothy Radcliffe.
27. Quoted in Rodney Stark, *The Victory of Reason: How Christianity led to freedom, capitalism and western success*, New York, Random House, 2005, p. 15.
28. "Lecture of the Holy Father," University of Regensburg, 12 September 2006, available at: http://www.vatican.va/holy_father/benedict_xvi/speeches/2006/september/documents/hf_ben-xvi_spe_20060912_university-regensburg_en.html
29. John Paul II, *Entrez dans l'espérance*, p. 154.
30. Benedict XVI, *Africae Munus*, Vatican City, Libreria Editrice Vaticana, 2011, p. 89.
31. Church Central Statistics Office, *Statistical Yearbook of the Church, 2009*, Vatican City, Libreria Editrice Vaticana, 2011, pp. 17, 34–43, 77, 365.
32. Exhibition on "Sisters and Spirit," organized by the Leadership Conference of Women Religious, Smithsonian Institution, January–April 2010.
33. Conversation with Andrea Riccardi (February 1999), cited in Riccardi, *Sant'Egidio, Roma e il Mondo*, Milan, Edizioni San Paolo, 1997, p. 39. (Translated from the Italian by the author.)
34. Interview with Dr Flaminia Giovanelli, Undersecretary, Pontifical Council for Justice and Peace, 12 October 2010.

Chapter 3: Social Teaching: From Caesar to *Centesimus Annus*

1. Jacques Leclercq, *Christianity and Money*, London, Burns & Oates, 1959, p. 35.
2. Albert Nolan, *Jesus before Christianity*, Maryknoll, Orbis Books, 2010, pp. 124–7.
3. Jean-Vincent Ondo, "La place de l'Église dans le processus démocratique en Afrique," dissertation, Institut Catholique de Paris, July 1996, pp. 35–6.
4. Nolan, *Jesus before Christianity*, p. 88.
5. Eliza Griswold, *The Tenth Parallel: Dispatches from the fault line between Christianity and Islam*, New York, Farrar, Straus and Giroux, 2010, p. 59.
6. Kraemer, *The Christian Message in a Non-Christian World*, pp. 93–4.
7. McCabe, *The Social Record of Christianity*, p. viii.
8. ibid., pp. 23–4, 120–33.
9. ibid. p. 112; Diarmaid MacCulloch, *A History of Christianity*, London, Penguin, 2010, pp. 710–11.
10. Leclercq, *Christianity and Money*, pp. 45–6.
11. MacCulloch, *A History of Christianity*, p. 592.
12. Leclercq, *Christianity and Money*, p. 39.
13. MacCulloch, *A History of Christianity*, p. 701.
14. Jean Pirotte, *Churches and Health Care in the Third World: Past and present*, Leiden, E.J. Brill, 1991, p. 23.
15. Quoted in Barbara Ward, *Faith and Freedom*, New York, W.W. Norton & Company, 1954, p. 82.
16. Joseph De Torre, *Politics and the Church: From Rerum Novarum to liberation theology*, Manila, Vera Reyes, 1987, pp. 3–4.
17. Cahill, *Pope John XXIII*, pp. 38, 57.
18. René Fülöp-Miller, *Leo XIII and Our Times*, New York, Longmans, Green and Co., 1937, p. 39.
19. Paul Christopher Manuel (ed.), *The Catholic Church and the Nation-State: Comparative perspectives*, Washington, DC, Georgetown University Press, 2006, p. 7.
20. Linden, *Global Catholicism*, p. 5.

21. Fülöp-Miller, *Leo XIII and Our Times*, p. 41.
22. ibid., p. 121.
23. Michael Fleet, *The Catholic Church and Democracy in Chile and Peru*, Notre Dame, University of Notre Dame, 1997, pp. 1–2.
24. J.B. McLaughlin, *The Immortal Encyclical*: Rerum Novarum *and the developments of Pius XI*, London, Burns, Oates & Washbourne, 1932, pp. 3, 20, 44, 60, 91, 95–6.
25. Quoted in Yves Ledure (ed.), *Rerum Novarum en France: Le Père Dehon et l'engagement social de l'Église*, Éditions Universitaires, 1991, p. 73.
26. Joseph Husslein, *The Christian Social Manifesto*, New York, Bruce, 1931, p. xii.
27. ibid., pp. xiii–xiv.
28. ibid., p. xii.
29. Donald J. Dietrich, *Human Rights and the Catholic Tradition*, London, Transaction, 2007, pp. 100–2.
30. Brooke F. Westcott, *Christian Social Union Addresses*, London, Macmillan, 1903, p. 4.
31. McCabe, *The Social Record of Christianity*, p. 143.
32. G.D.H. Cole, *Persons and Periods*, Harmondsworth, Penguin, 1945, p. 168.
33. Quoted in Ledure, *Rerum Novarum en France*, p. 79.
34. Rodolfo Cardenal, in Keogh (ed.), *Church and Politics in Latin America*, p. 176.
35. Kevin E. Schmiesing, *Within the Market Strife: American Catholic economic thought from Rerum Novarum to Vatican II*, Latham and Oxford, Lexington Books, 2004, p. 9.
36. Michel Lagrée, in Paul Furlong and David Curtis (eds), *The Church Faces the Modern World*: Rerum Novarum *and its impact*, Hull, Earlsgate Press, 1994, p. 153.
37. Vitalis Anaehobi, "Le Pere Lebret, Paul-VI et *Populorum Progressio*: Enjeux pour une approche théologique du développement," dissertation, Université de Paris-Sorbonne (Paris IV), Institut Catholique de Paris, 2006, p. 20.
38. ibid., pp. 31–2.
39. ibid., p. 13 (author's translation).
40. Paul Poupard, *Le développement des peuples: Entre souvenirs et espérance*, Paris, Parole et Silence, 2008, pp. 69–75.
41. Linden, *Global Catholicism*, p. 107.
42. Pius XI, *After Forty Years*, New York, Barry Vail, 1931, p. 33.
43. Etchegaray, *J'ai senti battre le cœur du monde*, p. 58.
44. James O'Connell in Furlong and Curtis (eds), *The Church Faces the Modern World*, p. 80.
45. De Torre, *Politics and the Church*, p. 18.
46. Pius XII, *Humani Generis*, revised edition, London, Catholic Truth Society, 1961, p. 7.
47. See http://www.vatican.va/holy_father/pius_xii/speeches/1941/documents/hf_p-xii_spe_19410601_radiomessage-pentecost_it.html
48. See "Church's concern for economic life" in Robert Kennedy and Stephanie Rumpza, *Pius XII on Work and Commerce*, University of St Thomas, Saint Paul, Minnesota, 2011, available at: http://www.stthomas.edu/cathstudies/cst/publications/piusxii/Pius_Section_II_51–53.pdf
49. Cahill, *Pope John XXIII*, p. 147.
50. John XXIII, *New Light on Social Problems*, London, Catholic Truth Society, 1961, pp. 46–8, 59, 63.
51. John XXIII, *Pacem in Terris*, para. 92.
52. Philip S. Land, *Catholic Social Teaching: As I have lived, loathed, and loved it*, Chicago, Loyola University Press, 1994, p. 34.
53. ibid., p. 25.
54. ibid., pp. 33–5.
55. Poupard, *Le développement des peuples*, p. 83 (author's translation).
56. *Populorum Progressio*, para. 66.
57. ibid., para. 6.
58. ibid., para. 31.

59. Michael Schultheis, *Catholic Social Teaching and the Church in Africa*, Gweru, Zimbabwe, Centre of Concern, 1984, p. 5.
60. David Brooks, "Bigger than the Nobel," *New York Times*, 11 October 2003.
61. Interview of 6 February 2012.
62. Andreas Widner, *The Pope and the CEO: John Paul II's leadership lessons for a young Swiss Guard*, Steubenville, Ohio, Emmaus Road, 2011, pp. 136–8.
63. Etchegaray, *J'ai senti battre le cœur du monde*, p. 178.
64. *Sollicitudo Rei Socialis*, para. 39.
65. John Sniegocki, *Catholic Social Teaching and Economic Globalization: The quest for alternatives*, Milwaukee, Marquette University Press, 2009, pp. 157–64.
66. Interview of 31 July 2012.
67. Peter Bauer, *From Subsistence to Exchange and Other Essays*, Princeton, Princeton University Press, 2000, p. 107.
68. Sniegocki, *Catholic Social Teaching and Economic Globalization*, pp. 157–64.
69. Alain Brezault and Gerard Clavreuil, *Missions: En Afrique, les Catholiques face à l'Islam, aux sectes, au Vatican*, Paris, Éditions Autrement, 1987, pp. 20–2 (author's translation).
70. Samuel Moyn, *The Last Utopia: Human rights in history*, Cambridge and London, Harvard University Press, 2010, p. 50.
71. Ward, *Faith and Freedom*, p. 85.
72. Jacques Maritain, *Christianisme et démocratie*, Paris, Desclée de Brouwer, 1989, pp. 11–12 (author's translation).
73. ibid., p. 90 (author's translation).
74. Interview with Dr Carlos Hoevel, Director, Center for Economic and Cultural Studies, Pontifical Catholic University, Buenos Aires, 6 February 2012.
75. Moyn, *The Last Utopia*, p. 66.
76. John S. Nurser, *For All Peoples and All Nations: The ecumenical church and human rights*, Washington, DC, Georgetown University Press, 2005, p. 27.
77. The exact numbers were 13 bishops, 4,000 priests, 2,500 brothers, 280 nuns, and 240 seminarians.
78. Etchegaray, *J'ai senti battre le cœur du monde*, p. 76 (author's translation).
79. Nurser, *For All Peoples and All Nations*, pp. 22, 27.
80. Jacques Maritain, *Les Droits de l'Homme*, Paris, Desclée de Brouwer, 1989, pp. 135–6 (author's translation).
81. Moyn, *The Last Utopia*, pp. 130–1.
82. Quoted in ibid., p. 127.
83. Quoted in Kearney, *Guardian of the Light*, p. 32.

Chapter 4: Religion and Development: "A Task of Fraternity"

1. Wade Davis, *The Wayfinders: Why ancient wisdom matters in the modern world*, Toronto, House of Anansi Press, 2009, p. 196.
2. Maathai, *The Challenge for Africa*, p. 40.
3. Matthew Parris, "As an atheist, I truly believe Africa needs God," *The Times*, 27 December 2008.
4. World Values Survey, Question: "How important is religion in your life?" (source: poll. orspub.com).
5. See http://www.gallup.com/poll/142727/Religiosity-Highest-World-Poorest-Nations.aspx
6. Mark Malloch-Brown, *The Unfinished Global Revolution: The limits of nations and the pursuit of a new politics*, London, Allen Lane, 2011, p. 81.
7. James D. Wolfensohn, *A Global Life*, New York, Public Affairs, 2009, p. 290.
8. Peter Bauer, *Equality, the Third World and Economic Delusion*, London, Weidenfeld and Nicolson, 1981, p. 88.
9. Quoted in Moyn, *The Last Utopia*, p. 87.
10. Martin Wolf, "Hopes in emerging countries," *Financial Times*, 11 January 2012.

11. "World Bank sees progress against extreme poverty, but flags vulnerabilities," Press Release No. 2012/297/DEC, 29 February 2012.
12. Interview of 22 October 2011.
13. "World Bank sees progress against extreme poverty, but flags vulnerabilities," Press Release No. 2012/297/DEC, 29 February 2012.
14. Dani Rodrik, *The Globalization Paradox: Why global markets, states, and democracy can't coexist*, Oxford, Oxford University Press, 2011, pp. 148–9.
15. Abhijit Banerjee and Esther Duflo, *Poor Economics: A radical rethinking of the way to fight global poverty*, New York, Public Affairs, 2011, p. 40; Charles Kenny, *Getting Better: Why global development is succeeding and how we can improve the world even more*, New York, Basic Books, 2011, p. 14.
16. Leandro Prados de la Escosura, "World Human Development, 1870–2007," lecture delivered at Oxford, 22 May 2012.
17. Kenny, *Getting Better*, p. 96.
18. Ian Buruma, *Taming the Gods: Religion and democracy on three continents*, Princeton and Oxford, Princeton University Press, 2010, p. 23.
19. Timur Kuran, *The Long Divergence: How Islamic law held back the Middle East*, Princeton, Princeton University Press, 2011.
20. Richard W. Timm, *Forty Years in Bangladesh: Memoirs of Father Timm*, Dhaka, Caritas Bangladesh, 1995, pp. 348–9.
21. Lesslie Newbigin, *A South India Diary*, London, Edinburgh House Press, 1951, pp. 48, 54.
22. Michael Ramsey, *The Gospel of the Catholic Church*, London, SPCK, 1990, pp. 2–3.
23. Penny Lernoux, *Hearts on Fire: The story of the Maryknoll Sisters*, Maryknoll, Orbis, 1995, p. 149.
24. Robert A. Sirico, *The Entrepreneurial Vocation*, Grand Rapids, Michigan, Acton Institute for the Study of Religion and Liberty, 2001, p. 8.
25. Robert Sarah, *Culture, démocratie et développement à la lumière de Centesimus Annus*, Conakry, Éditions IMC, 1998, "Introduction".
26. Joseph Bouchaud, *L'Église en Afrique noire*, Paris and Geneva, La Palatine, 1958, pp. 181–2 (author's translation).
27. Quoted in David Jones, "The redemption of economics: the political thought of Eric Gill and Vincent McNabb," *Allan Review: An Oxford Journal of Catholic Thought*, 7 (1992), pp. 29–30.
28. G.K. Chesterton, *The Outline of Sanity*, Norfolk, Virginia, IHS Press, 2001, pp. 15–17.
29. Thomas M. McFadden (ed.), *Liberation, Revolution, and Freedom: Theological perspectives*, New York, Seabury Press, 1975, pp. 57–8.
30. Quoted by Peter Hebblethwaite, in Keogh (ed.), *Church and Politics in Latin America*, p. 57.
31. Interview of 13 February 2012.
32. See http://www.goodreads.com/author/quotes/151379.Gustavo_Guti_rrez
33. Quoted in Djereke, *L'Engagement politique du clergé catholique en Afrique noire*, p. 15 (author's translation).
34. Quoted in McFadden, *Liberation, Revolution, and Freedom*, p. 4.
35. De Torre, *Politics and the Church*, pp. 62–8.
36. John Paul II to the bishops of Ecuador, 23 October 1984.
37. Emilio Mignone, in Keogh (ed.), *Church and Politics in Latin America*, p. 369.
38. Interview of 8 February 2012.
39. Interview with Luis Mendiola, 7 February 2012.
40. Donal Dorr, "Themes and theologies in Catholic social teaching over fifty years," *New Blackfriars*, 93:1044 (March 2012), p. 152.
41. Fleet, *The Catholic Church and Democracy in Chile and Peru*, pp. 224–5.
42. Interview of 27 February 2012.
43. Interview of 7 March 2011.
44. John W. O'Malley, *The First Jesuits*, Cambridge and London, Harvard University Press, 1993, pp. 15, 27, 51, 142, 208–9.

45. Alexander Hetherwick, *The Gospel and the African*, Edinburgh, T. & T. Clark, 1932, pp. 136–7.
46. Norman Etherington (ed.), *Missions and Empire*, Oxford, Oxford University Press, 2005, p. 273.
47. ibid., pp. 265–73.
48. ibid., p. 261.
49. Interview of 21 October 2011.
50. Banerjee and Duflo, *Poor Economics*, pp. 54–5, 74, 83.
51. Etherington, *Missions and Empire*, p. 273.
52. Harry Johnstone, "Review of *Adventures in Aidland: The anthropology of professionals in international development*, edited by David Mosse," *Times Literary Supplement*, 9 September 2011, p. 26.
53. Quoted in de Torre, *Politics and the Church*, p. 46.
54. Etchegaray, *J'ai senti battre le cœur du monde*, pp. 208, 288.
55. Michael Swan, "Dominicans set bar high on human rights," *Catholic Register*, 23 January 2012, p. 15.
56. Lernoux, *Hearts on Fire*, pp. 221–2.

Chapter 5: Africa: "No One is Opposed to a School"

1. Bouchaud, *L'Église en Afrique noire*, p. 22 (author's translation).
2. ibid., p. 24 (author's translation).
3. Chinua Achebe, *The Education of a British-Protected Child*, London, Penguin, 2011, p. 7.
4. Desmond Forristal, *The Second Burial of Bishop Shanahan*, Dublin, Veritas, 1990, p. 80.
5. Bouchaud, *L'Église en Afrique noire*, p. 34.
6. John P. Jordan, *Bishop Shanahan of Southern Nigeria*, Dublin, Clonmore and Reynolds, 1949, p. 19.
7. ibid., p. 23.
8. ibid., pp. 22–3.
9. ibid., p. 55.
10. ibid., p. 118.
11. ibid., p. 105.
12. ibid., pp. 208–9.
13. Forristal, *The Second Burial of Bishop Shanahan*, p. 214.
14. ibid., p. 271.
15. Ian Linden, *The Catholic Church and the Struggle for Zimbabwe*, London, Longman, 1980, pp. 8, 26.
16. Quoted in Marcus Ndongmo, *Éducation scolaire et lien social en Afrique noire*, Mbalmayo, Cameroon, ICERh, 2004, p. 33 (author's translation).
17. ibid. (author's translation).
18. ibid., p. 34 (author's translation).
19. Marie-Noelle Ezeh, "La reconnaissance de la dignité de la femme dans la rencontre de la société Igbo du Nigéria avec le christianisme de 1885 à 1965," dissertation, Université de Paris-Sorbonne (Paris IV), Institut Catholique de Paris, April 2002, p. 131 (author's translation).
20. ibid., p. 173 (author's translation).
21. ibid., pp. 167–9.
22. Bouchaud, *L'Église en Afrique noire*, p. 91 (author's translation).
23. Yves Tourigny, *So Abundant a Harvest*, London, Darton, Longman and Todd, 1979, pp. 79–80.
24. ibid., pp. 49–50.
25. ibid., p. 68.
26. Jan Christiaan Smuts, *Africa and Some World Problems*, Oxford, Clarendon Press, 1930, pp. 87–8.

27. Etherington, *Missions and Empire*, pp. 268–9.
28. Ezeh, "La reconnaissance de la dignité de la femme," p. 120 (author's translation).
29. Jordan, *Bishop Shanahan of Southern Nigeria*, p. 91.
30. Ndongmo, *Éducation scolaire et lien social en Afrique noire*, p. 38 (author's translation).
31. ibid., pp. 68–9 (author's translation).
32. Cheikh Hamidou Kane, *Ambiguous Adventure*, New York, Walker, 1963, pp. 45–7.
33. Ndongmo, *Éducation scolaire et lien social en Afrique noire*, p. 21 (author's translation).
34. Société africaine de culture, *Civilisation noire et Église catholique: Colloque d'Abidjan 12–17 septembre 1977*, Paris, Présence africaine, pp. 41–5 (author's translation).
35. Missionnaires d'Afrique, *Le Cardinal Lavigerie: Apôtre de l'Afrique*, Bobo-Dioulasso, Burkina Faso, Imprimerie de la Savane, 1991, pp. 10–11 (author's translation).
36. Griswold, *The Tenth Parallel*, pp. 30–2.
37. Ndongmo, *Éducation scolaire et lien social en Afrique noire*, p. 25 (author's translation).
38. Venerable F.M.P. Libermann, quoted in ibid., p. 25 (author's translation).
39. Quoted in ibid., p. 26 (author's translation).
40. "Bishop Joseph Shanahan," The Spiritans website, available at: http://spiritanroma.org/world/wwwroot/cssphistmission/Joseph%20Shanahan.html
41. Lernoux, *Hearts on Fire*, p. 54.
42. Quoted in Ezeh, "La reconnaissance de la dignité de la femme," p. 203 (author's translation).
43. ibid., p. 204 (author's translation).
44. ibid., pp. 206–7 (author's translation).
45. Pierre Ryckmans, *Dominer pour Servir*, Brussels, Librairie Albert Dewit, 1931.
46. Bouchaud, *L'Église en Afrique noire*, pp. 124–5 (author's translation).
47. ibid., pp. 180–1 (author's translation).
48. Interview with Bishop Amadeus Msarikie, 21 August 2011.
49. Ezeh, "La reconnaissance de la dignité de la femme," p. 16 (author's translation).
50. Bouchaud, *L'Église en Afrique noire*, pp. 101–2 (author's translation).
51. William J. Wilson (ed.), *The Church in Africa: Christian mission in a context of change*, Maryknoll, Maryknoll Publications, 1967, p. 3.
52. ibid., pp. 4–7.
53. Djereke, *L'Engagement politique du clergé catholique en Afrique noire*, p. 23 (author's translation).
54. ibid., pp. 70–1 (author's translation).
55. Personal communication to the author, November 1991.
56. Djereke, *L'Engagement politique du clergé catholique en Afrique noire*, pp. 220–1 (author's translation).
57. Paul Gifford, *The Christian Churches and the Democratisation of Africa*, Leiden, E.J. Brill, 1995, p. 4.
58. Cardinal Malula, in "Essai de profit des prêtres de l'an 2000 au Zaïre," *La Documentation catholique*, 1961 (1 May 1988), pp. 463–9. Quoted in Djereke, *L'Engagement politique du clergé catholique en Afrique noire*, pp. 54–5 (author's translation).
59. Brezault and Clavreuil, *Missions*, p. 31 (author's translation).
60. Ministry of Education and Sports, *Uganda Education Statistical Abstract*, Vol. 1, Kampala, 2009, p. 41.
61. ibid., pp. 21, 31.
62. National Planning Authority, *National Development Plan (2010/11–2014/15)*, Kampala, 2010.
63. Séverine Deneulin, *Religion in Development: Rewriting the secular script*, London, Zed Books, 2009, p. 84.
64. Interview with Louis Shayo, 20 August 2011.
65. Bishop Bernardin Francis Mfumbusa, *The Guardian* (Dar es Salaam), 14 August 2011.
66. Interview of 6 September 2011.
67. John Sivalon, "Roman Catholicism and the defining of Tanzanian socialism, 1953–1985," dissertation, St Michael's College, University of Toronto, November 1990, pp. 220–9.

68. Marie J. Giblin, "Toward justice, equality and participation: Issues for the Church concerning Tanzanian women and men peasants," dissertation, Union Theological Seminary, New York City, May 1986, p. iii.

69. Tanzanian Episcopal Conference, *Manifesto: Proposal of national priorities*, Dar es Salaam, 2009, pp. 3–4.

70. ibid., p. 17.

71. Interview of 5 September 2011.

72. Interview of 16 August 2011.

Chapter 6: Asia: A Determined Minority

1. Kraemer, *The Christian Message in a Non-Christian World*, pp. 51, 58.

2. Antoine Tran Van Toàn, in Philippe Delisle (ed.), *Les relations Églises-État en situation postcoloniale: Amériques, Afrique, Asie, Océanie, XIX-XXe siècles*, Paris, Karthala, 2003, pp. 104–5.

3. C.R. Boxer, *The Christian Century in Japan, 1549–1650*, Berkeley and Los Angeles, University of California, 1951, p. 137.

4. "Matteo Ricci," New Advent online Catholic encyclopedia, available at: http://www.newadvent.org/cathen/13034a.htm

5. Quoted in Buruma, *Taming the Gods*, p. 63.

6. Lernoux, *Hearts on Fire*, p. 12.

7. ibid., pp. 16–17.

8. Kraemer, *The Christian Message in a Non-Christian World*, p. 45.

9. Newbigin, *A South India Diary*, p. 56.

10. Interviews of 19–20 February 2011.

11. Interview of 24 February 2011.

12. Antoine Tran Van Toàn, in Delisle, *Les relations Églises-État en situation postcoloniale*, p. 112.

13. Interview of 25 February 2011.

14. Interview of 28 February 2011.

15. Interview of 28 February 2011.

16. Deneulin, *Religion in Development*, p. 84.

17. "Indian government threatens independence of Catholic schools," CatholicCulture.org website, 18 March 2010, available at: http://www.catholicculture.org/news/headlines/index.cfm?storyid=5767

18. Manuel (ed.), *The Catholic Church and the Nation-State*, p. 215.

19. Loreta N. Castro, *Poverty and Development: The call of the Catholic Church in Asia*, Rome, International Jacques Maritain Institute, 1995, pp. 54–6.

20. Edward LeJoly, *Servant of Love* (1977), p. 58, quoted in Timothy Radcliffe, *Take the Plunge: Living baptism and confirmation*, London, Bloomsbury, 2012.

21. Kenny, *Getting Better*, p. 98.

22. François Houtart and Geneviève Lemercinier, *Church and Development in Kerala*, Bangalore, Theological Publications of India, 1979, p. 320.

23. Webster and Webster, *The Church and Women in the Third World*, pp. 76–7.

24. Interview of 4 March 2011.

25. "Red flags in Kerala?" *Indian Express*, 11 March 2011.

26. Richard Timm, *The Church and Development in Bangladesh*, Dhaka, Caritas Bangladesh, 1994, pp. 6, 55, 58.

27. Richard Timm, *On Building a Just Society*, Dhaka, Caritas Bangladesh, 1994, pp. 66–74.

28. Timm, *Forty Years in Bangladesh*, 1995, p. 385.

29. ibid., pp. 1, 10, 24, 181–2, 222, 249, 276–7, 354, 285, 296, 416.

30. Interview of 11 March 2011.

31. Interview of 2 March 2011.

32. Interview of 12 March 2011.

33. Email of 16 January 2013.

34. Lernoux, *Hearts on Fire*, p. 200.

35. Interview of 2 March 2011.
36. Richard Timm, *Father of the Credit Unions in Bangladesh: Life of Father Charles J. Young, CSC*, Dhaka, Holy Cross, 2010, p. 91.
37. Castro, *Poverty and Development*, p. 16.
38. *Financial Times*, 17 February 2009.
39. *The Independent*, 21 February 2009.
40. Lernoux, *Hearts on Fire*, p. 206.

Chapter 7: Latin America: From Las Casas to Romero

1. Jared Diamond, *Guns, Germs, and Steel: The fates of human societies*, New York, W.W. Norton, 1999, pp. 67–81.
2. Bartolomé de Las Casas, *Witness*, ed. and trans. by George Sanderlin, Maryknoll, Orbis Books, 1993, pp. 66–7.
3. Personal communication of Timothy Radcliffe.
4. Edwin Williamson, *The Penguin History of Latin America*, London, Penguin Books, 2009, pp. 64–5.
5. MacCulloch, *A History of Christianity*, p. 692; personal communication from Timothy Radcliffe; Helen Rand Parish (ed.), *Bartolomé de Las Casas: The only way*, Mahwah, Paulist Press, 1992, p. 203.
6. Williamson, *The Penguin History of Latin America*, pp. 102–3.
7. Luis Quintanilla, *The Other Side of the Mexican Church Question*, Washington, DC, 1935, p. 24.
8. ibid., pp. 89–103, 119, 133–4.
9. Manuel Prieto, *The Church Problem in Mexico*, New York, Academy Press, 1926, p. 8.
10. Quintanilla, *The Other Side of the Mexican Church Question*, p. 43.
11. National Conference of Catholic Bishops, *The Church in the Present-Day Transformation of Latin America in the Light of the Council: Conclusions of the Second General Council of Latin American Bishops*, Washington, DC, Secretariat for Latin America, National Conference of Catholic Bishops, 1979, pp. 32, 40–1.
12. Conor Cruise O'Brien, in Keogh (ed.), *Church and Politics in Latin America*, p. 132.
13. Emile Poulat, in Keogh (ed.), *Church and Politics in Latin America*, pp. 17–18.
14. Manuel (ed.), *The Catholic Church and the Nation-State*, p. xiii.
15. Linden, *Global Catholicism*, p. 128.
16. Christine Kearney, in Manuel (ed.), *The Catholic Church and the Nation-State*, p. 158.
17. ibid., pp. 161–5.
18. Virginia Marie Bouvier, *Alliance or Compliance: Implications of the Chilean experience for the Catholic Church in Latin America*, Syracuse, Syracuse University, 1983, pp. 34–5.
19. Linden, *Global Catholicism*, pp. 124–5.
20. Bouvier, *Alliance or Compliance*, p. 58.
21. Ricardo Lagos, *The Southern Tiger: Chile's fight for a democratic and prosperous future*, New York, Palgrave Macmillan, 2012, p. 61.
22. ibid., p. 62.
23. Fleet, *The Catholic Church and Democracy in Chile and Peru*, pp. 116, 132, 156.
24. Susan Fitzpatrick-Behrens, *The Maryknoll Catholic Mission in Peru, 1943–1989: Transnational faith and transformation*, Notre Dame, University of Notre Dame, 2012, p. 140.
25. Interview of 14 February 2012.
26. Interview of 6 February 2012.
27. Emilio Mignone, in Keogh (ed.), *Church and Politics in Latin America*, pp. 365–6.
28. John J. Kennedy, *Catholicism, Nationalism, and Democracy in Argentina*, Notre Dame, University of Notre Dame, 1958, p. 107.
29. Mario Aguilar, *The History and Politics of Latin American Theology*, London, SCM Press, 2007, pp. 114–15.
30. Anna L. Peterson, *Seeds of the Kingdom: Utopian communities in the Americas*, Oxford and New York, Oxford University Press, 2005, p. 51.

31. Fleet, *The Catholic Church and Democracy in Chile and Peru*, p. 156.
32. Interview of 8 February 2012.
33. Obituary in *Daily Telegraph*, 16 July 2012.
34. Interview of 6 October 2010.
35. Interview of 20 October 2011.
36. Interview of 6 February 2012.
37. Interview of 9 February 2012.
38. Interview with José Panades, 21 February 2012.
39. Óscar Rodríguez Maradiaga, *De la difficulté d'évoquer Dieu dans un monde qui pense ne pas en avoir besoin*, Paris, Robert Laffont, 2008, pp. 123–4, 137, 158, 164, 201; Enzo Romeo, *Cardinal Oscar Rodriguez Maradiaga: La voix de l'Amérique latine*, Quebec, Éditions Anne Sigier, 2007, p. 168 (author's translation).
40. Deneulin, *Religion in Development*, p. 80.
41. Gustavo Gutiérrez, *A Theology of Liberation: Fifteenth anniversary edition*, Maryknoll, Orbis Books, 1990, p. xviii.

Chapter 8: Horror in Rwanda

1. Interview of 22 August 2011.
2. Interview of 23 August 2011.
3. Vénuste Linguyeneza (ed.), *Verité, Justice, Charité: Lettres pastorales et autres déclarations des évêques catholiques du Rwanda, 1956–1962*, Waterloo, 2001, p. 8 (author's translation).
4. ibid., pp. 62–76 (author's translation).
5. Bernardin Muzungu, "Église Catholique pendant le génocide," *Cahiers Lumière et Société*, 43 (2010), p. 32 (author's translation).
6. ibid., p. 6 (author's translation).
7. Interview of 24 August 2011.
8. Interview of 26 August 2011.
9. Nicolas Poincaré, *Gabriel Maindron, un prêtre dans la tragédie*, Paris, Éditions ouvrières, 1995, pp. 27, 40–1, 51–2, 113, 105, 124–5 (author's translation).

Chapter 9: Tilting at Condoms

1. Interview of 14 October 2011.
2. John L. Allen, "Think again: the Catholic church," *Foreign Policy*, 15 October 2008, p. 7.
3. Joseph McCabe, *The Catholic Church and the Sex Problem: The stupidity, futility and insolence of its ethic*, first published 1949, reprinted by The Black Cat Press, London, 2009, p. 25.
4. Thomas C. Fox, *Sexuality and Catholicism*, New York, George Braziller, 1995, pp. 33–4.
5. ibid., pp. 34–5.
6. Garry Wills, *Papal Sin: Structures of deceit*, New York, Doubleday, 2000, p. 90.
7. Fox, *Sexuality and Catholicism*, p. 63.
8. *Humanae Vitae*, paras 28, 30.
9. John J. Carroll, *A Balancing Act: Social and Catholic perspectives on population and development*, Manila, Philippine Center for Population and Development, 2007, p. 48.
10. Wills, *Papal Sin*, pp. 89–98.
11. Fox, *Sexuality and Catholicism*, p. 71.
12. ibid., pp. 72–3.
13. ibid., p. 81.
14. Interview with Pierre Hurtubise, St Paul's University, Ottawa, 23 September 2011.
15. Fox, *Sexuality and Catholicism*, p. 81.
16. The speaker prefers to remain anonymous.
17. Marilen J. Dañguilan, *Women in Brackets: A chronicle of Vatican power and control*, Manila, Philippine Center for Investigative Journalism, 1997, pp. 20–1.
18. ibid., p. 26.

19. ibid., p. 38.
20. ibid., p. 42.
21. ibid., p. 83.
22. ibid., pp. 86–8.
23. ibid., pp. 98–9.
24. Interview of 10 October 2010.
25. "Vatican officials fear resignation domino effect," *Conscience*, 31:3 (2010), p. 9.
26. Interview with Jon O'Brien of 5 October 2011.
27. Summary of findings on back page of *Conscience*, 32:1 (2011).
28. Mary Jo Iozzio (ed.), *Calling for Justice throughout the World: Catholic women theologians on the HIV/AIDS pandemic*, New York, Continuum, 2008, pp. 63–4.
29. ibid., p. 158.
30. Interview of 17 February 2011.
31. Interview with Fely Rixhon, Philippine Center for Population and Development, 18 February 2011.
32. Interview of 20 February 2011.
33. Interview of 23 February 2011.
34. Interview of 21 February 2011.
35. Personal communication from Jeanne Haji.
36. Catholic Bishops' Conference of Nigeria, *The Catholic Church in an Independent Nigeria: Joint pastoral letter of the Nigerian hierarchy, 1 October 1960*, Ibadan, Clarendon Press, 1960, p. 17.
37. Interview of 17 February 2012.
38. Kathryn Joyce, *Seeing is Believing: Questions about faith-based organizations that are involved in HIV/AIDS prevention and treatment*, Washington, DC, Catholics for Choice, 2010, p. 17.
39. ibid., p. 13.
40. ibid., p. 11.
41. Gail Collins, "Tales from the kitchen table," *New York Times*, 8 February 2012.
42. Bauer, *From Subsistence to Exchange*, p. 30.
43. ibid., p. 31.
44. Interview of 13 October 2010.
45. Sarah, *Culture, démocratie et développement à la lumière de Centesimus Annus*, p. 7 (author's translation).
46. Statement of Cardinal Peter K.A. Turkson, President of the Pontifical Council for Justice and Peace, New York, 20 September 2010.
47. Interview of 7 December 2011.
48. Personal communication of Andrew Mwenda, publisher of the Ugandan news magazine *The Independent*.
49. "HIV and AIDS in Uganda," AVERT website, available at: www.avert.org/aids-uganda
50. Interview with Musa Bungudu, 31 August 2011.
51. Interview of 5 September 2011.
52. Interview of 18 August 2011.
53. *The Citizen* (Dar es Salaam), 15 August 2011, p. 28.
54. Interview with Emmanuel Kolini, 23 August 2011.
55. Linden, *Global Catholicism*, p. 267.
56. Manuel (ed.), *The Catholic Church and the Nation-State*, pp. 215–16.
57. Personal communication to the author in Washington, DC, October 1986.
58. Interview of 14 October 2011.
59. Email from Diane Rubino, Office of Public Information, Population Council, 17 October 2011.
60. Denis Meadows, *A Popular History of the Jesuits*, New York, Macmillan, 1958, p. 37.

Chapter 10: Catholic Charity: "A Network to Die For"

1. Pirotte, *Churches and Health Care in the Third World*, pp. 59–61.
2. Hetherwick, *The Gospel and the African*, p. 141.

3. Etherington, *Missions and Empire*, p. 275.
4. Linden, *Global Catholicism*, p. 9.
5. ibid., p. 29.
6. *Deus Caritas Est*, paras 22, 31c.
7. Griswold, *The Tenth Parallel*, pp. 91–2.
8. Interview of 14 August 2012.
9. Pontifical Council *Cor Unum, Religion and Charitable Activity*, Proceedings of the plenary assembly, Vatican City, 2003, p. 65.
10. Interview of 5 October 2011.
11. Timm, *Father of the Credit Unions in Bangladesh*, p. 121.
12. Pontifical Council *Cor Unum, Acts of the World Congress on Charity: Rome, 12–15 May 1999*, Vatican City, 1999, p. 90.
13. *Rerum Novarum*, para. 30.
14. Pontifical Council *Cor Unum, Acts of the World Congress on Charity*, pp. 187–8.
15. Interview with Peter Howard, Food for the Hungry, 14 August 2012.
16. Monsignor Jean Rodhain, quoted in Etchegaray, *J'ai senti battre le cœur du monde*, p. 118 (author's translation).
17. Interview of 2 December 2011.
18. Second Vatican Council, "*Gaudium et Spes*: Pastoral constitution on the Church in the modern world," Vatican City, 1965, available at: http://www.vatican.va/archive/hist_councils/ii_vatican_council/documents/vat-ii_cons_19651207_gaudium-et-spes_en.html, paras 25, 43, 57, 65.
19. Timm, *Father of the Credit Unions in Bangladesh*, pp. 119, 124.
20. Independent evaluation provided to the author by Caritas Internationalis.
21. Pontifical Council *Cor Unum, Deus Caritas Est: Acts of the World Conference on Charity*, Vatican City, 2006, pp. 35–6.
22. Kenneth Hackett, President of Catholic Relief Services, in Pontifical Council *Cor Unum, Religion and Charitable Activity*, pp. 61–3.
23. R. Scott Appleby, *The Ambivalence of the Sacred: Religion, violence and reconciliation*, Lanham, Maryland, Rowman and Littlefield, 2000, p. 52.
24. ibid., pp. 292–3.
25. Caritas Uganda, *Strategic Plan, 2009–2014*, Kampala, Caritas, 2009, pp. 44–9.
26. Kerala Social Service Forum, *Annual Report, 2009–2010*, Kottayam, Kerala, KSSF, 2010.
27. Independent evaluation provided to the author by Caritas Internationalis.
28. Interview of 8 August 2012.
29. Interview of 5 October 2011.
30. Interview of 3 September 2011.
31. Karoline Mayer, *El Secreto siempre es el amor: En los suburbios de Chile*, Barcelona, Plataforma, 2008, p. 22.
32. ibid., p. 36.
33. Interviews of 19–20 August 2011.
34. Interview of 20 August 2011.
35. Interview of 18 May 2012.
36. Michel Arseneault, *Un Rêve pour la vie*, Montreal, Libre Expression, 2011, pp. 36, 102, 170, 236–7, 273, 295–6 (author's translation).
37. Interview of 30 August 2011.
38. Interview of 20 September 2011.
39. Interview of 2 September 2011.
40. Email of 16 January 2013.
41. Interviews of 21–23 February 2011.

Chapter 11: Looking Ahead: A Fading Social Mission?

1. Andrea Riccardi, *Sant'Egidio: L'Évangile au-delà des frontières*, Paris, Bayard, 2001, pp. 41–2.
2. ibid., p. 73.

3. Interview of 6 December 2011.
4. Cottier, *Église et pauvreté*, p. 203 (author's translation).
5. Timm, *Forty Years in Bangladesh*, pp. 348–9.
6. Massimo Faggioli, *Vatican II: The battle for meaning*, New York, Paulist Press, 2012, p. 69.
7. Fitzpatrick-Behrens, *The Maryknoll Catholic Mission in Peru*, p. 235.
8. Address to the Community of St Martin, 25 June 2011, translated from the French by the author.
9. Leclercq, *Christianity and Money*, pp. 14–15.
10. Pontifical Council for Justice and Peace, *Towards Reforming the International Financial and Monetary Systems in the Context of Global Public Authority*, Vatican City, 2011.
11. Benedict XVI, *Africae Munus*, pp. 55, 88.
12. National Catholic Commission for Justice and Peace, *A Call for Sustainable Constitutionalism and Rule of Law in Uganda*, Kampala, NCCJP, 2009, p. 3.
13. Interview of 14 February 2012.
14. Etchegaray, *J'ai senti battre le cœur du monde*, p. 296 (author's translation).
15. Interview with Adhemir Caceres, 14 February 2012.
16. Lecomte, in Cottier, *Église et pauvreté*, p. 225 (author's translation).
17. Vatican Information Service, 14 March 2013.
18. Quoted in Jim Wallis, "Rebuild My Church", 14 March 2013, http://sojo.net/blogs/2013/03/14/rebuild-my-church.
19. Email from Nithiya Sagayam, 16 January 2013.
20. In Cottier, *Église et pauvreté*, pp. 203–4 (author's translation).

Chapter 12: Conclusions: "Everyone Who Fights for Justice Upsets People"

1. Personal communication to the author, 13 June 2011.
2. Pirotte, *Churches and Health Care in the Third World*, p. 25.
3. http://sojo.net/blogs/2013/03/14/rebuild-my-church.
4. Quoted in John W. O'Malley, *Vatican II: Did anything happen?* New York and London, Continuum, 2008, pp. 25–6.
5. Interview of 31 July 2012.
6. Interview of 20 February 2012.
7. Quoted in Wills, *Papal Sin*, p. 11.
8. Etchegaray, *J'ai senti battre le cœur du monde*, p. 193 (author's translation).

Bibliography

Achebe, Chinua, *The Education of a British-Protected Child*, London: Penguin, 2011

Agathangelus, Fr., *The Catholic Church and Southern Africa*, Cape Town: Catholic Archdiocese of Cape Town, 1951

Aguilar, Mario, *The History and Politics of Latin American Theology*, London: SCM Press, 2007

Allen, John L, "Think again: the Catholic Church," *Foreign Policy*, 15 October 2008

Anaehobi, Vitalis, "Le Pere Lebret, Paul-VI et *Populorum Progressio*: Enjeux pour une approche théologique du développement," dissertation, Université de Paris-Sorbonne (Paris IV), Institut Catholique de Paris, 2006

Appleby, R. Scott, *The Ambivalence of the Sacred: Religion, violence and reconciliation*, Lanham, Maryland: Rowman and Littlefield, 2000

Arseneault, Michel, *Un Rêve pour la vie*, Montreal: Libre Expression, 2011

Aurenche, Guy, *Le souffle d'une vie*, Paris: Albin Michel, 2011

Banerjee, Abhijit and Esther Duflo, *Poor Economics: A radical rethinking of the way to fight global poverty*, New York: Public Affairs, 2011

Bauer, Peter, *Equality, the Third World and Economic Delusion*, London: Weidenfeld and Nicolson, 1981

——, *From Subsistence to Exchange and Other Essays*, Princeton: Princeton University Press, 2000

Benedict XVI, *Africae Munus*, Vatican City: Libreria Editrice Vaticana, 2011

——, *Light of the World: A Conversation with Peter Seewald*, San Francisco, Ignatius Press, 2010

Blouin, Francis X., Jr. (ed.), *Vatican Archives: An inventory and guide to historical documents of the Holy See*, New York and Oxford: Oxford University Press, 1998

Bouchaud, Joseph, *L'Église en Afrique noire*, Paris and Geneva: La Palatine, 1958

Bouvier, Virginia Marie, *Alliance or Compliance: Implications of the Chilean experience for the Catholic Church in Latin America*, Syracuse: Syracuse University, 1983

Boxer, C.R., *The Christian Century in Japan, 1549–1650*, Berkeley and Los Angeles, University of California, 1951

Brezault, Alain and Gerard Clavreuil, *Missions: En Afrique, les Catholiques face à l'Islam, aux sectes, au Vatican*, Paris: Éditions Autrement, 1987

Buruma, Ian, *Taming the Gods: Religion and democracy on three continents*, Princeton and Oxford: Princeton University Press, 2010

Cahill, Thomas, *Pope John XXIII: A life*, New York: Penguin, 2008

Câmara, Hélder, *Church and Colonialism*, London: Sheed and Ward, 1969

Caritas Uganda, *Strategic Plan, 2009–2014*, Kampala: Caritas, 2009

Carroll, John J., *A Balancing Act: Social and Catholic perspectives on population and development*, Manila, Philippine Center for Population and Development, 2007.

Castro, Loreta N., *Poverty and Development: The call of the Catholic Church in Asia*, Rome, International Jacques Maritain Institute, 1995

Catholic Bishops' Conference of Nigeria, *The Catholic Church in an Independent Nigeria: Joint pastoral letter of the Nigerian hierarchy, 1 October 1960*, Ibadan: Clarendon Press, 1960

Chesterton, G.K., *Autobiography*, London: Hutchison, 1936

——, *Orthodoxy* (first published 1908), London: Hodder & Stoughton,1999

——, *The Outline of Sanity*, Norfolk, Virginia: IHS Press, 2001

Chuchiak, John F., "Writing as resistance: Maya graphic pluralism and indigenous elite strategies for survival in colonial Yucatan, 1550–1750," *Ethnohistory*, 57:1, 2010

Church Central Statistics Office, *Statistical Yearbook of the Church, 2009*, Vatican City: Libreria Editrice Vaticana, 2011

Cole, G.D.H., *Persons and Periods*, Harmondsworth: Penguin, 1945

Cottier, Georges, *Église et pauvreté*, Paris: Les Éditions du Cerf, 1965

Coulton, G.G., *Two Saints: St Bernard and St Francis*, Cambridge: Cambridge University Press, 1932

Dañguilan, Marilen J., *Women in Brackets: A chronicle of Vatican power and control*, Manila: Philippine Center for Investigative Journalism, 1997

Davis, Wade, *The Wayfinders: Why ancient wisdom matters in the modern world*, Toronto: House of Anansi Press, 2009

de Las Casas, Bartolomé, *Witness*, ed. and trans. by George Sanderlin, Maryknoll: Orbis Books, 1993

De Torre, Joseph M., *Politics and the Church: From Rerum Novarum to liberation theology*, Manila: Vera Reyes, 1987

Dear, John SJ, "Dom Helder Camara, Presente!" *National Catholic Reporter*, 28 April 2009

Delisle, Philippe (ed.), *Les relations Églises-État en situation postcoloniale: Amériques, Afrique, Asie, Océanie, XIX-XXe siècles*, Paris: Karthala, 2003

Deneulin, Séverine, *Religion in Development: Rewriting the secular script*, London: Zed Books, 2009

Diamond, Jared, *Guns, Germs, and Steel: The fates of human societies*, New York: W.W. Norton, 1999

Dietrich, Donald J., *Human Rights and the Catholic Tradition*, London: Transaction, 2007

Dixon, Thomas, *Science and Religion: A very short introduction*, Oxford: Oxford University Press, 2009

Djereke, Jean-Claude, *L'Engagement politique du clergé catholique en Afrique noire*, Paris: Karthala, 2001

Dorr, Donal, "Themes and theologies in Catholic social teaching over fifty years," *New Blackfriars*, 93:1044, March 2012

Etchegaray, Roger, *J'ai senti battre le cœur du monde*, Paris: Fayard, 2007

Etherington, Norman (ed.), *Missions and Empire*, Oxford: Oxford University Press, 2005

Ezeh, Marie-Noelle, "La reconnaissance de la dignité de la femme dans la rencontre de la société Igbo du Nigéria avec le christianisme de 1885 à 1965," dissertation, Université de Paris-Sorbonne (Paris IV), Institut Catholique de Paris, April 2002

Faggioli, Massimo, *Vatican II: The battle for meaning*, New York: Paulist Press, 2012

Fitzpatrick-Behrens, Susan, *The Maryknoll Catholic Mission in Peru, 1943–1989: Transnational faith and transformation*, Notre Dame: University of Notre Dame, 2012.

Fleet, Michael, *The Catholic Church and Democracy in Chile and Peru*, Notre Dame: University of Notre Dame, 1997

BIBLIOGRAPHY

Forristal, Desmond, *The Second Burial of Bishop Shanahan*, Dublin: Veritas, 1990

Fox, Thomas C., *Sexuality and Catholicism*, New York: George Braziller, 1995

Fülöp-Miller, René, *Leo XIII and Our Times*, New York: Longmans, Green and Co., 1937

Furlong, Paul and David Curtis (eds), *The Church Faces the Modern World: Rerum Novarum and its impact*, Hull: Earlsgate Press, 1994

Gamley, Anthony M. (ed.), *Denis Hurley: A portrait by friends*, Pietermaritzburg: Cluster Publications, 2001

Giblin, Marie J., "Toward justice, equality and participation: Issues for the Church concerning Tanzanian women and men peasants," dissertation, Union Theological Seminary, New York City, May 1986

Gifford, Paul, *The Christian Churches and the Democratisation of Africa*, Leiden: E.J. Brill, 1995

Griswold, Eliza, *The Tenth Parallel: Dispatches from the fault line between Christianity and Islam*, New York: Farrar, Straus and Giroux, 2010

Gutiérrez, Gustavo, *A Theology of Liberation: Fifteenth anniversary edition*, Maryknoll: Orbis Books, 1990

Haggard, H. Rider, *King Solomon's Mines*, London: Cassell, 1933

Hartley, Olga, *Women and the Catholic Church: Yesterday and today*, London: Burns Oates & Washbourne, 1935

Hetherwick, Alexander, *The Gospel and the African*, Edinburgh: T. & T. Clark, 1932

Houtart, François and Geneviève Lemercinier, *Church and Development in Kerala*, Bangalore, Theological Publications of India, 1979

Husslein, Joseph, *The Christian Social Manifesto*, New York: Bruce, 1931

Iozzio, Mary Jo (ed.), *Calling for Justice throughout the World: Catholic women theologians on the HIV/AIDS pandemic*, New York: Continuum, 2008

John XXIII, *New Light on Social Problems*, London: Catholic Truth Society, 1961

John Paul II, *Entrez dans l'espérance*, Paris: Plon, 1994

Johnstone, Harry, "Review of *Adventures in Aidland: The anthropology of professionals in international development*, edited by David Mosse," *Times Literary Supplement*, 9 September 2011

Jones, David, "The redemption of economics: the political thought of Eric Gill and Vincent McNabb," *Allan Review: An Oxford Journal of Catholic Thought*, 7, 1992

Jordan, John P., *Bishop Shanahan of Southern Nigeria*, Dublin: Clonmore and Reynolds, 1949

Joyce, Kathryn, *Seeing is Believing: Questions about faith-based organizations that are involved in HIV/AIDS prevention and treatment*, Washington, DC: Catholics for Choice, 2010

Kane, Cheikh Hamidou, *Ambiguous Adventure*, New York: Walker, 1963

Kearney, Paddy, *Guardian of the Light: Denis Hurley – renewing the church, opposing apartheid*, New York and London: Continuum, 2009

Kennedy, John J., *Catholicism, Nationalism, and Democracy in Argentina*, Notre Dame: University of Notre Dame, 1958

Kennedy, Robert and Stephanie Rumpza, *Pius XII on Work and Commerce*, University of St Thomas, Saint Paul, Minnesota, 2011, available at: http://www.stthomas.edu/cathstudies/cst/publications/piusxii.html

Kenny, Charles, *Getting Better: Why global development is succeeding and how we can improve the world even more*, New York: Basic Books, 2011

Keogh, Dermot (ed.), *Church and Politics in Latin America*, London: Macmillan, 1990

Kerala Social Service Forum, *Annual Report, 2009–2010*, Kottayam, Kerala: KSSF, 2010

Kraemer, Hendrik, *The Christian Message in a Non-Christian World*, London: Edinburgh House Press, 1938

Küng, Hans, *The Catholic Church: A short history*, London: Weidenfeld and Nicolson, 2001

Kuran, Timur, *The Long Divergence: How Islamic law held back the Middle East*, Princeton: Princeton University Press, 2011

Lagos, Ricardo, *The Southern Tiger: Chile's fight for a democratic and prosperous future*, New York: Palgrave Macmillan, 2012

Land, Philip S., *Catholic Social Teaching: As I have lived, loathed, and loved it*, Chicago: Loyola University Press, 1994

Leclercq, Jacques, *Christianity and Money*, London: Burns & Oates, 1959

Ledure, Yves (ed.), *Rerum Novarum en France: Le Père Dehon et l'engagement social de l'Église*, Éditions Universitaires, 1991

Lernoux, Penny, *Hearts on Fire: The story of the Maryknoll Sisters*, Maryknoll: Orbis, 1995

Linden, Ian, *The Catholic Church and the Struggle for Zimbabwe*, London: Longman, 1980

——, *Global Catholicism: Diversity and change since Vatican II*, New York: Columbia University Press, 2009

Linguyeneza, Vénuste (ed.), *Verité, Justice, Charité: Lettres pastorales et autres déclarations des évêques catholiques du Rwanda, 1956–1962*, Waterloo, 2001

Maathai, Wangari, *The Challenge for Africa*, New York: Pantheon Books, 2009.

MacCulloch, Diarmaid, *A History of Christianity*, London: Penguin, 2010

Malloch-Brown, Mark, *The Unfinished Global Revolution: The limits of nations and the pursuit of a new politics*, London: Allen Lane, 2011

Manuel, Paul Christopher (ed.), *The Catholic Church and the Nation-State: Comparative perspectives*, Washington, DC: Georgetown University Press, 2006

Maradiaga, Oscar Rodríguez, *De la difficulté d'évoquer Dieu dans un monde qui pense ne pas en avoir besoin*, Paris: Robert Laffont, 2008

Maritain, Jacques, *Christianisme et démocratie*, Paris: Desclée de Brouwer, 1989

——, *Les Droits de l'Homme*, Paris: Desclée de Brouwer, 1989

Mayer, Karoline, *El Secreto siempre es el amor: En los suburbios de Chile*, Barcelona: Plataforma, 2008

McCabe, Joseph, *The Social Record of Christianity*, London: Watts & Co., 1935

——, *The Catholic Church and the Sex Problem: The stupidity, futility and insolence of its ethic* (first published 1949), London: Black Cat Press, 2009

McFadden, Thomas M. (ed.), *Liberation, Revolution, and Freedom: Theological perspectives*, New York: Seabury Press, 1975

McLaughlin, J.B., *The Immortal Encyclical: Rerum Novarum and the developments of Pius XI*, London: Burns, Oates & Washbourne, 1932

Meadows, Denis, *A Popular History of the Jesuits*, New York: Macmillan, 1958

Ministry of Education and Sports, *Uganda Education Statistical Abstract*, Vol. 1, Kampala, 2009

Missionnaires d'Afrique, *Le Cardinal Lavigerie: Apôtre de l'Afrique*, Bobo-Dioulasso, Burkina Faso: Imprimerie de la Savane, 1991

Moyn, Samuel, *The Last Utopia: Human rights in history*, Cambridge and London: Harvard University Press, 2010

Muzungu, Bernardin, "Église Catholique pendant le génocide," *Cahiers Lumière et Société*, 43, 2010

Nagle, Robin, *Claiming the Virgin: The broken promise of liberation theology in Brazil*, New York and London: Routledge, 1997

National Catholic Commission for Justice and Peace, *A Call for Sustainable Constitutionalism and Rule of Law in Uganda*, Kampala: NCCJP, 2009

National Conference of Catholic Bishops, *The Church in the Present-Day Transformation of Latin America in the Light of the Council: Conclusions of the Second General Council of Latin American Bishops*, Washington, DC: Secretariat for Latin America, National Conference of Catholic Bishops, 1979

National Planning Authority, *National Development Plan (2010/11–2014/15)*, Kampala, 2010

Ndongmo, Marcus, *Éducation scolaire et lien social en Afrique noire*, Mbalmayo: Cameroon, ICERh, 2004

Newbigin, Lesslie, *A South India Diary*, London: Edinburgh House Press, 1951

Nolan, Albert, *Jesus before Christianity*, Maryknoll: Orbis Books, 2010

Nurser, John S., *For All Peoples and All Nations: The ecumenical church and human rights*, Washington, DC: Georgetown University Press, 2005

O'Malley, John W., *The First Jesuits*, Cambridge and London: Harvard University Press, 1993

——, *Vatican II: Did anything happen?* New York and London: Continuum, 2008

Ondo, Jean-Vincent, "La place de l'Église dans le processus démocratique en Afrique," dissertation, Institut Catholique de Paris, July 1996

Parish, Helen Rand (ed.), *Bartolomé de Las Casas: The only way*, Mahwah: Paulist Press, 1992

Peterson, Anna L., *Seeds of the Kingdom: Utopian communities in the Americas*, Oxford and New York: Oxford University Press, 2005

Pirotte, Jean, *Churches and Health Care in the Third World: Past and present*, Leiden: E.J. Brill, 1991

Pius XI, *After Forty Years*, New York: Barry Vail, 1931

Pius XII, *Humani Generis*, revised edition, London: Catholic Truth Society, 1961

Poincaré, Nicolas, *Gabriel Maindron, un prêtre dans la tragédie*, Paris: Éditions ouvrières, 1995

Pontifical Council Cor Unum, *Acts of the World Congress on Charity: Rome, 12–15 May 1999*, Vatican City, 1999

——, *Religion and Charitable Activity*, Proceedings of the plenary assembly, Vatican City, 2003

——, *Deus Caritas Est: Acts of the World Conference on Charity*, Vatican City, 2006

Pontifical Council for Justice and Peace, *Towards Reforming the International Financial and Monetary Systems in the Context of Global Public Authority*, Vatican City, 2011

Poupard, Paul, *Le développement des peuples: Entre souvenirs et espérance*, Paris: Parole et Silence, 2008

Prieto, Manuel, *The Church Problem in Mexico*, New York: Academy Press, 1926

Quintanilla, Luis, *The Other Side of the Mexican Church Question*, Washington, DC, 1935

Radcliffe, Timothy, *Take the Plunge: Living baptism and confirmation*, London: Bloomsbury, 2012

Ramsey, Michael, *The Gospel of the Catholic Church*, London: SPCK, 1990

Riccardi, Andrea, *Sant'Egidio, Roma e il Mondo*, Milan: Edizioni San Paolo, 1997

——, *Sant'Egidio: L'Évangile au-delà des frontières*, Paris: Bayard, 2001

Rodrik, Dani, *The Globalization Paradox: Why global markets, states, and democracy can't coexist*, Oxford: Oxford University Press, 2011

Romeo, Enzo, *Cardinal Oscar Rodriguez Maradiaga: La voix de l'Amérique latine*, Quebec: Éditions Anne Sigier, 2007

Russell, Bertrand, *Why I Am Not a Christian*, New York: Simon and Schuster, 1957

Ryckmans, Pierre, *Dominer pour Servir*, Brussels: Librairie Albert Dewit, 1931

Sarah, Robert, *Culture, démocratie et développement à la lumière de Centesimus Annus*, Conakry, Éditions IMC, 1998

Schmiesing, Kevin E., *Within the Market Strife: American Catholic economic thought from Rerum Novarum to Vatican II*, Latham and Oxford: Lexington Books, 2004

Schultheis, Michael, *Catholic Social Teaching and the Church in Africa*, Gweru: Zimbabwe, Centre of Concern, 1984

Second Vatican Council, "*Gaudium et Spes*: Pastoral constitution on the Church in the modern world," Vatican City, 1965, available at: http://www.vatican.va/archive/hist_councils/ii_vatican_council/documents/vat-ii_cons_19651207_gaudium-et-spes_en.html

Sen, Amartya, *Development as Freedom*, New York: Anchor Books, 1999

Sirico, Robert A., *The Entrepreneurial Vocation*, Grand Rapids, Michigan, Acton Institute for the Study of Religion and Liberty, 2001

Sivalon, John, "Roman Catholicism and the defining of Tanzanian socialism, 1953–1985," dissertation, St Michael's College, University of Toronto, November 1990

Smuts, Jan Christiaan, *Africa and Some World Problems*, Oxford: Clarendon Press, 1930

Sniegocki, John, *Catholic Social Teaching and Economic Globalization: The quest for alternatives*, Milwaukee: Marquette University Press, 2009

Société africaine de culture, *Civilisation noire et Église catholique: Colloque d'Abidjan 12–17 septembre 1977*, Paris: Présence africaine, 1978

Soupa, Anne and Christine Pedotti, *Les Pieds dans le bénitier*, Paris: Presses de la Renaissance, 2010

Stark, Rodney, *The Victory of Reason: How Christianity led to freedom, capitalism and western success*, New York: Random House, 2005

Tanzanian Episcopal Conference, *Manifesto: Proposal of national priorities*, Dar es Salaam, 2009

Timm, Richard W., *On Building a Just Society*, Dhaka: Caritas Bangladesh, 1994

——, *The Church and Development in Bangladesh*, Dhaka: Caritas Bangladesh, 1994

——, *Forty Years in Bangladesh: Memoirs of Father Timm*, Dhaka: Caritas Bangladesh, 1995

——, *Father of the Credit Unions in Bangladesh: Life of Father Charles J. Young, CSC*, Dhaka: Holy Cross, 2010

Tourigny, Yves, *So Abundant a Harvest*, London: Darton, Longman and Todd, 1979

Ward, Barbara, *Faith and Freedom*, New York: W.W. Norton & Company, 1954

Weber, Max, *The Protestant Ethic and the Spirit of Capitalism* (first published 1905), London: Allen and Unwin, 1930

Webster, John and Ellen Webster (eds), *The Church and Women in the Third World*, Philadelphia: Westminster Press, 1985

Westcott, Brooke F., *Christian Social Union Addresses*, London: Macmillan, 1903

Widner, Andreas, *The Pope and the CEO: John Paul II's leadership lessons for a young Swiss Guard*, Steubenville, Ohio: Emmaus Road, 2011

Williamson, Edwin, *The Penguin History of Latin America*, London: Penguin Books, 2009

Wills, Garry, *Papal Sin: Structures of deceit*, New York: Doubleday, 2000

Wilson, William J. (ed.), *The Church in Africa: Christian mission in a context of change*, Maryknoll: Maryknoll Publications, 1967

Wolfensohn, James D., *A Global Life*, New York: Public Affairs, 2009

Chronological List of Papal Encyclicals Mentioned in the Book

De Rerum Novarum, Encyclical Letter of Pope Leo XIII, 15 May 1891

Casti Connubii, Encyclical Letter of Pope Pius XI, 31 December 1930

Quadragesimo Anno, Encyclical Letter of Pope Pius XI, issued 15 May 1931

Mit brennender Sorge, Encyclical Letter of Pope Pius XI, issued 10 March 1937

Humani Generis, Encyclical Letter of Pope Pius XII, 12 August 1950

Evangelii Praecones, Encyclical Letter of Pope Pius XII, 2 June 1951

Mater et Magistra, Encyclical Letter of Pope John XXIII, 15 May 1961

Pacem in Terris, Encyclical Letter of Pope John XXIII, 11 April 1963

Populorum Progressio, Encyclical Letter of Pope Paul VI, 26 March 1967

Humanae Vitae, Encyclical Letter of Pope Paul VI, 25 July 1968

Laborem Exercens, Encyclical letter of Pope John Paul II, 14 September 1981

Sollicitudo Rei Socialis, Encyclical Letter of Pope John Paul II, 30 December 1987

Centesimus Annus, Encyclical Letter of Pope John Paul II, 1 May 1991

Deus Caritas Est, Encyclical Letter of Pope Benedict XVI, 25 December 2005

Caritas in Veritate, Encyclical Letter of Pope Benedict XVI, 29 June 2009

Index

INDEX